I HAVE AN ANSWER

"In *I Have An Answer*, Dr. Bowman provides answers to a great many questions about the teachings and history of The Church of Jesus Christ of Latter-day Saints that people often use to dissuade investigators of the LDS Church from continuing to study its teachings and new members from maintaining their affiliation with it. He ran into these questions as he served as a full-time missionary in the Missouri Saint Louis Mission and as a part-time stake and ward missionary at home.

"Sensing the unevenness of such encounters, Dr. Bowman has tried to level the playing field by telling his readers why some people ask intentionally misleading questions about the LDS Church, its history, and its teachings, and then by offering answers to those questions, which he has gained from a lifetime of studying and associating with the Church. He expressly states in the Introduction that this book is intended to help investigators gain and new members maintain faith in the Church and its teachings by offering answers to them that have helped him sustain his own faith in and service to it.

"*I Have An Answer* will help many people find the truth about the teachings of The Church of Jesus Christ of Latter-day Saints."

Dr. Charles D. Tate, Jr.
Emeritus Professor of English and Ancient Scripture
Brigham Young University

I HAVE AN ANSWER

A POWERFUL REFERENCE GUIDE CONCERNING THE BELIEFS AND DOCTRINES OF THE LDS CHURCH

DR. DAVID PRESSLEY BOWMAN

Springville, Utah

ISBN: 1-55517-708-5
e. 2

Published by Cedar Fort, Inc.
www.cedarfort.com

Distributed by:

Cover design by Nicole Cunningham
Cover design © 2003 by Lyle Mortimer

Printed in the United States of America
10 9 8 7 6 5 4 3 2 1

Printed on acid-free paper

Library of Congress Control Number: 2003109765

Dedicated to my angel wife, Kim,
whom I have loved forever.

Also to my three gifts from heaven:
Jens, Jacob, and Anna.

"If ye are prepared ye shall not fear."
(D&C 38:30)

CONTENTS

ACKNOWLEDGEMENTS

I would like to acknowledge my wife Kimberly Bowman who spent many hours assisting, and proof reading, also for her patience and love. She helped me and at the same time was busy as a mother and writing her own book. Thanks to my former mission President Charles D. Tate who provided invaluable support in analyzing key doctrines. I will always look up to him.

I would also like to thank Casie Wehrli for her many hours of typing. Also Brett Bagley for his help with questions on the Chinese language.

Finally I wish to express appreciation to Cedar Fort for their excellent staff and all their expertise.

PREFACE

This book has two purposes:

1. For LDS Church members who want to strengthen their testimony and be prepared for the questions that will likely be asked at some point in their life.

2. To be used as a reference for LDS "member missionaries" and fulltime missionaries who know an investigator who has a question. It can also be used as a source of information for lessons, talks etc. I encourage copying of this book at will. Feel free to copy any question/answer an investigator may have.

I have found that many people who are sincerely interested in the LDS Church often have a "friend" or acquaintance sew seeds of doubt in their mind. These investigators can easily be deceived "like a wave of the sea driven with the wind and tossed" (James 1:6). These sincere investigators need to be provided with an answer.

When we talk to investigators about their questions I feel it is best to just answer their questions at hand and then move on to the principles of the gospel. In that regard for the investigators sake I feel it would be best to only use portions of this book at a time. The scriptures say:

> I have fed you with milk, and not meat: for hitherto
> ye were not able to bear it neither yet now are ye able.
> (1 Cor. 3:2)

INTRODUCTION

I heard an analogy that a testimony is like cement. When fresh, a small bird can land on it and leave an impression. When the cement has had time to harden, an elephant can walk across it and not leave a mark.

The Savior stated that even the "very elect" would be deceived in the last days (Matt. 24:24). Following are some quotes concerning the importance of strengthening ones testimony.

> Unless every member of this Church gains for himself an unshakable testimony of the divinity of this Church, he will be among those who will be deceived in this day when the 'elect according to the covenant' are going to be tried and tested. Only those will survive who have gained for themselves this testimony.[1]

> Look out for the great sieve, for there will be a great sifting time, and many will fall; for I say unto you there is a test, a test, a TEST coming, and who will be able to stand? To meet the difficulties that are coming, it will be necessary for you to have a knowledge of the truth of the work for yourselves. The difficulties will be of such a character that the man or woman who does not possess this personal knowledge or witness will fall . . . Remember these sayings, for many of you will live to see them fulfilled. The time will come when no man or woman will be able to endure on borrowed light. Each will have to be guided by the light within himself.[2]

> God grant that we may all seek for that testimony, because we are living in a day when, unless we have a strong testimony, we are in danger of falling by the wayside, for the principle of revelation is on trial in this Church. Those who don't believe it and haven't a

testimony are going to be sorely tried; but those who believe and have faith and follow the leaders will be safe on Zion's hill when destruction shall come upon the wicked.[3]

We shall have to pass through trials, sorrows, and afflictions of various kinds. We shall have to be tested and tried and proved; the dross of our nature must necessarily be cleansed and purified by affliction. If Jesus had to be made perfect through suffering, what shall we expect.[4]

We are here in mortality, and the only way to go is through; there isn't any around . . . including having our faith and patience tried in order to be strengthened.[5]

"Receiving a testimony requires a trial of our faith . . . And only after we have had a trial of our faith and we have proved ourselves, then only can we receive the witness—that means testimony. Living the gospel, if you would receive a testimony, is the essential.[6]

This book will give you knowledge that will strengthen your testimony. The day will come when a friend or acquaintance will ask you a sincere question about the Church. Without an answer to the question, your testimony can be "shaken" as you contemplate the unknown answer. This "trial" of your testimony is resolved as you gain an understanding of the sometimes—twisted question and the Holy Ghost bears witness that the Church is true. Joseph Smith said, "Would to God, brethren, I could tell you who I am! Would to God I could tell you what I know! But you would call it blasphemy, and there are men upon this stand who would want to take my life."[7] Thus, if you are a new member of the Church, it would be better to start first by reading *Gospel Doctrine* and other books before reading this book, although you may find it useful to look up answers to questions you may have.

I request that this book be used to answer questions of the pure in heart and not for arguing with others about points of doctrine. You will find, if you haven't already, that those who ask insincere questions about gospel doctrine, in an attempt to prove you wrong, will generally never listen to your explanation no matter how right.

In General Conference, Elder Loren C. Dunn stated:

> There is a need for us, perhaps more than ever before, to reach within ourselves and allow the qualities of mutual respect, mingled with charity and forgiveness; to influence our actions with one another; to be able to disagree without becoming disagreeable; to lower our voices and build on common ground with the realization that once the storm has passed, we will still have to live with one another.[8]

With this thought in mind, let's proceed to analyze some of the doctrines and questions that may some day be presented to you. It will be apparent as you read through the passages that follow, that Satan is harder at work to deceive members and investigators of the Church of Jesus Christ of Latter Day Saints than any other religion.

Aaronic Priesthood

(see PRIESTHOOD)

Adam-God Theory

Question 1

Did Brigham Young once state that our God is actually Adam, and that we have nothing to do with God the Father mentioned in the Bible?

Answer 1

Nearly every enemy of the LDS Church brings up the Adam-God theory, as if the LDS Church believes it. These enemies know full well that we don't believe the doctrine that Adam is our God and that this doctrine is not taught within our Churches or temples. Nevertheless they make statements as if we do. The original misunderstanding comes from a written quote from Brigham Young that was transcribed in error. They did not have tape recorders at the time of Brigham Young's discourses and of his thousands of speeches that were hand transcribed an occasional error was made just as when the Bible was transcribed. Brigham Young's statement says this:

> Michael, the Archangel, the Ancient of days, about whom holy men have written and spoken—He is our father and our God, and the only God with whom we have to do.[9]

The most important thing the reader can learn about the "Adam God Theory" as stated by a prophet of God is this:

We denounce that theory and hope that everyone will be cautioned against this and other kinds of false doctrine.[10]

Be assured that President Brigham Young also did *not* believe that Adam was over God the Father and Jesus Christ, nor did he believe that we have nothing to do with God the Father Elohim. Brigham Young stated in the very same discourse: "Then the Lord by his power and wisdom organized the mortal tabernacle of man. We were made first spiritual and afterwards temporal." Brigham Young also stated "It is true that the earth was organized by three distinct characters, namely, Elohim, Jehovah, and Michael." Notice that President Young puts Michael or Adam third in line. Again he said, "The greatest desire in the bosom of our Father *Adam, or of his faithful children who are co-workers with God, our Father in Heaven,* is to save the inhabitants of the earth."[11] This statement certainly reflects Brigham Young's knowledge that Adam is not our God. However, it is important to realize that (a) Adam is the Father of us all; (b) Adam will be a God (see GODS). The prophet Joseph Smith said: "Our Father Adam, Michael, will call his children together and prepare them for the coming of the Son of Man. He (Adam) is the father of the human family, and presides over the spirits of all men, and all that have had the keys must stand before him in this grand council. The Son of Man (Christ) stands before him, and there is given him glory and dominion. Adam delivers up his stewardship to Christ."[12]

Thus, the prophet Joseph believed even as the prophet Brigham Young.

ANIMAL SACRIFICE

(see PROPHECY; SACRIFICE)

ALCOHOL

(see WORD OF WISDOM)

APOSTASY AND AUTHORITY

(see also PRIESTHOOD; REVELATION)

Question 1

In Matthew 28:19–20, the Savior stated to his apostles "lo I am with you always." Does this mean Jesus would always be with the apostles, and that they would have no harm? Does this mean there would be no apostasy, as the LDS Church believes?

Answer 1

The words "lo I am with you always" are the words of the Savior. He had been resurrected at the time and was giving instructions to his apostles before his departing. These verses do not mean there would not be an apostasy. These words were addressed to the apostles only, not to the whole Church. The Savior is basically telling the apostles that he will always be with them, to ease their burdens. He tells them this knowing that persecutions will eventually take all of their lives. Any Bible scholar can tell you that the apostles were killed. Even Peter himself was crucified.[13]

Question 2

In the book of Ephesians 3:21, it says that Christ would be with the Church throughout all ages. If Christ is always with the Church, how could there be an apostasy?

Answer 2

Let's take a look at the verse:

> Unto him be glory in the Church by Christ Jesus
> throughout all ages, world without end. Amen. (Eph. 3:21)

This verse is a good example of the importance at looking at the entire verse, and not just part of it. Ephesians 3:21 speaks of glory in the Church at a time when there would be a "world without end" as it states at the end of the verse. This will occur after the earth has been transformed into its celestial state (Rev. 21:1–5; Matt. 5:5).

Question 3

In Hebrews 13:5, Christ speaking to the apostles said, "I will never leave thee nor forsake thee." Does this mean there would be no apostasy?

Answer 3

This statement doesn't say there would not be an apostasy. This is a general statement meaning the Lord will be with and comfort when in need.

Question 4

Jesus was speaking to Peter and said,

> And I say also unto thee, that thou art Peter, and upon *this* rock I will build my Church; and the gates of hell shall not prevail against it. (Matt. 16:18; italics added)

The Catholic Church and some other religions claim the "rock" is Peter, and that their line of authority has come from the time of Peter with no apostasy. Others have used this scripture to say the gates of hell could not prevail against the Church, so there was no apostasy. Is the rock spoken of Peter? And, if so, does that mean the Church would be solid like a rock, and there would be no apostasy?

Answer 4

No, the rock spoken of is revelation. Let's look at the

whole concept Christ was stating to Peter rather than just one verse:

> When Jesus came into the coasts of Caesarea Philippi, he asked his disciples, saying, Whom do men say that I the Son of man am?
>
> And they said, Some say that thou art John the Baptist: some, Elias; and others, Jeremias, or one of the prophets.
>
> He saith unto them, But whom say ye that I am?
>
> And Simon Peter answered and said, Thou art the Christ, the Son of the living God.
>
> And Jesus answered and said unto him, Blessed art thou, Simon Bar-jona: for flesh and blood hath not *revealed it unto thee,* but *my Father which is in heaven.*
>
> And I say also unto thee, That thou art Peter, and *upon this rock* I will build my Church; and the gates of hell shall not prevail against it. (Matt. 16:13–18; italics added)

The rock is not Peter. Christ would not build his Church upon one man. A look at all the verses makes it clear that Jesus was telling Peter that Heavenly Father had *revealed* to Peter that Jesus was the Christ. It is through this revelation that the Church is built. And the gates of hell have not prevailed against revelation. Even with the dark ages and death of every apostle and prophet, Satan was unable to keep revelation from again being on the earth. With the restitution of all things, revelation to prophets was restored. Just as the Lord said he would do nothing unless he revealed his secrets to his servants the prophets (see Amos 3:7). Today, Jesus himself is the head of the Church of Jesus Christ of Latter Day Saints and that is why the Church is named after him. The nickname "Mormon" was given by our enemies, because we believe in the Book of Mormon, but the Lord in his wisdom has turned it from a negative into a positive. But it is still only a nickname.

Question 5

In Hebrews 12:28 it states, "We receiving a kingdom which cannot be moved, let us have grace." Does this verse mean there would be no apostasy?

Answer 5

No it does not. The kingdom spoken of is not the Church itself. Paul is speaking of the kingdom of heaven (see also Matt. 21:43).

Question 6

In the book of Luke 16:16 (as well as Matt. 11:13) it states, "The law and the prophets were until John." Does this mean there would be no prophets after John?

Answer 6

No it does not. The proper interpretation of this verse is that all the prophets *foretold the coming of Christ until* John the Baptist (see the Joseph Smith Translation below). The answer to this question is obvious because there were many prophets after John including Jesus (Acts 3:22), Peter, James, John, Paul, and yes, Joseph Smith and others. The scriptures say there will be prophets until there is a unity of the faith (Eph. 4:11–15), and that God would do nothing except He reveal to the prophets (Amos 3:7). Some have tried to say that the parable stated in Matthew 21:37–39 meant Jesus would be the last prophet. As stated in Ephesians and Amos, we know this in not the correct interpretation of Matthew 21. There is a prophet on the earth today; a wise person listens to today's prophet just as if they were listening to the ancient prophet Noah.

The correct interpretation of the above verse is this:

> And they said unto him, We have the law, and the prophets; but as for this man we will not receive him to be our ruler. . . .

Then said Jesus unto them, The law and the prophets testify of me; yea, and all the prophets who have written, even until John, have foretold of these days. (Luke 16:16–17, Joseph Smith Translation)

COMMENTS AND EVIDENCES OF THE APOSTASY:

Even without scriptural reference you can look around at the world today and see quite obviously that there was an apostasy. That is why there are so many different denominations. When Christ organized his Church he *set it up one way:* "One Lord, one faith, one baptism" (Eph. 4:5). Without a prophet and revelation, different ideas result in different Churches (see fig. 1). Christ's Church was built upon a certain foundation. That foundation was apostles and prophets with Jesus Christ himself as the chief cornerstone (see Eph. 2:20). What happens if you take the foundation out from under a building? It crumbles. That is exactly what happened to Christ's original Church and that is called an apostasy.

Following is scriptural evidence of the apostasy:

For I know this, that after my departing shall grievous wolves enter in among you, not sparing the flock. (Acts 20:29).

For the time will come when they will not endure sound doctrine; but after their own lusts shall they heap to themselves teachers, having itching ears;

And *they shall turn away their ears from the truth,* and shall be turned unto fables. (2 Tim. 4:3–4; italics added)

Now we beseech you, brethren, by *the coming of our Lord Jesus Christ,* and by our gathering together unto him,

That ye be not soon shaken in mind, or be troubled, neither by spirit, nor by word, nor by letter as from us, as that the day of Christ is at hand.

CHRIST FORMS HIS ORIGINAL CHURCH

Built upon a foundation of apostles and prophets, with Christ as the chief cornerstone *(Ephes. 2:19-20)* The intention was that if an apostle died, he would be replaced with another apostle. *(Acts 1:23-26, Ephes. 4:11-14)* After Judas died Matthias was put in as an apostle to keep a continuing number of 12 apostles.

APOSTASY

Christ's original church was built upon a foundation of apostles and prophets. Just as with a building, if you remove the foundation the building crumbles. This is exactly what happened to Christ's original organization. The apostles and prophets *(the foundation)* were killed and the church crumbled. *(the apostasy)(1Tim. 4:1 2, 2 Tim. 4:3-4, Heb. 13:20, Acts 20:29-30, 2 Peter 3:3-7, Amos 8: 11-12, 2 Thess. 2:3-4, Matt. 21:41-46, Matt. 24:4-12.)*

CATHOLIC CHURCH FORMED

Catholics mistakenly claim direct apostolic priesthood authority today through an unbroken chain of Bishops in Rome who took the place of Peter. But the succession they claim is impossible because after Peter died the priesthood did not go to a Pope. It went to John who was still alive. After all the Apostles died, authority was lost.

DIVISION 1054 CE

ROMAN CATHOLIC CHURCH
(Center in Rome — Western)
(Reformation begins, council of Trent)

EASTERN ORTHODOX
(Center in Constantinople)

THE PROTESTANT REFORMATION BEGINS

CHURCH OF ENGLAND 1534
(Known as Episcopalian Churches in the U.S.)
Forms after tension builds between the English crown and Rome. Tudor reformation takes place and Henry VIII Divorces Catherine of Argon and Henry returns to the older standard that the king is the head of the English Church. He left church doctrine basically the same.

ANGLICAN CHURCH
Formed from Englanders who came to American in 1607. Established in Jamestown Virginia.
War of Independence 1607

PROTESTANT EPISCOPAL CHURCH 1789
Reverend Samuel Seabury receives Episcopal succession from the Bishops of the Anglican Church in Scotland, and forms this autonomous organization. This church is specifically separate from the Church of England but has a strong resemblance. A lot of the liturgy is identical.

RADICALS

SEVENTH DAY ADVENTISTS
Believe the Sabbath is Saturday

MENNONITES
Menno Simmons, Dutch reformer
Reject church organization

UNITARIANS
Martin Cellarius, Unipersonality of God

BAPTISTS
John Smyth, a separatist exiled in Amsterdam, and Roger Williams in Rhode Island. Evangelical in their approach. Congregations are basically independent. They call and ordain their own pastors. In the U.S. there are two major Baptist Communions; Southern Baptist Convention, and American Baptist. Others include Free Will Baptists, Primitive Baptists, and Old Regular Baptists. They all baptize by immersion.

MARTIN LUTHER
In 1517 as an ordained Catholic Priest he nailed ninety-five theses to the door of the Church in Wittenberg, Germany. He challenged the sale of "Indulgences," which promised the release of a certain number of years in Purgatory, if the buyer would contribute to varying papal projects. Luther had challenged the authority of the Papacy, and expressed the belief that Priests were not necessary to save the people.

EVANGELICAL REFORMED CHURCH & CONGREGATIONAL CHRISTIAN CHURCHES
Join to form

UNITED CHURCH OF CHRIST

NUMEROUS LUTHERAN FELLOWSHIPS
(Germany, Denmark, Norway, U.S.) 1526
In the U.S. they are: Evangelical Lutheran Church, Missouri Synod Lutheran and other minor bodies.

METHODIST (promoted 1729)
John Wesley, a priest in the Church of England, wanted to bring back some of the necessary spiritual dimensions of the gospel. John Wesley set apart Thomas Coke in 1784. After Wesley's death the Methodist Church became acknowledged as a separate denomination. Methodists still have an Episcopal organization present.

SALVATION ARMY 1888

REFORMED GROUPS 1536
Martin Luther, John Calvin and others
Churches: **Presbyterian Congregational** and **Dutch Reformed** believe that everyone is called to be priests of God. There is no hierarchy of Priests. All people believe everyone is called to the priesthood, and the people elect the Ministers. Some Presbyterians believe the doctrine of predestination.

Figure 1. Apostasy Branches

Let no man deceive you by and means: *for that day shall not come except there come a falling away first,* and that man of sin be revealed, the son of perdition. (2 Thes. 2:1–3; italics added)

After the apostasy, a restoration of the truth was foretold. Following are evidences of the restoration:

Repent ye therefore, and be converted, that your sins my be blotted out, when the *times of refreshing shall come* from the presence of the Lord;

And he shall send Jesus Christ which before was preached unto you:

Whom the heaven must receive until *the times of restitution of all things,* which God hath spoken by the mouth of all his holy prophets since the world began. (Acts 3:19–21; italics added)

And Jesus answered and said unto them, Elias truly shall first come, and *restore all things.* (Matt. 17:11).

And in the days of these kings shall the God of heaven *set up a kingdom,* which shall never be destroyed: and the kingdom shall not be left to other people, but it shall break in pieces and consume all these kingdoms, and it shall stand forever. (Dan. 2:44; italics added)

And I saw another angel fly in the midst of heaven, *having the everlasting Gospel* to preach unto them that dwell on the earth, and to every nation, and kindred, and tongue, and people,

Saying with a loud voice, Fear God, and give glory to Him, for the hour of His judgment is come" (Rev. 14:6–7; italics added).

God would not send an angel to bring the everlasting gospel if it was already present on the earth.

There are many Churches that claim to trace their existence back to Peter and the apostles; yet none of them are the same as the Church set up in the New Testament (see also GOSPEL and see fig. 1).

COMMENTS ABOUT AUTHORITY

When the apostasy took place, the priesthood was taken from the earth and ordinances, such as baptism could not be performed. Although there were those that went ahead and performed the ordinances, they were not binding. Ordinances that took place during New Testament times were also not recognized as binding and were repeated (see Acts 19:1–8). Just as in ancient times, when the priesthood was taken from the earth it could not be purchased with money nor could one go to school and buy the authority (see Acts 8:14–20). The authority given to the ancient apostles does not authorize just anyone to start their own Church. When all is said and done and we stand at the judgment seat, the Lord will not recognize baptisms done by those Churches that do not have the authority. Just as a court today would not recognize a ticket given by an ice cream truck driver who decides to suddenly start giving out tickets instead of ice cream. Sounds absurd but it is just as absurd for a man to suddenly start his own Church and start baptizing people without priesthood authority. There is only one way to get authority, by the laying on of hands by a worthy appointed member who himself has the authority. That is the way it was done in Old and New Testament times; this is the way it is done today. Following are some scriptural evidences of the need for authority.

> Ye have not chosen me but I have chosen you. (John 15:16)

> And no man taketh this honour unto himself, but he that is called of God, as was Aaron. (Heb. 5:4)

Though Paul had a vision and saw the resurrected Lord. He did not actually get the priesthood until the apostles laid their hands on his head and conferred him to the priesthood. And Paul did not get the Holy Ghost until Ananias laid his hands upon his head and gave it to him (Acts 9:3–18; 13:1–3).

Cornelius had a visitation from an angel but he still had to go to Peter for baptism because Peter had the authority (Acts 10:1–48).

BAPTISM FOR THE DEAD

(see also GOSPEL PREACHED TO THE DEAD)

Question 1

1 Corinthians 15:29 discusses baptism for the dead. Why is it in the form of a question?

Answer 1

Let's take a look at the verse:

> Else what shall they do which are baptized for the dead, if the dead rise not at all? Why are they then baptized for the dead? (1 Cor. 15:29)

The reason Paul formed this scripture into a question is that he is answering a question about resurrection with a question, i.e., a rhetorical question. The saints were wondering if there would be a resurrection (1 Cor. 15:21–22). Paul in essence is saying to the saints of that time, yes, there is a resurrection and that is why you are performing baptism for the dead.

BAPTISM NECESSITY

Question 1

In 1 John 1:7 it states, "the blood of Jesus Christ, His Son, cleanseth us from all sin." If this is the case, why do Mormons believe that baptism gives a remission of sins?

Answer 1

Mormons believe the blood of Jesus Christ cleanses sin through repentance, for all sins except a sin against the Holy Ghost and murder (see MURDER). Mormons also believe that baptism gives a remission of sins. A look at the scriptures reveals that Christ's atonement for sins and baptism for the remission of sins are related. The apostle Paul said, *"without shedding of blood is no remission"* (Heb. 9:22; italics added). By being baptized is the shedding of Christ's blood available to us for the remission of sins. Let's take a look at the verses that reveal baptism is for the remission of sins.

> Then Peter said unto them, Repent, and be baptized every one of you in the name of Jesus Christ for the remission of sins, and ye shall receive the gift of the Holy Ghost. (Acts 2:38)

There have been enemies of the Church that have tried to rephrase Acts 2:38 and say that the Greek meaning of *for* is *because of* and thus, they claim baptism is because of remission of sins and not for the remission of sins. This is an obvious twisting of the scriptures to try and get it to say what you want it to say. Can you imagine if we took every word "for" in the scriptures and changed it to "because of?" Needless to say, there would be a lot of confusion.

The fact baptism gives a remission of sins is seen throughout the scriptures, lets take a look at some of the verses.

> John did baptize in the wilderness, and preach the baptism of repentance for the remission of sins. (Mark 1:4)

> John preached the baptism of, repentance, *for the remission of sins.* (Luke 3: 3; italics added)

> arise and be baptized and *wash away your sins.* (Acts 22:16; italics added) that he might *sanctify and*

cleanse it with the washing of water. (Eph. 5:26; italics added)

by the *washing* of regeneration. (Titus 3: 5; italics added)

the like figure whereunto *even baptism* doth also now save us. (1 Peter 3: 21; italics added)

Question 2

The apostle Paul stated:

For Christ sent me not to baptize, but to preach the gospel. (1 Cor. 1:17)

Paul also said this about baptism:

I thank God that I baptized none of you, but Crispus and Gaius.

Lest any should say that I baptized in my own name.

And I baptized also the house of Stephanas: besides, I know not whether I baptized any other. (1 Cor. 1:14–16)

Do these verses prove that baptism is not a necessary ordinance?

Answer 2

There are numerous scriptures showing the necessity of baptism. In this question we have a few verses from the entire Bible that only appear to say differently. But in reality, it only needs to be looked at in the true context of the situation.

The reason for Paul's statement is because he is having problems with factions. Part of what Paul did was work to resolve conflict, and correct when needed. Paul *seems* to minimize baptism for one reason. The Corinthian's were using *Paul's personal baptisms* to promote their factions. The fact is, Paul was *not* minimizing the importance of baptism, but *who* baptized them. That is why in these verses Paul states he was glad he was not the one who baptized all of them. He was only glad that he had baptized Crispus and Gaius. He even emphasized the fact it was not important who baptized them by stating he could not remember baptizing many of them except Stephanas's household. Paul stated *the reason* in 1 Corinthians 1:15, *"Lest any should say that I baptized in mine own name."* Paul was obviously trying to solve a problem if he had to worry that *a rumor was going around that he was baptizing in his name.* I would also thank God, just as Paul did, if this were happening to me ("I thank God that I baptized none of you"). Paul had seen that the Corinthian saints were *turning to there own wisdom* and not to Christ's. He further reprimands them by saying in 1 Corinthians 1:19, "I will destroy the wisdom of the wise and will bring to nothing the understanding of the prudent."

Paul knew and believed that baptism was a necessary ordinance. In fact, he later told the Corinthian saints,

> For by one Spirit are we *all* baptized into one body.
> (1 Cor. 12–13; italics added)

Paul would not teach a useless unessential principle of salvation, and then require *all* to receive it. A look through the scriptures reveals that not only Paul knew this, but John the Baptist, Peter, James, John, and Jesus as well. Jesus said this to his apostles:

> And he said unto them, Go ye into all the world, and preach the gospel to every creature. He that believeth *and is baptized* shall be saved; but he that believeth not shall be damned. (Mark 16:15–16; italics added)

Note that the savior did not say *"or is baptized."* The Savior meant both "believe *and* be baptized" by proper authority (see APOSTASY AND AUTHORITY). Now let's take a look at *a few of the many* scriptures revealing that baptism is essential for salvation in addition to those already listed:

Jesus answered, Verily, verily, I say unto thee, Except a man be born of water [baptized] and of the Spirit, he cannot enter into the kingdom of God. (John 3:5)

even baptism doth also now save us. (1 Pet. 3:21)

if you are not baptized you reject the counsel of God. (Luke 7:30)

For as many of you as have been baptized into Christ have put on Christ. (Gal. 3:27)

And Jesus answered . . . The baptism of John, was it from heaven, or of men? Answer me. (Mark 11:29–30)

Without modern revelation, gospel doctrines degrade. In the fifth century, before the LDS Church ever came to be, it was universally agreed and accepted that every adult needed baptism in order to obtain salvation in the kingdom of heaven. In fact, there was such an assurance that baptism was a necessary ordinance that a different dispute arose. The dispute was whether babies should be baptized or not. Those who insisted that babies be baptized felt that if they were not, they would go to hell. Baptism of babies is not necessary because of Christ's atonement and children are not accountable for their sins until the age of eight (Moro. 8:19–22; Mark 10:13–16; D&C 68:27; Moro. 8:11). For centuries religions have known that baptism is essential for salvation. This is why both anciently and today baptisms are done vicariously in temples for those who have passed away without receiving the opportunity (1 Cor. 15:29; D&C 124:29).

BIRTH OF CHRIST

Question 1

The Book of Mormon states Christ was born in Jerusalem

and not in Bethlehem does this mean the Book of Mormon is false?

Answer 1

Let's take a look at the verse:

> And behold, he shall be born of Mary, at Jerusalem which is the land of our forefathers, she being a virgin, a precious and chosen vessel, who shall be overshadowed and conceive by; the power of the Holy Ghost, and bring forth a son, yea, even the Son of God. (Alma 7:10)

Enemies of the Church use this verse to say the Book of Mormon must be false because it states Christ was born in Jerusalem instead of Bethlehem. It actually is a testimony builder of the assurance of the truthfulness of the Book of Mormon. This is because Joseph Smith, as translator of the Book of Mormon, would have obviously known, as we all do, that Christ was born in Bethlehem. For Joseph Smith to record Jerusalem tells you that he wrote it like he saw it. What is the explanation for the record saying Jerusalem? The prophets in America at that time all had ancestors that *were from Jerusalem,* not Bethlehem. The Lord used a location that would make sense to them. Could the Lord have just given them the name Bethlehem? Yes, but it would not have had the meaning to the members at that time. Of course the two cities are so close; one is essentially a suburb of the other. Even today many of us live in a suburb, but often say we live in the city for purposes of people knowing the location. For example, it doesn't mean much to a foreigner to say someone lives in Pomona, but it does to say they live in Los Angeles.

The prophet Isaiah prophesied that a virgin would bear a son, and call his name Immanuel. Of course the virgin called his name Jesus, *not* Immanuel. Later he was known as Immanuel. Thus, there are times specifics are not necessary to get the point across. Even the Bible says Christ would be born in Jerusalem (City of David)

(Luke 2:11; 2 Sam. 5:7, 9; 1 Chr. 11:5, 7; etc.). In one section of the Bible even an angel said Jesus would be born in Jerusalem (City of David) (see Luke 2:11). The other important point is this, after the first publication of the Book of Mormon, and many people had read it some grammatical errors, etc., were found. Joseph Smith fixed many of the grammatical errors in the next addition. He did not change the name Jerusalem to Bethlehem because it is not a mistake (see also CHANGES TO THE BOOK OF MORMON).

BLACKS AND THE PRIESTHOOD

Question 1

The LDS Church has often been persecuted because the African Americans in the Church did not originally have the opportunity to hold the priesthood but later this rule was changed.

Did the change that allowed African Americans to receive the priesthood come because of persecution and not because of revelation?

Answer 1

The change in policy that occurred in the 1970s came for one reason—it was the Lord's desire. During the law of Moses only Levites could hold the Aaronic Priesthood. Was that prejudice? The Lord said, "Ye have not chosen me, but I have chosen you, and ordained you" (John 15:16). It is very apparent that the Lord chooses who and when the people can hold the priesthood.

It should be noted this instance of the Lord changing a policy is *not* the only time the Lord has done this. For example, it was also ruled that the Savior and his apostles would *not* go among the gentiles (Matt. 10:5–6, 15:24) *the gentiles* were even compared to as dogs by the Savior himself (Matt. 15:26). Yet later this ruling was *changed* and the apostles did go among the gentiles (Matt. 28:19–20, Acts 10:1-48).

Other examples, just to name a few, include:

1. God commanded circumcision *forever* (Gen. 17:10–11) and later revoked it (Acts 15, Gal. 5: 2-3).

2. At one time, women could not speak in the Churches (1 Cor. 14:34–35). Yet during other times they worked with Paul (Rom. 16:1–4), some women were even prophetesses (Luke 2:36).

3. The law of Moses was in full force during Old Testament times and withdrawn during New Testament times (Matt. 5:17).

4. At one time, divorce was not allowed then later under certain circumstances it was permitted (Matt. 19:8–9).

The fact is the LDS Church has been without prejudice from the beginning. When the Church was first organized, many other religions would allow African Americans to join their churches, but forced them to meet at different times or in different meeting places. African Americans have *always* been welcome in the LDS Church. Baptism for African Americans has been allowed since the Church's beginning. There were Mormon African Americans with the Saints when they crossed the plains. Did *the Lord* change the policy because of persecution? It is not known, but the Church survived much greater persecution because of the Book of Mormon than it ever did from the priesthood policy. It was time for the African Americans to receive the priesthood, the revelation was given and they have had the opportunity ever since. The Saints knew the African Americans would receive the priesthood much sooner than the persecution started. As early as 1852 Brigham Young said that the "time will come when they will have the privilege of all we have the privilege of and more."[14]

There was *no* revelation given on when it would happen. Many opinions of Church leaders and members were expressed concerning the date but again no revelation. When the word came, elation and happiness spread through the Church that a revelation had come from God above that our black brothers could hold the priesthood. The Book of Mormon says this:

> He inviteth them all to come unto him and partake of his goodness; and he denieth none that come unto him, *black and white,* bond and free, male and female. (2 Ne. 26)

Yes, changes are made in *policy,* just as with the times of Christ, but on the other hand the *gospel* itself is unchangeable. That is why, just as at the time of Christ, the Church still has apostles and prophets unlike most other religions on the earth today.

Question 2

Why did the Lord choose not to originally give the priesthood to the African Americans?

Answer 2

In the book of Isaiah, the Lord said this:

> For my thoughts are not your thoughts, neither are your ways my ways, saith the Lord. (Isa. 55:8)

The Lord has chosen when the African Americans could and could not hold the priesthood. The reason the African Americans could not originally hold the priesthood is revealed in the scriptures. It goes back to the time of Adam and his son Cain. The Bible tells us because of Cain's sin of killing his brother Abel, Cain was cursed with a "mark" (Gen. 4:15). This mark was black skin, and all the lineage of Cain inherited the same mark (Moses 7:22). With the flood of Noah, everyone on earth was killed that didn't get on the ark. Obviously for there to be black people on the earth today, there would have had to be a black person on Noah's Ark in order to carry forth the mark and lineage. This is exactly what happened. Ham, Noah's son, married a descendant of Cain, whose name was Egyptus. The curse continued through Ham's posterity. The word Ham means "swarthy" or "black" and the word Egyptus means, "that which is forbidden." Although Ham was forbidden to marry Egyptus, he did it anyway. Because of the curse given to Cain, he and all his posterity—through Ham were "despised among all people" (Moses 7:8). They were also forbidden to hold the priesthood. It may not seem fair that all of Cain's posterity received the curse when they were innocent of the sin, but it was not the Churches decision it was the Lord's decision, and his ways are not our ways. During ancient Bible times Enoch would not even teach the Gospel to Cain's posterity (Moses 7:12). The great prophet Abraham commanded his son Isaac not to marry anyone from Cain's posterity (Canaanites) because of this mark (Gen. 24:3). Was this prejudice? Those who question why the LDS Church did not originally give the priesthood to the African Americans are also questioning why God did not want Isaac to marry anyone with the mark of dark skin. Are you willing to question God on this doctrine?

BLOOD ATONEMENT

(see also MURDER; PROPHECY; and SACRIFICE)

Question 1

Does the LDS Church believe in a doctrine known as blood atonement? Is it true that according to this doctrine if a person murders he must atone for the sin himself with his own blood?

Answer 1

The doctrine of blood atonement as stated in 1 John 1:7 is as follows: "*If* we walk in the light, as he is in the light, we have fellowship one with another, and *the blood* of Jesus Christ his Son cleanseth us from *all* sin." Thus, the Savior's blood atoned for our sins but we need to be careful about the words "all sin" in the verse above. In 1 John 3:15 it states: "and ye know that no murderer hath eternal life abiding in him." The *Savior* himself *also* stated that those who willfully deny the Holy Ghost will have *no* forgiveness for sins in this life nor in the life to come (Matt. 12:31–32). Thus we see there are *exceptions* to the rule that the Savior's blood atonement cleanses us from *all* sin. Because of these exceptions, there are times the Savior's blood atonement does not atone for certain sins.

Murder, just as a sin against the Holy Ghost, has no forgiveness in this life or the life to come. However, there is an important difference between these two sins. Those who commit the unpardonable sin against the Holy Ghost will spend the rest of eternity in Outer Darkness. Murderers also do not have forgiveness in this life or the life to come. But a murderer's sin is a pardonable sin. Murderers can still inherit a level of salvation namely the Telestial Kingdom. In this life there is no forgiveness for murder, and as far as the earthly laws allow the murderer should atone for his own sin with his own blood.[15]

The LDS Church believes in capital punishment as handled by the laws and courts of the land and as declared in D&C 42:79.

Of course during New Testament and Old Testament times capital punishment was also practiced (Heb. 9:22; Gen. 9:6). Obviously, the laws of the land were different at that time. Those who think that capital punishment is wrong need only look at the scriptures. To say that capital punishment is wrong would be like saying God is wrong. To some it may not seem fair that God would ask this, but was it fair that Jesus had to die for your sins and mine?

BOOK OF MORMON

(see also CHANGES TO THE BOOK OF MORMON; SCRIPTURE)

Question 1

Was the idea for the Book of Mormon taken from a book called the "Spaulding Manuscript" that was written in the 1800s?

Answer 1

Those of you asking what the Spaulding Manuscript is are not alone. The reason most people have not heard of it is because this theory is so off base that even most enemies of the LDS Church have decided to let this one go. The Spaulding Manuscript is a fictional story published in the 1800s after the manuscript was found. In 1833, "Doctor" Philastus Hurlbut was excommunicated from the LDS Church for repeated acts of immorality. Hurlbut wanted to discredit the Book of Mormon and came up with a story that Joseph Smith had got the idea for the Book of Mormon from a book written by Solomon Spaulding. No one could find the manuscript until 1884. The story is about a group of Romans who were blown off course while traveling to England. They landed in North America and one of the Romans kept a history of his experiences among eastern American Indians. Once the manuscript was found and published, enemies of the Church, along with everyone else, realized there was absolutely no correlation. I bring up the question here only to show how far Satan will go to try and discredit the Book of Mormon. Satan wants little more than to keep mankind from finding the strait and narrow path.

Question 2

Did Joseph Smith write the Book of Mormon?

Answer 2

To anyone who thinks Joseph Smith could have written such a complex book of scripture, which coincides with the Bible in every way, must think of the challenge. If you were to do the same you would need to convince your own father, mother, and every brother and sister you have that the book is not a fraud. You would then need to convince millions of other people. Of these millions of people, there would have to be some of the most sophisticated scientists, doctors, and lawyers in the world that would be willing to give their lives for the book and the religion.

After you wrote the book, you would have to find eleven witnesses that would say they saw the plates you transcribed them from. Three of the witnesses would have to claim to have seen an angel of God. All eleven of your witnesses must never deny their testimony even unto death. Now think this through carefully—could you really write this book and find all of these people? Joseph Smith was willing to live through a life of persecution and torment and eventually die defending and sustaining the Book of Mormon and Christ's restored Church. Joseph's wife Emma did not go to Salt Lake with the rest of the saints. She stayed behind and remarried a Methodist.

Thus, her influences in the Church were all gone. It is more than interesting that Emma had lived through the torment and persecution with the prophet Joseph and had nearly all influences of the Church gone but she never denied her testimony and in fact was an instigator of getting things going again in Nauvoo. She encouraged her son to be president of a branch off known as the RLDS Church or more recently the Community of Christ. If Emma knew Joseph was faking the whole thing she certainly would have let it go.

Parents know their boys. If a mom and dad raised a boy, who lied and cheated and then one day at the age of fourteen, this boy came to his parents and said he had a vision and was going to translate a book of scriptures, the parent would say "right, go to your room." But Joseph Smith's parents believed him. They followed him where he went and died knowing that their son was telling the truth.

Another miraculous thing Joseph Smith accomplished was to translate an ancient papyrus. A man brought an ancient papyrus that he found from the catacombs in Egypt to Joseph Smith because he heard that the prophet had the ability to translate. The LDS Church placed fragments of these ancient writings *on display* and welcomed scholars to examine them. Thus, even if you could make an effort to make up your own book of scripture, you would have to be able to translate ancient Egyptian writings and put fragments from these original papyri for all to see and inspect.

Another important fact is, The Book of Mormon had many authors just as the Bible had many authors. For example, in the Bible, Matthew, Mark, Luke, John, Paul, etc., all have their own writing styles. In the Book of Mormon, Moroni, Alma, Nephi, Mormon, King Benjamin, and others had their own writing styles. C. Wade Brown in his book *The First Page of the Golden Plates* compares some of these styles.[16] You will see in the following examples it would be quite impossible for Joseph Smith to have forged the Book of Mormon. Dr. Wade divides the Book of Mormon by author and compares different phases unique to each author. For example, a statement used to express the action of lifting up your hand can be said many different ways. Let's take a look at how different authors like Nephi, King Benjamin, Mormon, and others use the following five phrases:

Lift Up His Hand

Dividing the Book of Mormon in this manner can help us understand the differences between authors. How does it help as to the use of word combinations? Consider how an ancient prophet might describe the action of a person lifting or raising up his hand or arm away from his body.

Nephi, expressed it this way; "lifted up his hand."

But Isaiah, quoted by Nephi and others from the Old testament, often used a different expression. Isaiah said "his hand is stretched out." Isaiah wrote "his hand is stretched out" six times.

But no one else used Isaiah's combination of words. In the Book of Mormon "his hand is stretched out" is a phrase unique to Isaiah.

King Benjamin never said "lifted up his hand" or "his hand stretched out." He used the word combination "extended his arm."

No other writer used Benjamin's word combination "extended his arm."

Mormon never wrote "lifted up his hand," "his hand is stretched out," or "extended his arm." Mormon expression was "stretched forth his hand" and he wrote it eight times in six separate sections.

The only other writer to use the phrase "stretched forth his hand" was Mormon son Moroni who used it just once. Moroni's speech patterns are very close to his father's, as would be expected from their relationship as father and son, fellow military leaders, authors, and prophets.

Alma never wrote "lifted up his hand," "his hand is stretched out," or "extended his arm." Instead he used "put forth his hand."

No one else used the same phrase.

As mentioned, Moroni followed the pattern of his father, saying "stretched forth his hand." He used the phrase while narrating the Jaredite history.

Each of these authors had his own unique word combination for describing the same actions of raising a hand or arm.

Began Again To

Occasionally the Nephites or Lamanites discontinued

an action and later returned to the same activity. In eleven separate sections Mormon described this recommencing of an activity. In all but one instance he used the word combination "began again to." The exception was when he described a certain mental instead of physical activity.

Again it was only his son and companion who used the phrase "began again to," and Moroni only used it once.

Here is a small but significant fact; other authors described the same renewal of action but reversed the word combination. For example, Nephi wrote *"again began* to."

And Zeniff also wrote *"again began* to."

Some other Nephite writers just said "again" to report the return to an activity.

I *Do* Know

Consider another example of this phenomenon. Alma the younger was emphatic in expressing his testimony. On over one hundred occasions Book of Mormon prophets expressed their beliefs by using such phrases as "I know." But Alma put special emphasis on his expression by stating "I *do* know."

In one of his sections Alma stated "Behold, I testify unto you that I *do* know that these things whereof I have spoken are true." In his next section, he again used the word combination, saying "This much I *do* know, that the Lord Go hath power to do all things which are according to his word.

Alma used the word combination "I *do* know" a total of eight times in four entirely separated sections.

No one else ever used it—except—his missionary junior companion Amulek. After working with Alma and hearing him say it many times, Amulek repeated the phrase " I *do* know" once himself.

When I think of Amulek using Alma's phrase, I can't help thinking of Elder Sewell.

He was my first missionary companion and he also had

a pet expression. Instead of swearing, because missionaries don't swear, he said "cottonpicker." When I heard that phrase during the first days of my mission I thought it was the silliest thing that could be said. After a few weeks I became used to it. By the time Elder Sewell went home the phrase stayed in our mission because . . . I used it—too often.

Instead of "I *do* know," the popular word combination repeated throughout the Book of Mormon is "I know." It extends from Nephi's first page "I know that the record which I make is true" to Moroni's "I know that thou [God] workest unto the children of men according to their faith." It is used so commonly in the Book of Mormon that we might sometimes be reminded of a Latter Day Saint testimony meeting.

Shaken from the Faith

Occasionally, uniqueness of authorship in the Book of Mormon is demonstrated not in the combination of words but in the context of how particular words are used. A word may be common to many authors but used in a specific thought pattern by only one.

For example, consider the phrase "shaken." In the Book of Mormon, "shaken" is utilized by several writers. But only Jacob used "shaken" in reference to testimony or faith. In one of his sections he stated "the righteous fear them not for they love the truth and are not shaken" (2 Ne. 9:40). In a second section he stated "I will unfold this mystery unto you if I do not by any means get shaken from my firmness in the spirit" (Jacob 4:18). In a third section he stated "Sherem . . . had hope to shake me from the faith. . . . I could not be shaken" (Jacob 7:5).

Thus Jacob used "shaken" in three of his four sections but only in reference to adherence to personal faith. All other authors who used the phrase wrote it in reference to things or people being physically moved or rattled.

These are just a few examples of word combinations that identify particular authors in the Book of Mormon. Eventually several hundred word combinations were identified as unique to particular authors or groups of authors.

Moroni's Preface to the Book of Mormon

After several years of studying differences in word combinations it became easy with just a few sentences to identify various Nephite authors. For example, historically it has been understood that the preface to the Book of Mormon was translated from the plates and was written by Moroni. An early edition even had his name attached to it. However, in recent years some have questioned his authorship and have suggested that it was composed by someone else.

But the preface contains nearly a dozen word combination which are characteristic of Moroni. This makes it difficult to believe that someone else could have composed the text but included Moroni's personal language patterns. The study of word combinations reinforces the historic claims of this and other issues.[17]

Other comparisons are noted in the FARMS *Review of Books* as follows:

> "Holy One of Israel" is frequently used by Jacob in a discourse explaining Isaiah passages. "Lord of Hosts" is used extensively in another discourse by Jacob on a *different* subject. "Lord of the vineyard" is found *only* in the prophecy of Zenos. "The Lord God Omnipotent" is found *only* in King Benjamin's speech. "Lamb of God" is used *almost exclusively* in Nephi's writings. This looks suspiciously like evidence for *independent authorship* of Nephi, Zenos, Jacob, and King Benjamin's speech.[18]

There are many other evidences that the Book of Mormon is true. Here are some examples:

1. Even today there are ancient traditions in Mesoamerica that a white God had once come to their

people and taught and healed them just as recorded in the Book of Mormon (3 Ne. 11–26). This is why the Indians worshiped Cortez when he first arrived. Quetzalcoatl (Jesus) became the symbol of this white God to the Mayans. The Mayans believed Quetzalcoatl created all things, had a virgin birth, healed the sick, and performed miracles ("The Common Source of Religious Truth," *Improvement Era*, 1939, Vol. xxxii. December, 1939. No. 12).

2. Dark-skinned and light-skinned people existed in ancient America just as recorded in the Book of Mormon. In the Book of Mormon they were separated as "Lamanites" (Indians) and "Nephites." The Lamanites were dark-skinned and the Nephites were light-skinned. There are colored murals drawn on walls in ancient American ruins showing this known fact (Hunter, Milton R. *Archaeology and the Book of Mormon* [Salt Lake City: Deseret Book Co., 1956], 181, 188, 202, 209, 211-214).

3. In the Book of Mormon Alma set forth the coinage (Alma 11). The smallest coin was known as a "senine." In Jerusalem the smallest coin was the "farthing." When Jesus visited the Americas he did not teach a different gospel! He taught the same principles. Part of what he taught was very similar to what Jesus had taught in Jerusalem known as the Sermon on the Mount (Matt. 5). It is interesting that when Jesus taught in America he used a language that would be familiar to them. If Jesus had said "farthing" the Nephites would not have known what he was talking about. Jesus used the word "senine" which was familiar to the people (3 Ne. 12:26). As mentioned above it was in Alma of the Book of Mormon when coinage was set

forth. If Joseph Smith had written the Book of Mormon it would have been nothing short of phenomenal that he would have remembered such a small detail that was only described briefly nearly two hundred pages prior. Those who transcribed for Joseph Smith stated that Joseph would verbally state the translation of the plates and the scribe would write what he said he did not take notes as he went, Joseph never asked for a sentence to be repeated back to him. Knowing the Book of Mormon was transcribed in this manner shows how absolutely impossible it would have been for Joseph Smith to keep straight all the civilizations, buildings, geographic locations, tools, animals, names, rivers, and roads. The Book of Mormon also fulfills Bible prophecies recorded in Ezekiel 37:15–19 and Isaiah 29:4, 11–14 and others. Bible characters like King Zedekiah and his sons are also harmonized in the Book of Mormon time line, along with the prophet Jeremiah and others.

4. Ancient writings have been found and published by a man who grew up in South America. This man's name was Fernando de Alva Ixtlilxochitl. He lived from 1578 to 1650. He recorded a history of his ancestors. His writings are similar to the Book of Mormon. Milton R. Hunter writes:

> Next to the Book of Mormon, the *Works of Ixtlilxochitl* gives the most reliable and complete account of the history and culture of the early Toltecs (Nephites) and the Lamanites, the ancestors of the American Indians. Ixtlilxochitl wrote the history of the inhabitants of ancient America—the Jaredites who came from the Tower of Babel, the Nephites, Lamanites, and Mulekites, who came from Jerusalem—from written documents received from his ancestors and from oral traditions received from Indians who knew the traditions of their people. His

first work was written about A.D. 1600 and his second about 1608.[19]

Do you doubt that Joseph Smith translated the Book of Mormon from ancient golden plates? If I told you that I had the ancient plates in my possession, and I welcomed you and scholars to look through the plates, and to even date them by any means they see fit and it all checked out, then would you believe? The answer to this question is no you would not. There is no way I can persuade you. There is only one way to know if the Book of Mormon is true and that is to read it and *pray* and ask God (Moro. 10:3–5). Neither I nor anyone else has the plates because God wants you to find out for yourself.

In the parable of Lazarus and the rich man, the rich man wanted to go back to earth and warn his brethren so they didn't end up like him. Abraham said this to the rich man:

> Abraham saith unto him, They have Moses and the prophets; let them hear them. And he said, Nay father Abraham: but if one went unto them from the dead, they will repent. And he said unto him, If they hear not Moses and the prophets *neither will they be persuaded though one rose from the dead.* (Luke 16:29–31; italics added)

Joseph Smith did not write the Book of Mormon. He translated it from the gold plates.

Question 3

Did Joseph Smith read a book called *View of the Hebrews* and from this book get enough ideas and facts about Indians to write The Book of Mormon?

Answer 3

Ever since the Book of Mormon was published in 1830 enemies have tried to find an explanation to its coming forth except for the real one. Joseph Smith did not write the Book of Mormon. The task of writing your own Book of Mormon is impossible. Like the examples written above computerized word analysis of the Book of Mormon unmistakably reveals separate Book of Mormon writers.[20] The other very obvious point is that Joseph Smith received his vision from God the Father and Jesus Christ *three years before* the book *View of the Hebrews* was even written. Joseph Smith told others of this visitation and received persecution for it from the time he was *fourteen years old*. No one in the 1800s even questioned Joseph Smith about *View of the Hebrews* because they knew Joseph's claims occurred before. No one even brought up a similarity until the 1900s.

The Book of Mormon gives you the reader a promise. If you read and pray about the Book of Mormon and ask if it is true God will give you the answer (Moro. 10:3–5). I have done this myself and have received the answer that it is true. My answer was so powerful that no mortal man with a list of "reasons" could ever convince me otherwise. You can also receive this conviction but first you must read and pray.

Question 4

Did the book *View of the Hebrews* have a lot of the same conclusions and evidences that are written in the Book of Mormon?

Answer 4

There are many more dissimilarities between the Book of Mormon and *View of the Hebrews* than there are similarities. To answer this question let me give the reader some information about the book View of the Hebrews. It is a book about a theory. A minister in 1823 theorized that the American Indians were of the lost ten tribes. Remarkably his theory had areas of *some* truth. In order to prove areas of his theory he discussed Bible evidences as well as the evidences that have been found on the American continent.

Some of the evidences he found are discussed and are true evidences both scriptural and physical. A truth is a truth and can only be stated so many ways thus, some of the points he brought up "parallel" what is stated in the Book of Mormon. Because of this, enemies of the LDS Church say that Joseph Smith copied him. For reasons stated in question 3 as well as many other reasons it was impossible for Joseph to have copied from Ethan Smith, in fact there is absolutely no evidence on this earth that Joseph Smith even heard of the book *View of the Hebrews* while he was translating the Book of Mormon.

Theories are an easy thing to postulate. Enemies of the LDS Church have attempted to use the false theory that Joseph Smith copied from Ethan Smith. It would be just as easy for me to postulate that Ethan Smith himself, a minister, received guidance from Satan as he wrote the book *View of the Hebrews*. How would I defend this theory? Satan certainly knew the entire Indian history and that the prophet Mormon had kept a record. He also knew Moroni buried the record in the ground. Ethan Smith was a minister who had denied the existence of present-day miracles and new revelation.[21] Satan found it easy to use Ethan Smith as an instrument to bring forth a book with partial truths in order to deceive the elect into believing that Joseph Smith copied from him. See how easy it is.

The fact is many of the points that parallel those in the Book of Mormon don't parallel as closely as it may first seem. Those who fight against the LDS Church list the similarities between the books as proof the Book of Mormon is not true. To list similarities or parallels is possible for nearly everything. Even black and white are similar in the sense they are both colors. To show you how simple it is I have included a table showing the parallels between the Book of Mormon, the Bible, *View of the Hebrews* and *Star Wars*! (see Table 1 on the following page).

Making parallels is easy. Years ago, LDS Church

TABLE 1. PARALLELS

	View of the Hebrews	Holy Bible	Book of Mormon	*Star Wars*
Belief in Life after Death	X	X	X	X
Communication from the heavens	X	X	X	X
Deterioration of a nation	X	X	X	X
Wars and bloodshed	X	X	X	X
Use of different languages	X	X	X	X
Presence of good and evil	X	X	X	X
Contains the words *and, or, is*	X	X	X	X
Contains the words *of, the, if*	X	X	X	X
Prophecies foretold	X	X	X	X
Includes travel	X	X	X	X

leader B. H. Roberts made a list of the parallels between the Book of Mormon and View of the Hebrews. He did this as a preparation to defend the Church only. In all his reading he could only find around eighteen parallels. Nevertheless enemies of the LDS Church have attempted to use these parallels against the Church but they have been able to deceive very few. As mentioned above many of the parallels only appear to be similar to the Book of Mormon. For example, *View of the Hebrews* quotes prophesies from Isaiah concerning the scattering of Israel and so does the Book of Mormon. A close look reveals that a mere 13 percent of the quoted scriptures are the same. Any person would have to ask themselves when it comes to prophesies concerning the scattering and gathering of Israel is it possible to bring up Bible prophesies without bringing up Isaiah? Hugh Nibley stated the following regarding the book *View of the Hebrews.*

> So after all Ethan Smith turns in a perfect score; not a single blemish mars the target. In every case where the Book of Mormon might have borrowed from him, it might much more easily have borrowed from the Bible or prevailing popular beliefs. In the few cases where he deals in common with the Book of Mormon with matters not treated in those other sources, the two books are completely at variance.[22]

John W. Welch also discusses some interesting "unparallels" concerning *View of the Hebrews* and the Book of Mormon as follows:

View of the Hebrews: "An Unparallel"

> 2 Nephi 33:2 "Wherefore, they cast many things away which are written and esteem them as things of naught."

The claim has been made before, and has recently been raised again, that Joseph Smith specifically copied the main structure and many details in the Book of Mormon from Ethan Smith's 1823 *View of the Hebrews.* Alleged parallels between these two books have led some to esteem the Book of Mormon lightly, "as a thing of naught."

Since the alleged points of contact are scattered throughout *View of the Hebrews* and in some cases are claimed to be quite specific, this assertion becomes plausible only if we assume that Joseph knew *View of the Hebrews* quite well and implicitly accepted it as accurate. If he did so, then he should have followed it—or at least should have not contradicted it—on its major points.

But this does *not* turn out to be the case. Since several people have pointed out alleged "parallels" between the Book of Mormon and *View of the Hebrews,* consider the following "unparallels" that weaken, if not completely undermine, the foregoing hypothesis:

1. *View of the Hebrews* begins with a chapter on the destruction of Jerusalem by the Romans. It has nothing to say, however, about the destruction in Lehi's day by the Babylonians.

2. *View of the Hebrews* tells of specific heavenly signs that marked the Roman destruction of Jerusalem. Joseph Smith ignores these singular and memorable details.

3. Chapter 2 lists many prophecies about the restoration of Israel, including Deuteronomy 30; Isaiah 11, 18, 60, 65; Jeremiah 16, 23, 30–31, 35–37; Zephaniah 3; Amos 9; Hosea and Joel. These scriptures are essential to the logic and fabric of *View of the Hebrews,* yet, with the sole exception of Isaiah 11, none of them appear in the Book of Mormon.

4. Chapter 3 is the longest chapter in *View of the Hebrews*. It produces numerous "distinguished Hebraisms" as "proof" that the American Indians are Israelites. Hardly any of these points are found in the Book of Mormon, as one would expect if Joseph Smith were using *View of the Hebrews* or trying to make his book persuasive. For example, *View of the Hebrews* asserts repeatedly that the Ten Tribes came to America via the Bering Strait,

which they crossed on "dry land." According to *View of the Hebrews,* this opinion is unquestionable, supported by all the authorities.

From there *View of the Hebrews* claims that the Israelites spread from north to east and then to the south at a very late date. These are critical points for *View of the Hebrews,* since Amos 8:11–12 prophesies that the tribes would go from the north to the east. Population migrations in the Book of Mormon, however, always move from the south to the north.

5. *View of the Hebrews* reports that the Indians are Israelites because they use the word "Hallelujah." Here is one of the favorite proofs of *View of the Hebrews,* a dead giveaway that the Indians are Israelites. Yet the word is never used in the Book of Mormon.

   Furthermore, a table showing thirty-four Indian words or sentence fragments with Hebrew equivalents appears in *View of the Hebrews.* No reader of the book could have missed this chart. If Joseph Smith had wanted to make up names to use in the Book of Mormon that would substantiate his claim that he had found some authentic western hemisphere Hebrew words, he would have jumped at such a ready-made list! Yet not one of these thirty-four Hebrew/Indian words (e.g., *Keah, Lani, Uwoh, Phale, Kurbet,* etc.) has even the remotest resemblance to any of the 175 words that appear for the first time in the Book of Mormon.

6. *View of the Hebrews* says the Indians are Israelites because they carry small boxes with them into battle. These are to protect them against injury. They are sure signs that the Indians' ancestors knew of the Ark of the Covenant! How could Joseph Smith pass up such a distinguished and oft-attested Hebraism as this?! Yet in all Book of Mormon battle scenes, there is not one hint of any such

ark, box, or bag serving as a military fetish.

7. The Indians are Israelites because the Mohawk tribe was a tribe held in great reverence by all the others, to whom tribute was paid. Obviously, to Ethan Smith, this makes the Mohawks the vestiges of the tribe of Levi, Israel's tribe of priests. If Joseph Smith believed that such a tribe or priestly remnant had survived down to his day, he forgot to provide for anything to that effect in the Book of Mormon.

8. The Indians are Israelites because they had a daily sacrifice of fat in the fire and passed their venison through the flame, cutting it into twelve pieces. This great clue of "Israelitishness" is also absent from the Book of Mormon.

9. *View of the Hebrews* maintains that the Indians knew "a distinguished Hebraism," namely "laying the hand on the mouth, and the mouth in the dust." Had Joseph Smith believed this, why is the Book of Mormon silent on this "sure sign of Hebraism" and dozens of others like it?

10. According to *View of the Hebrews,* the Indians quickly lost knowledge that they were all from the same family. The Book of Mormon tells that family and tribal affiliations were maintained for almost one thousand years.

11. *View of the Hebrews* claims that the righteous Indians were active "for a long time," well into recent times, and that their destruction occurred about A.D. 1400, based upon such convincing evidence as tree rings near some of the fortifications of these people. The Book of Mormon implicitly rejects this notion by reporting the destruction of the Nephites in the fourth century A.D.

12. *View of the Hebrews* argues that the Indians are Israelites because they knew the legends of Quetzalcoatl. But the surprise here is that

View of the Hebrews proves beyond doubt that Quetzalcoatl was none other than—not Jesus—but Moses! "Who could this be but *Moses,* the ancient legislator in Israel?" Quetzalcoatl was white, gave laws, required penance (strict obedience), had a serpent with green plumage (brazen, fiery-flying serpent in the wilderness), pierced ears (like certain slaves under the law of Moses), appeased God's wrath (by sacrifices), was associated with a great famine (in Egypt), spoke from a volcano (Sinai), walked barefoot (removed his shoes), spawned a golden age (seven years of plenty in Egypt—which has nothing to do with Moses, by the way), etc. Besides the fact that the *View of the Hebrews*'s explanation of Quetzalcoatl as Moses is inconsistent with the Book of Mormon, none of these hallmark details associated with Quetzalcoatl are incorporated into the account of Christ's visit to Bountiful in 3 Nephi.

The foregoing twelve points could be multiplied literally seven times over. In the face of these differences, the few vague similarities pale. Both speak of long migrations for religious reasons; both report wars; both say the people knew how to write and work with metals; and both praise generosity and denounce pride. *View of the Hebrews* speaks of Indian lore that they left a "lost book" back in Palestine. But these points are rather general and inconsequential.

The question has been asked: "Can such numerous and startling points of resemblance and suggestive contact be merely coincidence?" The answer is "yes," not only because the points of resemblance are neither numerous nor startling, but also because the differences far outweigh the similarities. *Why would Joseph have contradicted and ignored* View of the Hebrews *at virtually every turn, if indeed he gave it basic credence?*

An expanded version of this October 1985 research by John W. Welch was published that same year by F.A.R.M.S., entitled "An Unparallel." It and Spencer Palmer's and William Knecht's 1964 article in BYU

Studies *are now available together under the title "View*
of the Hebrews: Substitute for Inspiration?"[23]

It is easy to see that Joseph Smith did not copy from
View of the Hebrews. Anyone searching for a reason not to
believe something can find it. This goes for Jesus, the Bible
and the Book of Mormon etc. Just try and convince many of
the Jews on the earth today to be Christian and they will
have many reasons Jesus is not the Son of God. They will
even show you scriptures about things Christians are not
doing that God commanded long ago like circumcision
(Gen. 17:10–11) and the feast of the Passover (Ex. 12:14).
They will tell you that these commands were meant to be
forever thus Christians are wrong. You can give many of
them answers but the answers often fall upon deaf ears. The
same is true for many people on the earth today regarding
the Book of Mormon. Now let's take a look at some of the
many verses in the scriptures that confirm that the Church
of Jesus Christ of Latter-day Saints and the Book of Mormon are true. It is quite obvious after looking at the following list of verses that Joseph Smith did much more than the
book *View of the Hebrews* ever dreamed of:

1. John 10:16 Jesus said he would visit his other
   sheep this surely would be recorded just as
   claimed in the Book of Mormon (3 Ne. 11–26).

2. Genesis 49:22–26 Jacob's son Joseph (coat of
   many colors) was told his lineage would travel
   over water to the American continent (everlasting
   hills) only the Book of Mormon fulfills the prophecy
   (1 Nephi 5:14). (View of the Hebrews said the
   Indians traveled to America over land).

3. Ezekiel 37:15–19 foretold two records would be
   written, one for Judah and one for Joseph (the
   Bible and the Book of Mormon).

4. Malachi 3:1–2 prophesies that Jesus will suddenly
   come to him temple. Mormons are one of the few

religions on the earth today that even has temples.

5. Malachi 4:5–6 prophesies Elijah the prophet coming to earth to turn our hearts to genealogy work. Elijah did come as prophesied and his visit is recorded in D&C 110:13–15. Mormons have the largest genealogy program in the world.

6. 1 Corinthians 15:29 speaks of baptism for the dead. With the apostasy it was lost but has been restored again because of Joseph Smith and the LDS Church (D&C 124:33–35).

7. Revelation 7:14–15 foretold that the saints would dress in white and work day and night in the temple. Even today the saints dress in white and work in the temple. Some temples are open day and night just as prophesied.

8. Isaiah 29:4 foretold a book that would come from the ground. The Book of Mormon was buried in the ground.

9. Isaiah 29:11–14 foretold that the book that came from the ground would be sealed. It also said it would be given to a man who is "not learned." The Book of Mormon had a seal on the gold plates and was given to Joseph Smith with a third-grade education (JS—H 1:64–65).

10. Revelation 14:6 foretold an angel would come to earth to restore the "everlasting gospel." The angel Moroni came to earth and visited Joseph Smith and is the angel spoken of.

11. Ephesians 4:11–14 states there will be apostles and prophets until there is a unity of all faiths. The LDS Church has apostles and prophets (see also Eph. 2:19–21).

12. Daniel 2:44 and Acts 3:19–22 foretold a restoration of the gospel. The LDS Church is a restored Church.

13. Matthew 24:14 foretells of the great missionary effort that "shall be preached in all the world." There is no greater missionary program in the world than that of the LDS Church.

Is there any other Church that fulfills all of these prophesies except the LDS Church? The answer is no. The Book of Mormon is much to complex to have been written by the prophet Joseph. I ask the reader, how old were you when you understood the Old and New Testament. How old were you when you understood the House of Israel, the scattering and gathering of Israel, King Zedekiah and his sons, the time table of Jeremiah, when Jerusalem was destroyed and how, the law of Moses, Jacob's blessing to his son Joseph, when the gospel would be preached to the gentiles, etc.? How old were you when you understood all these things? When the Book of Mormon was printed Joseph Smith was approximately twenty-five years old with a third grade education. And as mentioned above Joseph Smith was fourteen years old when the whole thing began. The book *View of the Hebrews* with its mere eighteen parallels is nothing compared to the restored Church of Jesus Christ and the Book of Mormon.

Question 5

Did Joseph Smith have access to the book *View of the Hebrews* at his local library?

Answer 5

It appears that Joseph Smith did not have access to the book *View of the Hebrews* at his local library. We know this because his local library required a fee and recorded the name of the person using the library. Neither Joseph Smith, nor any new member of the LDS Church at that time, had their names recorded. It is not surprising that Joseph is not listed as a patron considering the poverty his family was living in. The other point is that Joseph only had a third grade education and was not really into books. His mother said that Joseph, "seemed much less inclined to the perusal of books than any of the rest of our children, but far more given to meditation and deep study." By age eighteen, he still had not read the Bible all the way through.[24]

This statement by Joseph's mother once again brings up the point that Joseph did not have the personal knowledge of the Bible to write the Book of Mormon. Joseph was young with little knowledge, so why would the Lord choose him? Simple,

> No man putteth a piece of new cloth unto an old garment, for that which is put in to fill it up taketh from the garment, and the rent is made worse.
>
> Neither do men put new wine into old bottles: else the bottles break, and the wine runneth out, and the bottles perish: but they put new wine into new bottles, and both are preserved. (Matt. 9:16–17)

Joseph was young and green. The Lord knew Joseph would do it the Lord's way.

Question 6

Oliver Cowdery was from the same hometown as Ethan Smith, the author of *View of the Hebrews*. Could Oliver have brought a copy of the book to Joseph Smith and then the two of them conspire to write the Book of Mormon?

Answer 6

There are several things that make the above theory impossible. Oliver was not Joseph Smith's first scribe, Martin Harris was. Thus, the Book of Mormon transcribing was already underway before Joseph even met Oliver Cowdery. The other point is that after Oliver finished as scribe and the Book of Mormon was published Oliver was actually excommunicated over some unrelated points and was thus kicked out of the Church. What a perfect time it would have been for an angry Oliver to expose Joseph Smith as a fraud but he did not. Let's read the following statement regarding the excommunication of both Oliver Cowdery and another witness David Whitmer:

> It will be remembered that these two men, Oliver Cowdery and David Whitmer, were two of the three special witnesses to the Book of Mormon. It was, therefore, a bold move to excommunicate these men. Although this is outside of the theme we are following in these articles, suppose for a moment that the theory of the world relative to the origin of the Book of Mormon be true—that it was the production of some man—that Joseph Smith was put forward as a figure head—and the three witnesses were induced to become parties to and false witnesses of the fraud that was to be perpetrated on mankind—would Joseph Smith and Sidney Rigdon, under such circumstances, dare to withdraw their fellowship from these men? If the Book of Mormon were a huge scheme to deceive mankind, and Cowdery and Whitmer were parties with Smith and Rigdon to the deception—the latter would hardly venture to cast away the former, for fear they might deny their testimony, expose the fraud, and cause the whole Mormon Church fabric to collapse. If the Book of Mormon had been a mere human production, Joseph Smith and Sidney Rigdon would never have dared to break with these two important witnesses, whatever their wickedness might be. But the bold, independent course pursued in excommunicating them, when their conduct warranted the action, gives very good evidence to us that Joseph Smith and the Church knew that the existence of the Church did not depend on the testimony of these men. The Book of Mormon, being true, it would stand independent of these witnesses, and Joseph knew it. But the most gratifying part of it is, these witnesses to the Book of Mormon, though separated from the Church—excommunicated for unrighteousness—have never denied their testimony or changed it in the least. But the fact of their having uniformly adhered to their testimony, while disconnected with the Church, doubtless adds strength to that testimony, as they stand in the light of disinterested witnesses.[25]

While away from the Church, in front of a court of law, Oliver was called a liar concerning his work in bringing forth the Book of Mormon. Oliver defended the Book of Mormon and said it was true. After Joseph Smith's death Oliver returned to the LDS Church requesting only membership, no office, and was soon re-baptized into the Church. Let's read the following concerning the death of Oliver Cowdery.

> Oliver Cowdery died March 3, 1850, at Richmond, Ray county, Mo. Elder Phineas H. Young, who was present at his death, says: "His last moments were spent in bearing testimony of the truth of the gospel revealed through Joseph Smith, and the power of the holy Priesthood which he had received through his administrations." Oliver Cowdery's half-sister, Lucy P. Young a widow of the late Phineas H. Young, relates that Oliver Cowdery just before breathing his last, asked his attendants to raise him up in bed, that he might talk to the family and his friends, who were present. He then told them to live according to the teachings contained in the Book of Mormon, and promised them, if they would do this, that they would meet him in heaven. He then said, "Lay me down and let me fall asleep." A few moments later he died without a struggle.[26]

Now I would ask the reader if you were about to die and see God would your dying words be a lie? Martin Harris another witness to the Book of Mormon plates also died with a testimony of the Book of Mormon on his lips. The book *View of the Hebrews* had nothing to do with the coming forth of the Book of Mormon.

Question 7

Did B. H. Roberts leave the LDS Church after he learned about the book *View of the Hebrews*?

Answer 7

No, he did not. B. H. Roberts said himself in 1933 that Ethan Smith had nothing to do with the coming forth of the Book of Mormon. After writing the parallels and other documents, B. H. Roberts said:

> I am taking the position that our faith is not only unshaken but unshakable in the Book of Mormon, and therefore we can look without fear upon all that can be said against it.[27]

Question 8

The Book of Mormon says there was silk and linen (Alma 1:29). Is it true that that this is impossible since the silk worm is not in America and neither is the plant that is used to make "linen"?

Answer 8

Concerning the many things found in ancient America Milton R. Hunter states:

> From those graves have been taken the most finely woven, beautiful laces, the most gorgeous wool and cotton cloths, and "fine-twined linen." In fact, various archaeologists maintain that the world has known no races of people who surpassed the predecessors of the Inca civilization in these various handicrafts.[28]

It is not hard to make silk and linen if you know how. For example to make linen you get fibers from plants and you do a lot of soaking and pounding to make the product. Plants in Ancient America like the yucca; maguey and many others were like flax or hemp and have been used to make "linen."

To make silk you get shiny fiber produced by the larvae of certain insects. In ancient America you can use fiber from cocoons gathered from the wild to make "silk." In fact many of the fabrics found in ancient America feel silkier than silk. If you were a Nephite in the Book of Mormon and you made a garment from a shiny fiber gathered from the larvae of an insect that looked and felt like silk would you make up a new name or just call it "silk"? I think most of us would say "silk." And even if you did rename it in a different language a translator may use the word silk so that American's would know what was being referred to. This question is quite trivial but I state it here to show that enemies of the LDS Church, and thus Satan, try to find even insignificant things to lead others away from the truth.

Question 9

The Book of Mormon states there were "many horses" (Enos 1: 21). Were there horses in Ancient America before the Spaniards brought them? What about the words *cattle* and *swine*? Were there cows or pigs in Mesoamerica?

Answer 9

Years ago there was no evidence that horses existed in Mesoamerica until the Spaniards brought them. With more recent excavations along the Yucatan Peninsula definite horse remains, dating to Book of Mormon times, have been found.[29] There is no longer any question that there were horses during Book of Mormon times. Other evidences also exist, for example, there is an ancient building that was constructed many years before the Spaniards came to America with the carving of a horse carved into one of the stones. There is a picture of this horse in a book by Milton R. Hunter called *Archaeology and the Book of Mormon.* Obviously if there were no horses the people would not have carved a horse onto the building.

Enemies of the LDS Church often try to "pick apart" the Book of Mormon with insignificant detractions. Words like cattle and swine are easily explained. Anyone can pick out a word whether it is from the Book of Mormon or the Bible and bring up many different translation variations.

Whether it is Greek, or Reformed Egyptian. Words are translated for one reason—understanding. For example in the Bible Ezekiel 34:27 it states the phrase, "served themselves of them." The Hebrew word for served is "enslaved." You may ask yourself, which is it served or enslaved? We could start a huge discussion and contend with one another over this one word. The point is when a translator translates even by the gift and power of God he must make a decision on which word will have most meaning. Translation is not a process of just sitting and reading. Oliver Cowdery tried to translate and failed, so I doubt translation is an easy process (see D&C 9). Thus, whichever word the Lord chose to help us in our understanding should not be questioned. This goes for animals listed in the Book of Mormon including cattle and swine. It also must be remembered that Nephi may have named these animals with words that were familiar to him. He may have named these animals based upon similar looking animals that he knew names for. The other point is that just as recent excavations have found horses, cattle and swine may be found in the future. Concerning the words *cattle* and *swine* FARMS states,

> *Cattle*
>
> The term cattle is used in the Book of Mormon (Enos 1:21;3 1 Nephi 3:22). Generally we tend to think that this term refers only to cows. However, it is not clear from the Book of Mormon exactly what the term cattle has reference to. The Hebrew word b'hemah, sometimes translated as "cattle" in the Old Testament, can refer to "any large quadruped or animal." The Hebrew word s´eh, also translated as "cattle," usually refers to smaller domesticates such as sheep or goats. The Book of Mormon term could easily refer to any small or large quadruped. There are, of course, many New World species that could fall within this description (see Strong, *A Concise Dictionary of the Words in the Hebrew Bible,* 19).
>
> *Swine*
>
> The term swine is used only twice, once in the

Jaredite period (Ether 9:18) and once by Jesus during his sermon at the temple (3 Ne. 14:6). The Book of Mormon does not claim that the Nephites ate swine as did the Jaredites. (The Jaredites were not under the law of Moses.) Peccaries were well known in Mesoamerica and look very much like domesticated pigs and could easily fit the Book of Mormon designation of swine.[30]

Question 10

In the Book of Mormon it speaks of elephants. Is there proof that elephants existed?

Answer 10

The scripture referred to is in Ether 9:19. The book of Ether tells of a people that lived in America two thousand years before Christ. There were elephants at that time and there has been proof of this found. John L. Sorenson states this:

> Mastodons and mammoths once lived throughout North America and part of South America. They are unquestionably elephants in the eyes of zoologists. The question is how late they lived. Most experts assume they failed to survive down to the time of the Jaredites. The only place they are mentioned in the Book of Mormon is in the Book of Ether, near the beginning of that record (by my calculations of Jaredite chronology, the date must have been before 2500 B.C.). Experts agree that the mammoth, and mastodon could have survived in favored spots much later than the time normally assigned for their extinction. The mastodon has already been dated as late as 5000 B.C. at Devil's Den, Florida, and around the Great Lakes to 4000 B.C. Then there is the remarkable discovery of the remains of a butchered mastodon in Ecuador; pottery associated with the find is said to date to after the time of Christ. In its light, the radiocarbon date around 100 B.C. of horse, mammoth and mastodon remains at St. Petersburg, Florida, does not seem impossible. The Jaredite mention of the elephant a single time—very early in their lineage history—

hints that the creature became extinct in their area soon thereafter. Perhaps the Jaredites themselves killed off the last of the beasts within their zone. But the Jaredites might not have been the only people to record the presence of the big animal. Some North American Indians have recounted legends of "great stiff-legged beasts who could not lie down" and of an animal with a fifth appendage, which came out of its head. Possibly, tribes transmitted through oral tradition some vague remembrance of encounters with these "elephants." The later the beasts survived, the easier it is to accept the reliability of the tradition. In any case, it is possible that the mammoth or mastodon hung on in Mexico at least as late as 2500 B.C.[31]

Joseph Smith was raised in America and he did not see elephants roaming the land. Thus, he did not know that elephants were in South America. But they were, this is another evidence that the Book of Mormon is true.

Question 11

The Book of Mormon states:

And I did teach my people to build buildings, and to work in all manner of wood, and of iron, and of copper, and of brass, and of steel, and of gold, and of silver, and of precious ores, which were in great abundance. (2 Ne. 5:15)

Is there evidence that any of these substances actually existed in ancient America?

Answer 11

The answer is yes. Concerning this topic John L. Sorenson states this:

Of actual specimens found where an early date is positively indicated. Over a dozen of these significantly precede A.D. 900. The earliest piece so far probably dates back to around the first century B.C. It is a bit of copper sheathing found on top of an altar at Cuicuilco in the Valley of Mexico. In addition to surely early specimens, other finds, not firmly dated, could be pre–A.D. 900; a late date has been inferred for some of them mainly *because* metal was found and "everybody knows" that metal occurs only in late sites. When all current information is considered, it appears that archaeologists should now be asking a new question. The old query was, why was there no metal in early Mesoamerica? Now it ought to become, why do we recover so little evidence of the metallurgical skill that was surely there?[32]

Milton R. Hunter also described some of the items found in ancient America:

When one considers all of the wonderful archaeological remains in Mexico, Honduras, Guatemala, and other Central American countries, and also carefully studies those of South America, one comes to the conclusion that those of the northern hemisphere do not surpass the marvelous archaeological ruins found in Peru, Ecuador, Bolivia, and Colombia. Numerous buildings have been excavated and some of them reconstructed. Thousands of graves have been opened and from them have been taken the most beautiful and artistic workings in gold, silver, copper, and precious stones of various kinds.[33]

Question 12

The Book of Mormon states:

And we began to till the ground, yea, even with all manner of seeds, with seeds of corn, and of wheat, and of barley, and with neas, and with sheum, and with seeds of all manner of fruits; and we did begin to multiply and prosper in the land. (Mosiah 9:9)

Is there any evidence of wheat and barley in Mesoamerica like the Book of Mormon states?

Answer 12

FARMS states this:

Grains, as Sorenson has shown, a variety of New World grains were known to pre-Columbian peoples, which could easily fit the ambiguous Book of Mormon references to "grain." Two grains, however, which are mentioned by name, barley and wheat, suggest at least two possibilities: (1) The terms *wheat* and *barley* could refer to certain New World grains identified by Old World names, even though they were another species of grain, or (2) they could refer to barley and wheat of a New World variety. We will look at each of these possibilities.

1. "It is a well known fact," writes Hildegard Lewy, a Near Eastern specialist, "that the names of plants and particularly of [grains] are applied in various languages and dialects to different species." Lewy notes the challenge this poses in interpreting references to Assyrian cereals in Near Eastern documents. When doing so, "the meaning of these Old Assyrian terms must be inferred from the Old Assyrian texts alone without regard to their signification in sources from Babylonia and other regions adjacent to Assyria." In the Western Hemisphere, many Spanish names were applied to New World plants following the Conquest because of their apparent similarity to European ones, even though, botanically speaking, these were often of a different species or variety. A similar practice may have occurred when the Nephites or the Jaredites encountered New World culture for the first time.

2. In addition to the above suggestion, Book of Mormon references to "barley" and "wheat" may indeed be to varieties of those species which were found in the New World by Book of Mormon peoples. For example, while it has been generally assumed that barley was first introduced to the New World by Europeans

after 1492, we now know that pre-Columbian Americans knew of and domesticated barley long before this time. Daniel B. Adams, in describing recent discoveries at the Hohokam site of La Ciudad near Phoenix, Arizona, reports, "Perhaps the most startling evidence of Hohokam agricultural sophistication came last year when salvage archaeologists found preserved grains of what looks like domesticated barley, the first ever found in the New World." John Sorenson, who first brought this fact to the attention of the Latter Day Saint community, has reported additional samples that have turned up in Illinois and Oklahoma.

So here was a domesticated barley in use in several parts of North America over a long period of time. Crop exchanges between North America and Mesoamerica have been documented by archaeology making it possible that this native barley was known in that tropical southland and conceivably was even cultivated there. The key point is that these unexpected results from botany are recent. More discoveries will surely be made as research continues.

Still, as already mentioned above, an Old World term for wheat may simply have been applied to one of several other New World grains.[34]

Question 13

The Book of Mormon states:

And it came to pass that we did begin to till the earth, and we began to plant seeds; yea, we did put all our seeds into the earth, which we had brought from the land of Jerusalem. And it came to pass that they did grow exceedingly; wherefore, we were blessed in abundance. (1 Ne. 18:24)

If the Book of Mormon is true shouldn't we find many of the same plants in Mesoamerica that were found in Jerusalem? The above scriptures state that they had brought their seeds from Jerusalem and they grew exceedingly.

Answer 13

Just because a plant grows and thrives one season does not mean that the plants will grow and survive the next generation. If I plant a specific banana plant in Idaho it very well may produce for one season before it dies out, especially if the Lord is blessing it. With God all things are possible so I'm sure the Lord could bless the people of Nephi so that their seeds could thrive. They no doubt deserved the blessings after doing what the Lord commanded and sailing to the American continent from Jerusalem.

Question 14

The Book of Mormon states this about King Noah:

> And it came to pass that he planted vineyards round about in the land; and he built wine-presses, and made wine in abundance; and therefore he became a wine-bibber, and also his people. (Mosiah 11:15)

How can there be vineyards to make wine if there has been no evidence of grapes in Mesoamerica?

Answer 14

Go to any nearby grocery store and you will find a multitude of peach wines, pineapple wines, strawberry wines and many more. All of these wines come from vineyards. Thus the definition of wine is a fermented fruit juice. Wine is not and never has been exclusively from grapes. The evil King Noah was a wine-bibber. Notice the Book of Mormon does not say grapes were used to make the wine.

Question 15

The prophet Joseph Smith claimed to receive gold plates. If the plates were gold like he said wouldn't they be very heavy? At one time Joseph Smith claimed to have run from three different attackers with the plates, is this possible?

Answer 15

Joseph Smith himself gave us the dimensions of the plates in the Wentworth Letter. The whole set was 6x8x6 in. or .1666 ft^3. If the plates were pure twenty-four karat gold, which no one including the Prophet Joseph has ever claimed, they would weigh 200.8 lb. Of course many people besides Joseph saw the plates or at least carried the covered plates. William Smith, the prophet's brother carried the covered plates and claimed they weighed about 53 lb.[35]

He also stated that they were "a mixture of gold and copper."[36] This would make sense since pure gold would be much too soft to make plates that would not scratch off the characters that had just been written. If the plates weighted approximately 53 pounds it would be no problem for Joseph, who was a large and powerful man to ward off three attempted thieves. The story of Joseph avoiding these attackers also brings up the known evidence that he did in fact have the experience. While avoiding the assault Joseph dislocated his thumb. It was fixed by his Father, and the injury was witnessed by Joseph's mother, Joseph's brothers Carlos and Hyrum, Mr. Knight and Mr. Knight's friend Stoal.[37]

Question 16

The Book of Mormon has recorded many wars. Mormons claim that Mayans are the relatives of the people mentioned in the Book of Mormon, but doesn't Mayan history reveal that there were no wars.

Answer 16

Mayans did have wars and any suggestion that they did not is a falsehood. Yale Mayan expert Michael D. Coe stated this:

> The Maya were obsessed with war. The Annals of the Cakciquels and the Popol Vuh speak of little but intertribal conflict among the highlanders, while the

sixteen states of Yucatán were constantly battling with each other over boundaries and lineage honour.[38]

Question 17

The Book of Mormon records the name "Alma" as a man. Wasn't the name Alma a woman's name when Joseph Smith was alive, could he have copied it?

Answer 17

The name Alma is a man's name in the Hebrew language. FARMS points out this fact:

> In 1961 Yigael Yadin discovered a land deed with several names on it, dating to the time of the Bar Kokhba rebellion in Palestine. Yadin translated one of the names as "Alma the son of Judah." So it turns out not only that Alma is an authentic Hebrew name, but that it was used anciently as the name of an Israelite man. Did Joseph borrow from Professor Yadin?[39]

FARMS further stated this on the subject of Joseph Smith copying:

> Fabricating the nonbiblical names would have been guesswork at best. If Joseph was merely playing around with a few word combinations, imagination and creativity might possibly allow for getting a couple of names right. But the chance of making serious mistakes would increase with every new word combination. Languages are far more complicated than that. The Tanners misunderstand the problem. They must not only account for Joseph's creating new names, but also for his choosing so many nonbiblical names that actually existed in the world antedating Lehi. While there is still much to learn about Book of Mormon names, it is quite clear that many are used contextually in ways that make sense from their Old World background. These comparisons can sometimes add a depth to our understanding of the Book of Mormon that nineteenth-century explanations cannot provide.[40]

Question 18

Joseph Smith claimed that he brought some reformed Egyptian writing to professor Anthon (JS—H 1:64). And that professor Anthon said words that were a fulfillment to the prophecy given in Isaiah 29:11 concerning a sealed book. But didn't professor Anthon deny ever having the conversation.

Answer 18

FARMS answered this same question to the anti-Mormon Tanners as follows:

> The Tanners assert that Martin Harris's account of his visit with Charles Anthon is inaccurate. They cite Anthon's 1834 letter to E. D. Howe denying that he ever said that the Book of Mormon characters resembled Egyptian (p. 105). The Tanners are apparently unfamiliar with the latest research done on the Anthon episode. Contrary to what the Tanners claim, there are persuasive reasons for believing that Harris and not Anthon was telling the truth.
>
> In 1841 Anthon declared that he had never made a public statement regarding the visit previously, when in fact he already had in 1834. In 1834 he claimed that he never gave Harris a written statement, while in 1841 he admitted that he had. Aside from Anthon's own contradictory claims, there are other aspects of his story that do not make sense historically. For instance, Anthon's assertion that Harris left believing that the whole affair was a fraud is unconvincing. Whatever occurred between the two men, one thing we know: Harris returned to his home convinced that he should support the cause of the Book of Mormon. In fact, Harris had everything to lose and Anthon had everything to gain by lying about the affair. In light of Anthon's known reputation for dishonesty among his scholarly colleagues, it is not difficult to believe that he lied about his identification of the characters, since being associated with the Mormons might threaten his scholarly reputation.
>
> In 1834 E. D. Howe published a letter by W. W.

Phelps in which Phelps described Harris's claim that Anthon had described the Book of Mormon characters as resembling "ancient shorthand Egyptian." While Anthon later denied that the characters resembled Egyptian, it now seems clear that he probably did say just that. Anthon possessed enough information both to recognize and to make such an identification. "While the first Egyptian grammars were still in preparation, Anthon had access to enough published, preliminary data in his own personal library to enable him to assess rapidly the apparent nature of the facsimile of Book of Mormon characters." In December 1826 an article in the *Edinburgh Review* noted that "all hieratic manuscripts . . . exhibit merely a tachygraphy, i.e., shorthand, of the hieroglyphic writing." The June 1827 issue of the *American Quarterly Review* published an article which described Demotic as "a species of shorthand" Egyptian. Several other scholarly works also discussed "shorthand" Egyptian. Today we know that Anthon owned, read, and cited from these publications and would have been familiar with them at the time of Harris's visit, while the term "shorthand Egyptian" would have been completely unknown to Harris and the Mormons prior to that fateful meeting in New York City. It is likely that Anthon "imagined that he could perform the same feats of translation which European classicists were then managing to accomplish at an ever increasing pace." In any case, "the mention of 'shorthand Egyptian' in the Phelps letter of 1831 innocently places a seal of doom on any meaningful defense of Anthon."[41]

If Joseph Smith were planning a lie he would have simply written down some true characters of Egyptian and gone to Professor Anthon and got a document stating they were true. He would have never brought up the Book of Mormon and would have just kept the document. But Joseph Smith was not planning a lie so he brought the real thing and the prophecy in Isaiah 29:11–14 was fulfilled. It is no more surprising that Professor Anthon denied the meeting than it is surprising that the guards by Jesus' tomb denied what they saw for money (see Matt. 11–15).

Question 19

Did Joseph Smith plagiarize information from Josiah Priest's 1825 book *The Wonders of Nature and Providence Displayed*?

Answer 19

At this point I am sure the reader is saying how many times can Joseph Smith be accused of plagiarizing? I agree all the accusations do get rather ridiculous. Critics go to many efforts to find and explanation to the coming forth of such a complex book when the real answer is as simple as seeing that Christ is the Son of God. Nevertheless the answer to the above question is no Joseph did not plagiarize, FARMS says this on the subject:

> Another source which the Tanners suggest that Joseph Smith used is Josiah Priest's 1825 work, *The Wonders of Nature and Providence Displayed*. They notice several scattered parallels between passages in Priest's book and the destruction in 3 Nephi 8:5–14 (pp. 84–85). However, many of Priest's ideas are merely taken from biblical events. Three days of darkness (Ex. 10:22), a darkness that could be felt (Ex. 10:21), the description of the darkness as a vapor, thunder, lightning, earthquakes, storm, tempest, fire (Isa. 29:6) and shy;— all are seen by the Tanners as direct borrowing from Josiah Priest. Yet while Josiah Priest does describe some of these things, and several general parallels may be drawn between them and 3 Nephi, the Book of Mormon claim that this was a real event remains very plausible and convincing. Moreover, there are several elements of 3 Nephi 8 which, although not found in the Tanners' source, can be found in old Mesoamerican sources, some of which were unavailable to Joseph Smith. When Josiah Priest published his *American Antiquities* in *1835*, he was critical of the Book of Mormon, but never suggested that Joseph Smith plagiarized from his 1825 book. *Wouldn't he have been one of the first to notice if it had been among the Prophet's sources? The same may be said of Ethan Smith. In 1833, the author of View of the*

Hebrews received an endorsement from 23 prominent clergymen who praised his 1823 work. Apparently, neither Reverend Smith nor any of his friends saw any relationship between that work and the Book of Mormon. No critic ever suggested that Joseph Smith used the works of Josiah Priest or Ethan Smith until the twentieth century.[42]

Question 20

The Book of Mormon states that the prophet Lehi and his family came from Jerusalem and settled the American Continent. If this is true shouldn't the American Indian have a similar writing system to either Egyptian or Hebrew?

Answer 20

FARMS says this about the subject:

What is the relationship, if any, between Mesoamerican and Egyptian hieroglyphic writing systems? The distinction needs to be drawn between a conceptual and a direct causal relationship. There appears to be no direct causal relationship between Mesoamerican writing systems and Egyptian hieroglyphics—the language, grammar, and characters are all different. Nonetheless, there are some very remarkable conceptual similarities between the two writing systems. Joyce Marcus, one of the leading specialists in this field, believes that *"Meso-american writing is better compared with Egyptian hieroglyphic writing, both in its format and in its function,"* and "that Egyptian hieroglyphic writing thus constitutes a much more appropriate analogy to Mesoamerican texts than does Sumerian." Indeed, Marcus["find[s] it more productive to mention *a number of similarities shared by Egyptian and Mesoamerican writing, with Maya writing being particularly similar to Egyptian in several respects.*" Thus, in their social function, format, and basic logic, there are significant parallels between Egyptian hieroglyphics and Mesoamerican writing systems.[43]

For evidence that the Book of Mormon is true, see appendixes A and B.

Question 21

In the Book of Mormon Alma 22:32 it speaks of the timing of a journey from the east sea to the west sea taking a day and a half. Then in Helaman 4:7 it says a journey from the west sea to the east sea is only a day. Is this a contradiction in the Book of Mormon?

Answer 21

This is not a contradiction. Those traveling east could use part of the journey going downstream and therefore traveled faster. This question again shows that even the littlest detail is correct in the Book of Mormon. There is over a hundred pages between these two verses yet no contradiction.

BOOK OF REVELATION

(see also REVELATION)

Question 1

Is there a scripture in the New Testament that states there would be no other scripture added after the book of Revelation? Does this mean the Book of Mormon can't be true since it came after the book of Revelation was written?

Answer 1

Let's take a look at what the verse says:

> For I testify unto every man that heareth the words of the prophecy of this book, if any man shall add unto these things, God shall add unto him the plagues that are written in this book. (Rev. 21:18)

This verse has often been misinterpreted. It is an easy one to misunderstand because it is at the very end of the Bible, and it says no other books would follow. Thus enemies of the LDS Church use it to say there would be no Book of Mormon because it is adding to "these things." Elder Howard W. Hunter addressing the April 1981 general conference stated:

> The answer to this query is really very simple. A careful reading of the words makes it clear that the warning against adding to or taking away does *not* refer to the whole Bible or even to the New Testament, but to use John's words, only to the words of "the book of this prophecy." That is the prophecy contained in the book of Revelation. This is substantiated by the fact *that some of the book of the New Testament had not yet been written when John wrote the book of Revelation,* and even those that had been written and were in existence at that time had *not* yet been gathered into one compilation.[44]

Elder Hunter pointed out that the sixty-six books contained in the Bible were brought together and compiled long *after* John wrote the book of Revelation. John *himself* also added to scripture *after* writing the book of Revelation. (John was banished to the isle of Patmos by Domitian, and while there received and wrote the book of Revelation. When Domitian died, St. John returned to Ephesus, and it was there he wrote his gospel.) Elder Hunter further noted that the Old Testament had a similar statement.

> Ye shall not add unto the word which I command you, neither shall ye diminish ought from it, that ye may keep the commandments of the Lord your God which I command you. (Deut. 4:2)

Obviously the New Testament was added after this scripture was written. The fact is there are numerous verses in the Bible that speak of the coming forth of the Book of Mormon and *none* that deny it would come forth (see also Ezek. 37:15–19, Isa. 29:11, John 10:16).

CELESTIAL MARRIAGE

(see MARRIAGE, CELESTIAL)

CHANGES TO THE BOOK OF MORMON

Question 1

Joseph Smith said the Book of Mormon is the "most correct" book on the earth. If this is true, why have there been over four thousand grammar, punctuation, and other changes?

Answer 1

God does not expect perfect grammar in scriptures. Errors have been found in scriptures including the Old Testament, the New Testament, the Dead Sea Scrolls, the book of Jasher (referred to in the Bible) the Book of Mormon, the Doctrine and Covenants, and the Pearl of Great Price. Every single book has grammatical errors. So why did Joseph say it is the most correct book? First of all, he was not bragging about its spelling and punctuation, *he was speaking of the contents, teachings, and doctrines.* The only difference between the grammatical error in the Bible and that in the Book of Mormon is that the LDS Church fixed the grammatical errors in the Book of Mormon many years ago. Enemies of the LDS Church fault Mormons for fixing grammatical errors, etc., in the Book of Mormon, but they say nothing about those who have changed the King James Bible into other editions and as a result lost many important truths.

Many people don't believe that there are errors in the Bible, but to deny this simple truth it is like denying that we live on this earth. In fact, the errors in the Bible are much worse than those found in the Book of Mormon. For the most part, the errors in the Book of Mormon were simply grammar. The grammatical errors that were changed in the Book of Mormon have in no way changed the central message. The errors in the Bible often deal with points of an event. Here are only a few examples:

- Matt. 28:1–5 says there was only one angel at Christ's tomb.
- Luke 24:4–5 says there was two angels at Christ's tomb.
- Mark and Luke said that Jesus stayed with Peter in his house and later healed the leper (Mark 1:29–45; Luke 4:38; Luke 5:12–13), yet Matthew says the opposite; that Christ first healed the leper (Matt. 8:1–4, 14–16).
- Genesis 6:6 says God repented.
- Numbers 23:19 says God does not repent.

An entire book could be written on mistakes like the above and many more. Although these are mistakes in Holy Scripture it is okay. It is also okay that there were misspelled words and punctuation mistakes in the Book of Mormon. Humans who are influenced and inspired by God write Scriptures. They are not inspired on where to put the comma.

To print a book in the 1800s was no small undertaking. Typesetting was a slow, laborious manual task any many errors were made. But, the fact still remains; both the Bible and Book of Mormon are Holy Scripture. If any person denies the validity of the Book of Mormon because of these minor changes he or she must also deny the validity of the Bible. Any person who does so is choosing a path that leads to damnation.

CHRIST'S BIRTH

(see BIRTH OF CHRIST)

CREATION OF THE EARTH

Question 1

In the book of Moses in the Pearl of Great Price, it refers to *one God* creating the earth:

> And *I, God,* said: let there be light; and there was light. (Moses 2:3; italics added)

Yet in the book of Abraham in the Pearl of Great Price it refers *to more than one God* creating the earth.

> And *they (the Gods)* said: let there be light; and there was light. (Abraham 4:3; italics added)

Is this a contradiction?

Answer 1

The answer to this question is written in Moses 2:1. Let's read it:

> And it came to pass that the Lord spake unto Moses, saying: Behold, I reveal unto you concerning this heaven, and this earth; write the words which I speak. I am the beginning and the End the Almighty God; *by mine Only Begotten I created* the heaven and the earth upon which thou standest. (Moses 2:1)

Christ is the God of the Old Testament (Ex. 6:3). In Moses 2:1, our Heavenly Father is saying that he made the worlds through his son. In Hebrews 1:2, it states:

> [God] Hath in these last days spoken unto us by his Son, whom he hath appointed heir of all things, by whom also he made the worlds.

Thus, the Pearl of Great Price is correct in both verses

above. God the Father created the earth through his son Jesus Christ. When it says "Gods" it refers to both God the Father and God the Son. Of course the book of Genesis is also correct when it says "God created the heaven and the earth" (Gen. 1:1). It could have just as easily said "the Gods" again meaning Jesus under the direction of God the Father.

CROSS

(see SYMBOLS)

CRUCIFIX

(see SYMBOLS)

CULT

(see also GOSPEL)

Question 1

Is Mormonism a cult?

Answer 1

The answer to this question is simple, if Mormonism is a cult, so is Christianity. Synonyms for the word cult include "sect," "faction," "religious group," "party," and "out of the ordinary." In the Bible, Peter said:

> But ye are a chosen generation, a royal priesthood, an holy nation, *a peculiar people.* (1 Pet. 2:9; italics added)

In ancient days, members of Christ's Church were seen as peculiar. Members of the LDS Church have beliefs like no other religion on the earth today. Things like new scripture, living prophets, living apostles, and revelation. Does it seem strange or peculiar? It did at the time of Christ too. Nevertheless Mormons are no more a cult than Christ's ancient Church. A prophet of God has said:

> There are those who say that Mormonism began as a cult. You don't like to hear that. I don't know what that means, really. But if it has negative connotations, I don't accept it as applying to this Church. . . . There are only six Churches in America with more members than this Church. We are the second Church in membership in the state of California. We are reaching out across the world. We are in more than 150 nations. This is a great, strong, viable organization with a tremendous outreach across the world.[45]

I admonish the reader of this page to look deep inside and ask, "What if the LDS Church has the truth?" Are you willing to chance your salvation by not looking into it? Noah pleaded with the people of his time to get on the ark, yet few would listen. The prophet Jeremiah said:

> Let us search and try our ways, and turn again to the Lord. (Lam. 3:40)

I testify to you that the LDS Church is Christ's Church. When Christ started the ancient Church, it was a new idea that was out of mainstream. The people were use to practicing the law of Moses, and Jesus came and said the law is fulfilled. Mormons claim new scripture and follow a prophet and apostles who teach the gospel of Jesus Christ. Comparatively, Jesus gave new scripture and had prophets and apostles. After Jesus died, the saints followed their prophet leader Peter who taught the gospel of Jesus Christ, but very few believed him. Today there is a prophet on the earth, just as the saints of old followed Peter we can follow the current prophet.

DEGREES OF GLORY

(see SYMBOLS)

DIFFERENT GOD

(see GOSPEL)

DNA AND THE BOOK OF MORMON

Question 1

The Book of Mormon claims the Lamanites (American Indians) and the Nephites came from Jerusalem and are thus ancestors of the house of Israel. Does new research with DNA fingerprinting prove that they cannot be related?

Answer 1

There is no such evidence with DNA fingerprinting, and if there were it would in fact prove, the authenticity of the Book of Mormon. This question was brought up in an anti-Mormon video called *DNA vs. The Book of Mormon.* The video has several "scholars" who formerly believed in Mormonism that claim DNA fingerprinting proves the American Indian is from Asia and not the Jerusalem area. The video deceptively suggests that the men testifying have worked on ancient Indian DNA when in fact they have not. One of the men actually worked with plant DNA, but acted as if he knew all about ancient Indian DNA. On the video these "scholars" talk for approximately thirty minutes testifying that there is no way Indians can be from Jerusalem and that DNA fingerprinting proves it. Yet not one of the "scholars" gives even one shred of evidence to support their claim. Watching the video is like watching four men fervently testifying to you that gravity does not exist and that new gravity devices prove it, but they don't give you any real evidence at all. The entire premise of the video actually makes no sense from a Book of Mormon perspective. The Nephite population (light skinned) in the Book of Mormon are the actual genetic ancestors of ancient Israel and they are entirely *extinct,* so *it is absolutely impossible to even test today's ancestors.* The video states that Mormon's claim the people in the Book of Mormon are from the tribe of Judah or Jews but nowhere in the Book of Mormon is this claim made. The Book of Mormon people are from the tribe of Joseph, the same Joseph who was sold into Egypt (1 Ne. 5:14). The other hugely important fact is that the Lamanites (dark skinned) in the Book of Mormon *underwent a genetic change* (Alma 3:6–10) *just like Cain in the Bible* (Gen. 4:15). They were given a curse of dark skin. So we would have to ask, "When God gave the curse how did it change their genetic structure?" "Did the Lamanites inherit their own unique genetic structure, or are they similar to Asians, and if so which Asians? Japanese, Chinese, Koreans, Philippines, Indonesians, Malaysians, etc.?" Of course it doesn't matter, but even without genetics, by just using common sense, it is more than obvious that American Indians do not look like Asians. In the video they fabricate pictures to try and make them look the same, but the eye and nose structures, etc., of these dissimilar groups have distinct differences. In the video they claim Asians traveled just fifty miles across the ocean to get to South America. The problem with this theory is that it does not fulfill the prophecy foretold in the Bible that *Joseph's* ancestors would travel over the water, and inherit "everlasting hills" like those of South America. (Gen. 49:22–26; Deut. 33:16; and see appendix A).

There are many other evidences that the Book of Mormon is true. Here are some examples:

- There are ancient traditions in Mesoamerica that a white God had once come to their people and taught and healed them just as recorded in the Book of Mormon (3 Ne. 11–26). This is why the Indians worshiped Cortez when he first arrived. Quetzalcoatl (Jesus) became the symbol of this white God to the Mayans. The Mayans believed Quetzalcoatl created all things, had a virgin birth, healed the sick, and performed miracles ("The Common Source of Religious Truth," *Improvement Era*, 1939, Vol. xxxii. December, 1939. No. 12).

- Dark-skinned and light-skinned people existed in ancient America just as recorded in the Book of Mormon. In the Book of Mormon they were separated as "Lamanites" (Indians) and "Nephites." The Lamanites were dark-skinned and the Nephites were light-skinned. There are colored murals drawn on walls in ancient American ruins showing this known fact (Hunter, Milton R., *Archaeology and the Book of Mormon* [Salt Lake City: Deseret Book Co., 1956], 181, 188, 202, 209, 211-214).

- Ancient writings have been found and published by a man who grew up in South America. This man's name was Fernando de Alva Ixtlilxochitl. He lived from 1578 to 1650. He recorded a history of his ancestors. His writings are similar to the Book of Mormon. Milton R. Hunter writes:

  > Next to the Book of Mormon, the *Works of Ixtlilxochitl* gives the most reliable and complete account of the history and culture of the early Toltecs (Nephites) and the Lamanites, the ancestors of the American Indians. Ixtlilxochitl wrote the history of the inhabitants of ancient America—the Jaredites who came from the Tower of Babel, the Nephites, Lamanites, and Mulekites, who came from Jerusalem—from

written documents received from his ancestors and from oral traditions received from Indians who knew the traditions of their people. His first work was written about A.D. 1600 and his second about 1608.[46]

- John 10:16 Jesus said he would visit his other sheep this surely would be recorded just as claimed in the Book of Mormon (3 Ne. 11–26).

- Genesis 49:22–26 Jacob's son Joseph (coat of many colors) was told his lineage would travel over water to the American continent (everlasting hills) only the Book of Mormon fulfills the prophecy (1 Ne. 5:14).

- Ezekiel 37:15–19 foretold two records would be written, one for Judah and one for Joseph (the Bible and the Book of Mormon) (see also appendix A).

- Malachi 3:1–2 prophesies that Jesus will suddenly come to him temple. Mormons are one of the few religions on the earth today that even has temples.

- Malachi 4:5–6 prophesies Elijah the prophet coming to earth to turn our hearts to genealogy work. Elijah did come as prophesied and his visit is recorded in D&C 110:13–15. Mormons have the largest genealogy program in the world.

- 1 Corinthians 15:29 speaks of baptism for the dead. With the apostasy it was lost but has been restored again because of Joseph Smith and the LDS Church (D&C 124:33–35).

- Revelation 7:14–15 foretold that the saints would dress in white and work day and night in the temple. Even today the saints dress in white and work in the temple. Some temples are open day and night just as prophesied.

- Isaiah 29:4 foretold a book that would come from

the ground. The Book of Mormon was buried in the ground.

- Isaiah 29:11–14 foretold that the book that came from the ground would be sealed. It also said it would be given to a man who is "not learned." The Book of Mormon had a seal on the gold plates and was given to Joseph Smith with a third-grade education (JS—H 1:64–65).

- Revelation 14:6 foretold and angel would come to earth to restore the "everlasting gospel." The angel Moroni came to earth and visited Joseph Smith and is the angel spoken of.

- Ephesians 4:11–14 states there will be apostles and prophets until there is a unity of all faiths. The LDS Church has apostles and prophets (see also Eph. 2:19–21).

- Daniel 2:44 and Acts 3:19–22 foretold a restoration of the gospel. The LDS Church is a restored Church.

- Matthew 24:14 foretells of the great missionary effort that "shall be preached in all the world." There is no greater missionary program in the world than that of the LDS Church.

As mentioned above a genetic change overcame the Lamanites (American Indians), which permanently set them apart from the Nephites (Israelites). *Because of this DNA and genetics has no meaning whatsoever to the American Indian as far as likeness to other nationalities.*

The video claims that researchers have dug up ancient Indian bones and have done testing on them. But the truth is that DNA recovered from archaeological specimens is so degraded that the usual techniques associated with DNA fingerprinting cannot be used. If you watch the news you will hear forensic scientists stating that if they even find a badly decomposed body, they may have difficulty even identifying if it is the person in question, let alone bones that are thousands of years old.

FARMS states this:

> The rapid degradation of biomolecules begins immediately following death. Except in unusual circumstances, this process continues unabated until the molecules return to a native state. DNA, found in large quantities in living tissue, degrades rapidly after death, and in most instances only small amounts of short DNA molecules can be recovered from dead tissue. This normally prevents recovery and analysis of DNA sequences from ancient tissue.[47]

Beyond DNA fingerprinting there are newer techniques such as PCR and amplification of mitochondria that have proven useful in dating some ancient bones, teeth, etc. With this technology there has been absolutely no evidence found to suggest that the American Indian is not from Jerusalem. As mentioned above the "scholars" in the video have done no actual testing on Indians themselves, they have simply researched what others have done, but in the entire video they don't even give one reference. As you can imagine the real scholars who actually do these tests have to spend hours just trying to date the bones. FARMS states this:

> The advent of PCR in 1985 further opened the possibility of isolating DNA sequences in extracts in which the majority of the molecules are damaged and degraded. Theoretically, a single intact copy of a target DNA sequence, which only needs to be on the order of one hundred to two hundred base pairs in length, is sufficient for PCR, making it an ideal tool for aDNA studies. PCR products can be sequenced directly from a sample (this is preferable), or after cloning, making DNA sequence comparisons an extremely useful tool for the study of kinship relationships between individuals and populations. The amplification of mitochrondrial DNA (mtDNA) from ancient bones and teeth dated from 750 to 5450 years b.p. has been accomplished recently by a number of investigators.[48]

These "scholars" are mainly disgruntled former believers of Mormonism. Going to them is like going to a Pharisee and asking about Jesus. These types of former Mormons are not hard to find. They typically arise after committing a grievous sin. Not willing to confess their sins and turn to Christ, this type of person searches for a "reason" the Church isn't true. It is much easier to say the Church isn't true than face embarrassing themselves and their families. At the very end of the video the viewer is told "you can receive salvation right now, from where ever you are, by praying a simple prayer to God." They then give an example of a prayer that confesses the name Jesus. (What do they say about Matt. 7:21 and Gal. 6:7–8; see also WORKS.) Why all the effort to tell us about DNA if all you have to do is say Lord, Lord, save me?

The Real Truth about DNA Fingerprinting

Now let's discuss the real facts we have about DNA fingerprinting. The following information has been taken from   *http://www.biology.washington.edu/fingerprint/ dnaintro.html,* I invite the reader to view the website for themselves.

What Is DNA Fingerprinting?

The chemical structure of everyone's DNA is the same. The only difference between people (or any animal) is the order of the base pairs. There are so many millions of base pairs in each person's DNA that every person has a different sequence.

Using these sequences, every person could be identified solely by the sequence of their base pairs. However, because there are so many millions of base pairs, the task would be very time-consuming. Instead, scientists are able to use a shorter method, because of repeating patterns in DNA.

These patterns do not, however, give an individual "fingerprint," but they are able to determine whether two DNA samples are from the same person, related people, or non-related people. Scientists use a small number of sequences of DNA that are known to vary among individuals a great deal, and analyze those to get a certain probability of a match.

VNTRs (Variable Number Tandem Repeats)

Every strand of DNA has pieces that contain genetic information which informs an organism's development (exons) and pieces that, apparently, supply no relevant genetic information at all (introns). Although the introns may seem useless, it has been found that they contain repeated sequences of base pairs. These sequences, called Variable Number Tandem Repeats (VNTRs), can contain anywhere from twenty to one hundred base pairs.

Every human being has some VNTRs. To determine if a person has a particular VNTR, a Southern Blot is performed, and then the Southern Blot is probed, through a hybridization reaction, with a radioactive version of the VNTR in question. The pattern which results from this process is what is often referred to as a DNA fingerprint.

A given person's VNTRs come from the genetic information donated by his or her parents; he or she could have VNTRs inherited from his or her mother or father, or a combination, but never a VNTR either of his or her parents do not have.

Practical Applications of DNA Fingerprinting

1. Paternity and Maternity

Because a person inherits his or her VNTRs from his or her parents, VNTR patterns can be used to establish paternity and maternity. The patterns are so specific that a parental VNTR pattern can be reconstructed even if only the children's VNTR patterns are known (the more children produced, the more reliable the reconstruction). Parent-child VNTR pattern analysis has been used to solve standard father-identification cases as well as more complicated cases of confirming legal nationality and, in instances of adoption, biological parenthood.

2. Criminal Identification and Forensics

DNA isolated from blood, hair, skin cells, or other genetic evidence left at the scene of a crime can be compared, through VNTR patterns, with the DNA of a criminal suspect to determine guilt or innocence. VNTR patterns are also useful in establishing the identity of a homicide victim, either from DNA found as evidence or from the body itself.

3. Personal Identification

The notion of using DNA fingerprints as a sort of genetic bar code to identify individuals has been discussed, but this is not likely to happen anytime in the foreseeable future. The technology required to isolate, keep on file, and then analyze millions of very specified VNTR patterns is both expensive and impractical. Social security numbers, picture ID, and other more mundane methods are much more likely to remain the prevalent ways to establish personal identification.

Problems with DNA Fingerprinting

Like nearly everything else in the scientific world, nothing about DNA fingerprinting is 100% assured. The term DNA fingerprint is, in one sense, a misnomer: it implies that, like a fingerprint, the VNTR pattern for a given person is utterly and completely unique to that person. Actually, all that a VNTR pattern can do is present a probability that the person in question is indeed the person to whom the VNTR pattern (of the child, the criminal evidence, or whatever else) belongs. Given, that probability might be 1 in 20 billion, which would indicate that the person can be reasonably matched with the DNA fingerprint; then again, that probability might only be 1 in 20, leaving a large amount of doubt regarding the specific identity of the VNTR pattern's owner.

Problems with Determining Probability

A. Population Genetics

VNTRs, because they are results of genetic inheritance, are not distributed evenly across all of human population. A given VNTR cannot, therefore, have a stable probability of occurrence; it will vary depending on an individual's genetic background. The difference in probabilities is particularly visible across racial lines. Some

VNTRs that occur very frequently among Hispanics will occur very rarely among Caucasians or African-Americans. Currently, not enough is known about the VNTR frequency distributions among ethnic groups to determine accurate probabilities for individuals within those groups; the heterogeneous genetic composition of interracial individuals, who are growing in number, presents an entirely new set of questions. Further experimentation in this area, known as population genetics, has been surrounded with and hindered by controversy, because the idea of identifying people through genetic anomalies along racial lines comes alarmingly close to the eugenics and ethnic purification movements of the recent past, and, some argue, could provide a scientific basis for racial discrimination.

SUMMARY OF DNA AND THE BOOK OF MORMON

Even without science, it's easy to see Asians don't look like American Indians. Not only do Asians not look like American Indians, but also they don't act like them. American Indians are their own unique genetic race that God created from their Hebrew ancestors, the Nephites. They lived in teepees and shot bows and arrows. The Indians shaved their heads and wore animal skins around their waists. Do those in the video think that the Asians built a boat, traveled fifty miles, and then suddenly changed their manner of living? The only true and logical story is the one recorded in the Book of Mormon.

FIRST VISION

Question 1

There are at least eight versions of Joseph Smith's first vision of seeing God and Jesus Christ. The version written in Joseph Smith's own handwriting says he saw two separate beings namely God and Jesus. But the very first version only mentioned seeing Jesus. How do you account for this discrepancy?

Answer 1

There is no discrepancy, in fact in all eight versions *there are no contradictions.* The first version *doesn't* say God was not there. When Joseph Smith had his vision, God and Jesus appeared and God said, "This is my beloved Son. Hear him." The rest of the instructions were from Jesus. The first version did not include the detail that others did. As mentioned above, Joseph only handwrote one version himself. Scribes or those who heard the story and paraphrased wrote *all* the other versions. If the prophet Joseph would have prepared the first version for printing he would have included this important detail. This lack of detail is a common occurrence in scripture when more than one person writes the story. For example, in the Bible there are many versions of Christ's atonement. In Matthew 26:37 it states, Christ took "Peter and the two sons of Zebedee." In the book of Luke 22:39 it says, "his disciples also followed him." Luke's version did not give detail, but it does not mean Peter and the two sons of Zebedee were not there. Likewise, not mentioning God the Father does not mean he was not present at Joseph Smith's first vision.

Question 2

In the Bible it says, "Satan can appear as an angel of light" (2 Cor. 11:14). Was it Satan who appeared to Joseph Smith?

Answer 2

Satan can appear as an angel of light, but it was *not* Satan who *appeared* to Joseph Smith. *It was* God and Jesus Christ. Several points need to be considered when looking at this question. First, it does *not* say Satan can appear as God and Jesus Christ. Second, if Satan does appear as an angel of light, he is there to deceive, and when Satan deceives, it is not for good works. One verse prior to the one mentioned above states that there would be false apostles and deceitful workers (2 Cor. 11:13). So how do we know if the angel is Satan or if the apostles or prophet is false? The scriptures give us the answer.

> Because strait is the gate, and narrow is the way, which leadeth unto life, and few there be that find it.
>
> Beware of false prophets, which come to you in sheep's clothing, but inwardly they are ravening wolves.
>
> *Ye shall know them by their fruits.* Do men gather grapes of thorns, or figs of thistles?
>
> Even so every *good tree bringeth forth good fruit; but a corrupt tree bringeth forth evil fruit.*
>
> *A good tree cannot bring forth evil fruit,* neither *can* a corrupt tree bring forth good fruit.
>
> Every tree that bringeth not forth good fruit is hewn down, and cast into the fire.
>
> Wherefore by their fruits ye shall know them. (Matt. 7:14–20; italics added).

Joseph Smith and the Church today bring forth good fruit.

> "And if Satan cast out Satan, he is divided against himself; how shall then his kingdom stand?" (Matt 12:26).

This verse reminds us that Jesus, like Joseph Smith, was accused of being a devil and a false prophet. Joseph Smith was not a false prophet. Satan is much to smart to raise up a prophet that would support strong families, morality, marriage, gospel standards, baptism, self sufficiency, overcoming temptation, missionary service, obedience to the commandments, prayer, sacrament, repentance, resurrection, service, humility, and patience. The list goes on and on. Pick up any Mormon Sunday school manual and you cannot deny this fact. It can also be said for Joseph Smith's sake in Luke 6:22–23:

> Blessed are ye, when men shall hate you, and when they shall separate you, from their company, and shall reproach you, and cast out your name as evil, for the Son

of man's sake. Rejoice ye in that day, and leap for joy: for, behold, your reward is great in heaven: for in the like manner did their fathers unto the prophets. (Luke 6:22–23)

FLESH AND BONE

(see also GODHEAD)

Question 1

Mormons believe all people will be resurrected with a body. How can this be true if 1 Corinthians 15 says that *no* flesh and blood will be in the afterlife?

Answer 1

Let's take a look at the verse:

"Now this I say, brethren, that flesh and *blood* cannot inherit the kingdom of God; neither doth corruption inherit incorruption" (1 Cor. 15:50).

At Easter, we celebrate the resurrection of Christ. An easy way to explain the above verses is to ask yourself—do you believe in the resurrection, and if so, what is the resurrection? It is a uniting of a spirit body with a body of flesh and bones. The two at that time will never be divided again. The body at that time is immortal with no blood only flesh and bone. Thus, the scripture above in Corinthians is true— no flesh and *blood* will inherit the kingdom of God, but flesh and *bone* will. Job 19:26 states, "And though after my skin worms destroy this body, yet in my flesh shall I see God." In Luke 24:36–39 it tells us Christ was resurrected with a body. In Philippians 3:20–21 it states:

For our conversation is in heaven; from whence also we look for the Saviour, the Lord Jesus Christ: Who shall change our vile body, that it may be *fashioned like unto his glorious body.* (italics added)

Notice the scripture says *body*. For truly that is what the resurrection is about, getting an immortal perfect body *just like Jesus* did. *All* who have lived on this earth will be resurrected (1 Cor. 15:22).

Question 2

In the book of John it states that God is a spirit, so why do Mormon believe that God has a body of flesh and bones (D&C 130:22)?

Answer 2

Let's take a look at the verse:

> God is a spirit: and they that worship him must worship him in spirit and in truth. (John 4:24)

How do we explain this in an apparent contradiction to what is said in John above? Quite simply, the verse in John is one of many mistakes recorded when the Bible was translated. Thus, we believe the Bible "as far as it is translated correctly." A look at the verse the way it is recorded is also easily explained however. God does have a spirit and we don't have to become a spirit to worship him. As 1 Corinthians 6:17 states:

> But he that is joined unto the Lord is one spirit.

This verse is of course symbolic. Nevertheless the verse as written in the King James Version was translated incorrectly many years ago. The correct translation of John 4:26 is as follows:

> For unto such hath God promised his Spirit. And they who worship him, must worship in spirit and in truth. (JST).

Question 3

Doesn't the Book of Mormon say that God is a spirit? If so, why do Mormons believe God has a body?

Answer 3

The verse referred to in question 3 is in the book of Alma. Let's have a look at the verse:

> Believest thou that there is a God?
>
> And he [Lamoni] answered, and said unto him: I do not know what that meaneth.
>
> And then Ammon said: Believest thou that there is a Great Spirit?
>
> And he said, Yea.
>
> And Ammon said: This is God. (Alma 18:24–28)

There have been enemies of the Church who have used the verses in Alma to say our very own Book of Mormon contradicts LDS doctrine. We believe that God had a body of flesh and bones, yet Ammon refers to God as the Great Spirit. A careful look at the full story reveals no contradiction. Ammon was simply helping King Lamoni to understand that Lamoni's tradition of believing in a Great Spirit is actually the same God Ammon believed in. But Lamoni's tradition of God being a spirit was only correct in the sense that God does have a spirit. Ammon did not *correct* Lamoni, as seen in the scriptures, but instead *taught* Lamoni about God and Christ. Referring to Lamoni's belief in a Great Spirit, it is states in the Book of Mormon Alma 18:5.

> Now this was the *tradition of Lamoni*, which he had received from his father, that there was a Great Spirit. Notwithstanding they believed in a Great Spirit, they supposed that whatsoever they did was right. (Alma 18:3; italics added)

Note the explanation that it was just a tradition of Lamoni and not doctrine. And of course Lamoni was not a prophet and had no understanding of gospel doctrines, except for the traditions of the Lamanites.

Comments Concerning the above Questions:

It is not hard believe that God has a body when we consider the fact that the savior Jesus Christ was resurrected with *a body.* After Christ was resurrected, he visited his apostles. Let's take a look at the verse:

> And as they thus spake, Jesus himself stood in the midst of them, and saith unto them, peace be unto you.
>
> But they were terrified and affrighted, and supposed that they had seen a spirit.
>
> And he said unto them, Why are ye troubled? And why do thoughts arise in your hearts?
>
> Behold my hands and my feet, that it is I myself: handle me, and see; for a spirit hath not *flesh and bones, as ye see me have.* (Luke 24:36–39; italics added)

Of course the purpose of Christ's resurrection was to get a body. There would be no reason for him to get rid of it after getting it back. God the Father *also* has a body of flesh and bones.

Question 4

Is there scriptural evidence that God the Father has a body of flesh and bones or that his body looks like Christ's body?

Answer 4

Yes, there are many scriptures that show this fact. Hebrews 1:1–3 reveals that Christ is absolutely in the image of God. Comparing Christ to God the verse states this:

> Who being the brightness of his glory, and the *express image* of his person, and upholding all things by word of his power, when had by himself purged our sins, sat down on the right hand of the Majesty on high. (italics added)

The book of John tells us Christ looks like God, and in fact, they look so closely alike that seeing one is like seeing the other. Who could ever deny that to look at God is to look at a holy being that has a body just as Christ has a body! Let's take a look at the verse:

> If ye had known me, ye should have known my Father also: and from henceforth ye know him, and have seen him.
>
> Philip saith unto him, Lord shew us the Father, and it sufficeth us.
>
> Jesus saith unto him, have I been so long time with you, and yet hast thou not known me, Philip? He that hath seen me hath seen the Father; and how sayest thou then, shew us the Father? (John 14:7–9)

Another evidence that God has a body is stated in the book of Genesis.

> And God said, Let us make man in our image, after our likeness. (Gen. 1:26)

Our Heavenly Father and Jesus Christ are not a mass in space. We were made in their image. Just as we have bodies—they have bodies.

FRUITS

(see FIRST VISION)

GENEALOGY

Question 1

Does the Bible say to avoid genealogies because they are vain and unprofitable? If so why do Mormons spend so much time doing genealogy work and temple work for those who have died?

Answer 1

Let's read the verses referred to:

> Neither give heed to fables and endless genealogies, which minister questions, rather than godly edifying which is in faith: so do. (1 Tim. 1:4)

Richard Lloyd Anderson said this regarding this question:

> Today's anti-Mormon literature proclaims against genealogical work by quoting Paul: "Neither give heed to fables and endless genealogies" (1 Tim. 1:4). But that was not the interpretation of Paul and the New Testament writers, for *Matthew begins with Jesus' genealogy to Abraham, and Luke 3 takes it back to Adam, just as endless as an earthly genealogy can be.* Paul preached that Christ descended from David (Rom. 1:3), and the apostle knew his own descent from Benjamin (Rom. 11:1). Indeed, the Gentile convert Luke records the lineage of the prophetess Anna from the tribe of Levi (Acts 4:36). In short, true genealogy, a serious Latter-day Saint goal, is sustained by the practice of the Early Church. *Paul's phrases, however, show that he condemns only false genealogies.* Paul's term never appears alone, but as part of a pattern, which is translated literally in its two appearances as follows: "Myths and endless genealogies . . . questions . . . empty talk" (1 Tim. 1:4); "Foolish questions and genealogies and strifes, and warring about the law" (Titus 3:9). Similar Pastoral phrases crop up regularly to characterize the false teachings as unsubstantial, untrue, filled with "unholy and blabbering myths" (1 Tim. 4:7, literal trans.) or "unholy and empty talk" (1 Tim. 6:20, literal trans.). Paul is clearly condemning irresponsible theories and invented stories, the meaning of the Greek *muthos* of the above passages. The "genealogies" condemned by Paul are clearly those that are debatable and fictitious.[49]

Truly the Bible is full of genealogies, to deny them is like denying the Bible itself. The other obvious point is that Gods plan for our ancestors ("the fathers") was foretold in the Bible.

> Behold, I will send you Elijah the prophet before the coming of the great and dreadful day of the LORD:
>
> And he shall turn the heart of the fathers to the children, and the heart of the children to their fathers, lest I come and smite the earth with a curse. (Mal. 4:4-6)

Without genealogies there are many scriptures in the Bible that cannot be explained. Because of modern day revelation only the LDS Church understands many of these verses. Here are a few examples:

> Else what shall they do which are baptized for the dead, if the dead rise not at all? why are they then baptized for the dead? (1 Cor. 15:29)

> For for this cause was the gospel preached also to them that are dead, that they might be judged according to men in the flesh, but live according to God in the spirit. (1 Pet. 4:6)

> If in this life only we have hope in Christ, we are of all men most miserable. (1 Cor. 15:19)

> For Christ also hath once suffered for sins, the just for the unjust, that he might bring us to God, being put to death in the flesh, but quickened by the Spirit:
>
> By which also he went and preached unto the spirits in prison. (1 Pet. 3:18–19)

GOD'S DECREE

Question 1

In the Book of Mormon, Alma 41:8 it states, "Now, the decrees of God are unalterable." Yet in the Doctrine and Covenants it says: "Wherefore, I the Lord, command and revoke, as it seemeth me good" (D&C 56:4). Is this a contradiction?

Answer 1

At first glance this may seem like a contradiction, but it is not. Many scriptures from the Bible can be taken out of context and used to show a discrepancy that does not really exist. For example in Hebrew 13:8, it states, "Jesus Christ the same yesterday, and to day, and for ever." Then in Luke 24:36–34 it states that Christ has changed and now has an *immortal* body of flesh and bones. This is a wrong interpretation as is the above question.

The verse in Alma 41 is simply stating that an unpredictable God who changes his commandments from one person to the other does not exist. What God demands from one, he demands from all. In the Doctrine and Covenants 56:4, we see that the Lord deals with things modernly, just as he did anciently. For the Lord does command and revoke at his discretion. Some examples include the following:

1. God commanded circumcision (Gen. 17:10:11) and later revoked it (Acts 15).

2. Women at one time could not speak in the churches (1 Cor. 14:34–35) and during other times when they worked with Paul (Rom. 16:1–4). Some women were even prophetesses (Luke 2:36).

3. The law of Moses was in full force during Old Testament times and withdrawn during New Testament times (Matt. 5:17).

4. At one time divorce was not allowed then later under certain circumstances it was permitted (Matt. 19:8–9).

5. The gospel was not brought to the gentiles then later it was commanded (Acts 10: 1–48).

Alma 41:8 and Doctrine and Covenants 56:4 listed above are both correct.

GOD MAKERS

Question 1

Did the movie and book *The God Makers* state truths about the Mormons?

Answer 1

Gilbert Scharffs' book shows the facts. Following are a list of errors found in *The God Makers*:

Repetition of charges from once to several times ..169

Statements that were not true 141

Unwarranted conclusions based on known facts ...131

Misinterpreted statements 125

Exaggerated statements 119

Broad generalizations 48

Significant quotes or charges
without documentation 47

Historical material quoted out of context which
altered the meaning 39

Scriptures quoted out of context or paraphrased
incorrectly which altered the meaning 18

Footnote references that were not where they were
indicated 7

Wrong footnote because the source copied by the
authors had the wrong footnote also 5

(Scharffs, Gilbert W. *The Truth about "The God
Makers."* SLC: Publisher's Press, 1986).

Please ask yourself, why all the lies about the Mormons? Why not the Baptists, Catholics, or Methodists? When was the last time you saw an anti-Baptist book at your local Christian bookstore? Christ said "do unto others as you would have others do unto you" (Matt. 7:12), "and love your neighbor as yourself" (Mark 12:31). So why do Christian bookstores sell only anti-Mormon books? Is it because

Mormons believe in additional scripture that was foretold in the Bible? (Ezek. 37:15–19; Isa. 29:4, 11–14; John 10:16; etc.). Is it because Mormons believe in Jesus, apostles, prophets, missionaries, and priesthood, just as Christ setup in his original Church? The answer is obvious, the Mormons have the truth and Satan will do all that is in his power to influence the people to stray from the strait and narrow path that few will find (Matt. 7:14).

GOD (MAN'S ABILITY TO SEE)

Question 1

In the Bible it says "No man hath seen God at any time" (John 1:18). Yet, Joseph Smith claimed to have seen God. How is this possible?

Answer 1

A close look at the scriptures makes it more than obvious that it is possible to see God and that many people have seen God. In fact, the list of those who have seen God is so large only a few scriptural references are placed here.

Not that any man hath seen the Father, save he which is of God, *he hath seen the Father.* (John 6:46; italics added)

Beloved, follow not that which is evil, but that which is good. He that doeth good is of God: but he that doeth evil hath not seen God. (3 Jn. 1:11)

And the Lord spake unto Moses face to face, as a man speaketh unto his friend. (Ex. 33:11)

And when Abram was ninety years old and nine, *the LORD appeared to Abram,* and said unto him, I *am* the Almighty God; walk before me, and be thou perfect. (Gen. 17:1; italics added)

For I [Jacob] have *seen God face to face,* and my life is preserved. (Gen. 32:30; italics added)

> But he, [Stephen] being full of the Holy Ghost, looked up stedfastly into heaven, and *saw the glory of God,* and Jesus standing on the right hand of God. (Acts 7:55; italics added)

The scripture in John 1:18 was transcribed with a mistake. The correct translation is,

> And no man hath seen God at any time, *except* he hath borne record of the Son; for except it is through him no man can be saved. (JST John 1:19; italics added)

Joseph Smith like others did see God and God spoke to him.

Question 2

In Matthew 24:23, it states:

> For there shall arise false Christs, and *false prophets,* and shew great signs and wonders; insomuch that, if it were possible, *they shall deceive the very elect.*
>
> Behold, I have told you before.
>
> Wherefore if they shall say unto you, Behold, he is in the desert; go not forth: behold, he is in the *secret chambers;* believe it not.

Is this verse referring to Joseph Smith? Does the phrase "secret chambers" refer to Joseph Smith alone in grove when he saw Jesus and God?

Answer 2

No, this verse does not refer to Joseph Smith. It does refer to some of the "evangelists" who claim to do healings with the power of God. They show many "great signs and wonders" but they are false prophets with no priesthood authority. There are many who have been deceived. Many of these false prophets live lavish lifestyles from the money donated by poor widows.

The comment about "secret chambers" also has nothing to do with Joseph Smiths visitation by God and Jesus.

Moses saw God alone on the mount, as well as many other prophets. In fact, most recorded evidences of God appearing to man are to single individuals. We do know that at the second coming of Christ that "every eye shall see him" (Rev. 1:7). But this has nothing to do with visitations to prophets such as Moses, Abraham, Joseph Smith, and others.

GOD, OR GODS (MAN A GOD?)

Question 1

Do Mormons believe they can become Gods? If so isn't this belief blasphemy?

Do Mormons really believe the following scripture?

> And all those who are begotten through me are *partakers of the glory of the same,* and are the Church of the Firstborn. (D&C 93:22; italics added)

Answer 1

As members of Christ's true Church, we believe what the scriptures teach. An easy way to look at the question above is to ask yourself, do you believe there is more than one God in our endless universe? *The scriptures say* there is more than one God. Even Jesus himself stated it. This being the case, where did the other gods come from? These are some pretty deep questions. Let's take a look at what evidence there is that *some* of mankind can become Gods. You will find that it is no harder to believe that a god can be made than to believe that there is a life after death.

The first evidence is realizing that Jesus was the Son of God and that *we too* are literal children of God. Most religions today agree that Christ is a God. This is because of Christ's greatness and because he was the Son of God, as well as the fact that the scriptures tell us he is a God. The following Scriptures are evidences that we too are children of God:

> The spirit itself beareth witness with our spirit, that *we are the children of God.* (Rom. 8:16; italics added)

> Forasmuch then as *we are the offspring of God,* we ought not to think that the Godhead is like unto gold, or silver, or stone, graven by art and man's device. (Acts 17:29; italics added)

As evidenced above, we are *literally* the children of God. This being the case, it does not seem unreasonable that we would inherit the same thing Christ inherited. Of course Christ received the same persecution as members of the Church today receive for believing in such a doctrine. Isn't it interesting that the persecutors both then and now have never seen themselves as persecutors? The fact is those who do not believe in Godhood do not know the scriptures and are ignoring a belief in both Old and New Testament times. Christ himself would turn his persecutors to the scriptures as evidence of the plurality of gods.

> The Jews answered him, saying, for a good work we stone thee not; but for blasphemy; and because that thou, being a man, makest thyself God.

> *Jesus answered* them, is it not *written* in your law, *I said,* Ye are gods? (John 10:33–34; italics added; see also Ps. 82:6)

Now let's look at some of the scriptural evidences of man's potential to become like God. For we, if we are worthy, will truly receive everything that Christ received, namely Godhood.

> The spirit itself beareth witness with our spirit, that we are the children of God:

> And if children, then heirs; *heirs of God, and joint-heirs with Christ;* if so be that we suffer with him, that we may be also glorified together. (Rom. 8:16–17; italics added)

> Let this mind be in you, which was also in Christ Jesus:

Who, being in the form of God, thought it not robbery to be *equal with God.* (Philip. 2:5–6; italics added)

To him that overcometh will I grant *to sit with me in my throne, even as I* also overcame, and am set down *with my Father* in his throne. (Rev. 3:21; italics added)

For though there be that are called gods, whether in heaven or in earth, (as *there be gods many, and lords many,*)
But to us there is but one God, the Father, of whom are all things, and we in him; and one Lord Jesus Christ, by whom are all things and we by him. (1 Cor. 8:5–6; italics added)

Question 2

Are the statements made by Lorenzo Snow and Joseph Smith blasphemy?

Answer 2

Let's take a look at the statements mentioned above.

"As man now is, our God once was; As now God is, so man may be" (Lorenzo Snow).

"God himself was once as we are now, and is an exalted man, and sits enthroned in yonder heavens! That is the great secret.[50]

It is not hard to believe that God was once a man when we realize that Christ was a man and became a God. No one calls Christ becoming a God blasphemy but because Satan stirs up the wicked they go around saying what Mormons believe is blasphemy. It is obvious that Satan is harder at work to persecute the Mormons than any other Church. If it is acceptable for Christ to become a God, it is also acceptable for God to have been a man, the scriptures state:

The Son can do nothing of himself, but what he seeth the Father do: for what things so ever he doeth, these also doeth the Son like wise. (John 5:19.)

Jesus did what he saw the Father do. God was a man on this earth, just as Jesus was a man on this earth.

Of course not every human on earth will be a god.

> "Strive to enter in at the strait gate: for many, I say unto you, will seek to enter in, and shall not be able" (Luke 13:24).

When you think of the next life, what do you envision we will be doing? Angels will be serving and the gods will be creating. In general we will not be sitting around idling our time away for eternity.

Question 3

In the book of Alma 11:28–29, it states that there is only one God. How is this explained considering that Mormons believe in the plurality of Gods?

Answer 3

Let's take a look at the verse:

> Now Zeezrom said: Is there more than one God?
> And he answered, No. (Alma 11:28–29)

It is important to know *the context* of these verses to understand the answer given. Zeezrom is a crafty individual who is trying to trick Amulek. Their discussion is referring to one person who Amulek is preaching; that person is Jesus Christ. In essence Zeezrom is asking, *"Is there more than one Jesus Christ?"* The obvious answer is no. For to us there, is only one Jesus. Isaiah said the same thing in Isaiah 43:11 "I, even I am the Lord; and beside me there is no saviour." Of course we know Jesus is the God of the Old Testament (Ex. 6:3; Heb. 1:1–4; John 1:1–5). Thus, in the Old Testament when it says God appeared to Moses it was Jesus or Jehovah who appeared to Moses.

Jesus is a God and there is only one Jesus. It is important to understand that Jesus is both a God and the Son of

God, and this God (Jesus) is the only one who atoned for our sins. The fact still remains that there is more than one God in the universe.

Question 4

Mormons believe in the book of Moses in the Pearl of Great Price. Moses 1:6, it states:

> But there is no God beside me, and all things are present with me, for I know them all.

So why do Mormons believe in more than one God?

Answer 4

The answer to this question is this: "as there be gods many and lords many, *but to us there is but one God*" (1 Cor. 8:5–6). Moses was essentially told the same thing in the book of Exodus 20:2, "Thou shalt have no other gods before me." But, again this does not deny the fact that there is more than one God.

Question 5

In the Doctrine and Covenants it states:

> Which Father, Son and Holy Ghost are one God, infinite and eternal, without end. Amen. (D&C 20:28)

So why do Mormons believe in more than one God?

Answer 5

Again, this verse has nothing to do with the number of Gods in the universe. This verse is simply stating that the Godhead is one in purpose. It states this same thing in the Bible. In the Bible, it even compares the apostles to being one with God (John 17:21). It is more than obvious that the apostles are not our God. They are simply one in purpose with God.

Question 6

In the book of Moses in the Pearl of Great Price it states:

> And God spake unto Moses, saying: Behold, I am the Lord God Almighty, and Endless is my name; for *I am without beginning of days* or end of years; and is not this endless? (Moses 1:3; italics added)

The scriptures also state:

> For I am the Lord, I change not. (Mal. 3:6)

> Jesus Christ the same yesterday, and today, and forever (Heb. 13:8).

How can God be without beginning of days, and unchangeable and have once been a man?

Answer 6

The easiest way to explain this question is to compare God to Christ. Christ existed and lived with God before coming to this earth (John 1:1–5). Christ came down to this earth with a mortal body but his body was changed into a resurrected immortal body. Christ inherited all that God had, namely Godhood. (See John 10:33–34, Rom. 8:16–17, Rev. 3:21).

The other fact is this: we all existed before coming to this earth. Like God, we are all without beginning of days. Let's read some verses that show this fact:

> In hope of *eternal life,* which God, that cannot lie, promised *before* the world began" (Titus 1:2; italics added)

> Then the word of the Lord came unto me saying,

> *Before* I formed thee in the belly I knew thee; and *before* thou camest forth out of the womb I sanctified thee, and I ordained thee a prophet unto the nations. (Jer. 1:4–5; italics added)

> And no man hath ascended up to heaven, but he that came down from heaven. (John 3:13)

> Man was also in the beginning with God. Intelligence, or the light of truth, was not created or made, neither indeed can be. (D&C 93:29).

God existed like Christ (and all of us) before living a mortal life. By living in a premortal life God is "without beginning of days" yet came down as a man just as Jesus did.

So these questions could just as easily be asked:

- "How can Jesus be the same yesterday and today and forever, when he once had a mortal body capable of dying and after his resurrection he received an immortal body that would never die again?"
- "How can Jesus be "unchangeable" if his body changed after the resurrection?" (Luke 24:36–34).
- "How can Jesus be the same yesterday and today and forever if he 'increased in wisdom and stature, and in favour with God and man'" (Luke 2:52).

The answer is simple. Terms like "unchangeable," "the same" and "everlasting" are not referring to Godhood or immortal bodies, these terms refer to law, truth and preexistence.

Question 7

> In the book of Isaiah it states:

> Before me there was no God formed, neither shall there be after me. I, even I, am the Lord; and beside me there is no savior. (Isa. 43:10–11)

Why do Mormons believe in Godhood if there is "no God formed . . . after me?"

Answer 7

These verses from Isaiah refer to the formation of false gods and idols. God is telling the Israelites to them there is no other God, and that Jehovah is God. Jesus Christ (Jehovah) is the God referred to in the Old Testament. These verses are correct, beside Jesus there is no Savior. Jesus is the only Savior. It does *not* say there would be no more gods; if it did it would be contradicting other Bible scriptures already listed above.

Question 8

Does the Bible say that God was not a man? If so why do Mormons believe God was a man?

Answer 8

Let's read the verse referred to:

> God is not a man, that he should lie; neither the son of man, that he should repent: hath he said, and shall he not do it? or hath he spoken, and shall he not make it good (Num. 23:19)?

Notice that the verse does not say God *was* not a man. This verse is simply stating that God is not a mortal man that lies, and is in need of repentance. The LDS Church does not teach that God is a mortal man nor do they teach that man in his present state is a God. To say that Jesus is not a child does not mean that he was not a child. Likewise, to say God is not a mortal man does not mean that he was not a mortal man.

Now let's take a look at some evidences that God is an immortal man.

- God made us in his image (Gen. 1:26–27).
- Jesus Christ, as a man on this earth, was described as being in the "express image" of God (Heb. 1:1–3).

- In the book of Deuteronomy the Lord is described "as a man" (Deut. 1:31).
- Moses spoke with God "*face* to face *as a man* speaketh unto his friend" (Ex. 33:11).
- Moses at another time saw God's back (Ex. 33:23).
- God has hands, "finger of God" (Ex. 31:18).
- Moses also saw God's feet (Ex. 24:10).

Enemies of the Church often bring up other verses that simply say that God is not mortal, or not an idol. Examples are Psalm 50:21, Numbers 23:19, and Romans 1:22–30. We agree God is not mortal, nor should we worship idols.

COMMENTS ABOUT GODHOOD

Enemies of the LDS Church have tried to discredit the statements written above in every possible way they can think, but to no avail. They often pull scriptures from the Old Testament that deal with pagan gods that a person made with their own hands and say this is proof that man cannot become a god. They also refer to verses that essentially say there is no other God besides God the Father. We agree with this and again state the verse in 1 Corinthians 8:5–6 quoted above. There are many gods, but to us there is but one God. The verses often used without relevance include Isaiah 46:6–8, 44:8, 57:15, 45:5, Malachi 3:6; Hebrews 1:4–5, 2:11, 6:13; Hosea 11:9; 2 Samuel 7:22; Micah 5:2, Revelations 22:13; and John 1:1–5.

They will also at times bring up John 1:3, which actually refers to Christ creating the world and is not even referring to God the Father. One thing I have noticed with all enemies of the LDS Church is that they are *all* willing to *distort the truth,* just as Satan, in order to turn others from Christ's gospel. For some, godhood is not an easy doctrine to understand that is why the scriptures say: "I have fed you with milk, and not meat: for hitherto ye were not able to bear it neither yet now are ye able" (1 Cor. 3:2). If God himself appeared to you today and said this concept is true, would you believe it? This concept has been told through prophets.

Remember this very important point. Mormons believe we will always worship God. By becoming a "god" (note the lower case g) *we will never be above the master.*

This is what *Christ also* referred to:

> The disciple is *not* above his master: but every one that is perfect *shall be as his master.* (Luke 6:40)

If Christ said it, believe it.

GOD, SPIRIT BODY

(see FLESH AND BONE)

GOLD PLATES

Question 1

What happened to the original gold plates that Joseph Smith translated the Book of Mormon from? Why did the Lord have them taken from the earth?

Answer 1

I suppose it would be just as easy to say, "Where is the original Ark of the Covenant and stone tablets that Moses brought down from the mount?" Very few could see Moses' tablets or even touch the Ark of the Covenant. In fact, recorded in the Bible it states a man touched the Ark in an effort to stabilize it when it was falling and he was struck dead (2 Sam. 2:6–7). Only those whom the Lord selects can see or touch his sacred documents.

Even if the plates were here, persecution would not subside and there would be those willing to lie and say they were translated wrong. Remember what the Lord has told others who want a sign.

> But he answered and said unto them, An evil and adulterous generation seeketh after a sign. (Matt. 12:39)

If you want to know what was on the gold plates, all you have to do is pick up a Book of Mormon and start reading.

GODHEAD

(see also FLESH AND BONE)

Question 1

Does the Bible say that God, Jesus Christ, and the Holy Ghost are one? If so why do Mormons believe they are separate?

Answer 1

The Bible says God, Jesus, and the Holy Ghost are one in purpose. There is not even one verse, throughout all the scriptures, that says they are the same person, but there are many that say they are separate and distinct beings. There are a few scriptures that are minimally confusing, so let's take a look at some of these debated scriptures:

> I and my Father are one. (John 10:30)

> For there are three that bear record in heaven, the Father, the Word, and the Holy Ghost: and these three are one. (1 Jn. 1:5)

> Thus saith the LORD the King of Israel, and his redeemer the LORD of hosts; I am the first, and I am the last; and beside me there is no God. (Isa. 44:6)

> Philip saith unto him, Lord, shew us the Father, and it sufficeth us.

> Jesus saith unto him, Have I been so long time
> with you, and yet hast thou not known me, Philip? he that
> hath seen me hath seen the Father; and how sayest thou
> then, Shew us the Father?
>
> Believest thou not that I am in the Father, and the
> Father in me? the words that I speak unto you I speak not
> of myself: but the Father that dwelleth in me, he doeth
> the works. (John 14:8–10)

If you believe that Jesus, God, and Holy Ghost are the same person I ask you to clear your mind for a moment and ask yourself, "what if they are separate." This is an important question because if they are separate you have been taught the wrong gospel. You will notice that not one of the verses above says that God and Jesus are the same person. The verses recorded in John and 1 John refer to God, Jesus and the Holy Ghost being *one in purpose.* The verse above recorded in Isaiah refers to idols. "Beside me there is no God." The verses in John 14 above simply state that Jesus looks physically just like God and he does what God tells him to do. Philip obviously understood the principle or he would not have asked to see the Father. Jesus answers with frustration that Philip would ask to see the father. What function would seeing the Father serve when Jesus was one in purpose with the Father? Jesus was doing what the Father would do in the same situation (John 5:19). Jesus told Philip about the oneness of Jesus and the Father, but Jesus was also sure to clarify that he was no more one with God than Jesus was one with his disciples! Lets read the verse:

> At that day ye [his disciples] shall know that I am
> in my Father, and ye in me, and I in you. (John 14:20)

Now let's read some of the verses that attest that God, Jesus, and the Holy Ghost are indeed separate.

> But he, being full of the *Holy Ghost,* looked up
> steadfastly into heaven, and saw the glory of *God,* and
> *Jesus standing on the right* hand *of God,*
>
> And said, Behold, I see the heavens opened, and

the Son of man standing on the right hand of God. (Acts 7:55–56; italics added)

These verses refer to Stephen when he was being stoned. Notice he witnessed three distinct personages. He was full of the Holy Ghost, and he saw two separate and distinct persons. God would not try to confuse someone by showing up as two people at the same time. The next verse states this:

> While he yet spake, behold, a bright cloud over-shadowed them: and behold a voice out of the cloud, which said, This is my beloved Son, in whom I am well pleased; hear ye him. (Matt. 17:5)

This verse documents God visiting Jesus and the apostles. God even spoke to them from the clouds. Again, God would not try to confuse the apostles, and act like he was Jesus but speak to them from the clouds. Jesus would also not speak to himself from the clouds and say that he was pleased with himself. God is a separate being from Jesus and the Holy Ghost.

If after showing you these verses if you still doubt that God, Jesus, and the Holy Ghost are one I ask you not to take my word for it but to take Jesus'. Jesus said himself, that he is no more one with God, than are the apostles. He said this in a prayer to God, let's read it:

> Neither *pray* I for these [the apostles] alone, but *for them also which shall believe on me* through their word;

> That *they [the apostles] all may be one; as thou, Father, art in me, and I in thee,* that *they* also may be one in *us:* that the world may believe *that thou hast sent me.*

> And the glory which thou gavest me I have given them; that *they* may be one, even as we are one:

> I in them, and thou in me, that they may be made perfect in one; and that the world may know that thou hast sent me, and *hast loved them, as thou hast loved me.* (John 17:20–23; italics added)

Jesus would not pray to himself, to ask himself, that his apostles would be one with himself.

Other examples:

Jesus would *not* pray to himself to ask himself to remove the cup from himself (Luke 22:42).

Jesus would *not* appear to Mary and say, "touch me not; for I am not yet ascended to myself: but go to my brethren, and say unto them, I ascend unto myself" (John 20:17).

Joseph Smith's vision of God and Jesus Christ showed two distinct personages. It is very clear that Jesus, God, and the Holy Ghost are only one in purpose.

GOSPEL

(see also CULT)

Question 1

In the book of Galatians 1:8–9, it states:

> But though we, or an angel from heaven, preach any other gospel unto you than that which we have preached unto you, let him be accursed.

Is the Mormon gospel the one referred to?

Answer 1

Mormon Gospel is Christ's gospel. Our fourth Article of Faith states this:

> We believe that the first principles and ordinances of the Gospel are: first, Faith in the Lord Jesus Christ; second, Repentance; third, Baptism by immersion for the remission of sins; fourth, Laying on of hand for the gift of the Holy Ghost.

When Christ was on the earth he set up his gospel one way. "One Lord, one faith, one baptism" (Eph. 4:5). He set it up with apostles, prophets, evangelists, pastors, and teachers. These were to continue until all faiths came into unity (Eph. 4:11–14, Amos 3:7).

- Christ's gospel required baptism by proper authority (John 3:5; Heb. 5:4). This baptism was to be performed by immersion (Matt. 3: 13–16). The gift of the Holy Ghost was to be given by the laying on of hands (Acts 8:14–17).

- Christ's gospel had missionaries (Matt. 24:14; Matt. 28:19–20). It also had temples that performed ordinances such as baptism for the dead (1 Cor. 15:29; Mal. 3:1; Rev. 7:15; 1 Cor. 9:13).

- Christ preached a gospel that would be restored (Acts 3:19–20).

- Christ's gospel taught that his Church would have revelation from heaven (Amos 3:7).

- Christ's gospel had a plan for all mankind. This included a way for the gospel to even be preached to those who had died and not had a chance to hear the good word (1 Pet. 4:6).

- Christ's gospel taught that God, Jesus, and the Holy Ghost were separate and distinct individuals that were one in purpose (Acts 7: 55–56; John 17:20–23).

- Christ's gospel taught the law of tithing as 1/10 of your income (Mal. 3:8–12; Gen. 28:20–22).

- Christ's gospel taught fasting (1 Cor. 7: 5; Jer. 6:6).

- Christ's gospel fulfills Bible prophesies (Rev. 14:6; Mal. 4:5–6).

- Christ's gospel taught that there would be two books of scripture. One for Jerusalem (Judah) and one for Joseph (America) (Ezek. 37:15–19). He said that one book would be buried in the ground and then come forth (Isa. 29:4, 11–14).

- Christ's gospel taught that he knew of another group of people and that he would visit them after his resurrection (John 10:16; 3 Ne. 15:21–24).
- Christ's gospel taught that he died for our sins and was resurrected into a body of flesh and bones (Luke 24:36–39, 1 Cor. 15:1–4).

This is Christ's gospel; if your Church does not contain all of the above, you are being preached another gospel. I invite you, as Noah of old, to follow the teachings of God and the prophets. In ancient times, you needed to get on the ark, today all you have to do is call the missionaries and they will do the rest.

GOSPEL PREACHED TO THE DEAD

(see also BAPTISM FOR THE DEAD)

Question 1

Mormons believe that the gospel is also preached to those who have died. So why does the book of Alma in the Book of Mormon state those who have procrastinated are subject to the devil?

Answer 1

Let's take a look at the verse:

> For behold, if ye have *procrastinated* the day of your repentance *even until death,* behold, ye have become subjected to the spirit of the devil, and he doth seal you his; therefore, the Spirit of the Lord hath withdrawn from you, and hath no place in you, and the devil hath no place in you, and this is the final state of the wicked. (Alma 34:35; italics added)

Mormons do believe the gospel is preached to those who have died (1 Pet. 4:6; 1 Cor. 15:29). But, Mormons do not believe you can deny the truth of the gospel on this earth and then get to the other side and get *another* opportunity. The verse above in Alma is absolutely true. Note the verse above does not say you get a second chance. The point is, if you have an opportunity in this life and you have "procrastinated the day of your repentance even until death," you will not get a second chance and you will be in Satan's hold.

Question 2

Why do Mormons believe that after death some people may have the gospel taught to them? Doesn't the Bible in Hebrews 9:27 say there is no chance after death?

Answer 2

Let's look at Hebrews. 9:27 it states:

> And as is appointed unto men once to die, but after this the judgment.

This verse does not say the gospel isn't taught in the next life. To understand the answer to this question some basic gospel knowledge must be understood. Many religions believe that after you die you either go to heaven or hell. This is not the case; the *final* judgment, which determines our final degree of salvation, does *not* take place until *after* the resurrection. After death, there is a small judgment (not the final judgment) that will determine if we go to paradise or prison. (Catholics call this wait before the final judgment purgatory.) Those in prison are in a state of hell, but it only lasts until the final judgment, or until the last farthing has been paid (Matt. 5:25–26). There are actually two states of hell in the hereafter, prison and outer darkness (Matt. 8:12). Prison is temporary; and outer darkness is forever. When Christ was on the cross, he told the thief he would see him in paradise not heaven (Luke 23:43). Also, when Christ came to Mary he said, "touch me not" for *he had not yet ascended and seen the father* (John 20:17). After the second coming of Christ, the *final* judgment will occur and we will be assigned to one of three heavens—Celestial, Terrestrial, or Telestial (1 Cor. 15:35–42; "many mansions" John 14:2; "third heaven" 2 Cor. 12:2–5). Or if you deny the Holy Ghost, you will gain neither of the three heavens, but will be cast into "outer darkness" (Matt. 5:25–26; Alma 40:13–14). Thus, the verse above talks of judgment, it doesn't say the gospel will not be taught to the dead. Let's look at evidences that the gospel is taught to those who have died.

> For this cause was the *gospel preached also to them that are dead,* that they might be *judged according to men in the flesh,* but live according to God in the spirit. (1 Pet. 4:6; italics added)

This verse tells us that indeed the gospel is taught after we die. But you will still be judged according to how you lived on this earth in the flesh.

> For *Christ* also hath once suffered for sins, the just for the unjust, that he might bring us to God, being put to death in the flesh, but quickened by the Spirit:
>
> By which also he went and preached unto the spirits in prison. (1 Pet. 3:19; italics added)

This verse tells us that after Christ suffered for our sins, he was put to death (crucified), his spirit went and prepared a way for the gospel to be preached to those in prison.

When Christ was on the earth, he told the parable of Lazarus and the rich man recorded in Luke 16:19–31. This parable tells us that *until* Christ went to the spirit prison, the gospel was not taught to the dead because there was a gulf between prison and paradise (Luke 26) and people could not cross. But after Christ prepared the way he bridged the gulf. From that time on, the gospel has been taught to those who have died.

> Verily, verily, I say unto you, The hour is coming, and now is, when the dead shall hear the voice of the Son of God: and they that hear shall live. (John 5:25)

> If in this life only we have hope in Christ, we are of all men most miserable. (1 Cor. 15:19)

God gives the opportunity to all mankind to hear the gospel. There are other verses not listed here that reveal this fact.

GRACE

(see WORKS)

ISAIAH

(see SCRIPTURES)

JOSEPH SMITH

Question 1

Did Joseph Smith say that he had done more than any other prophet except Jesus? If so, doesn't this seem arrogant? The scriptures say "be clothed with humility: for God resisteth the proud" (1 Pet. 5:5).

Answer 1

The above *question* was fabricated by enemies of the LDS Church to try and deceive others. The truth is, the quote referred to was *not* written by Joseph Smith at all. John Taylor wrote it about Joseph Smith, and the statement is absolutely correct. If it was stated that John the Baptist was greater than Isaiah or Moses, would it be wrong to say? Jesus stated in Luke 7:28:

> For I say unto you, among those that are born of women there is not a greater prophet than John the Baptist.

At that time John was the greatest (next to Jesus). As John Taylor said it:

> Joseph Smith, the Prophet and Seer of the Lord, has done more, save Jesus only, for the salvation of men in this world, than any other man that ever lived in it. (D&C 135:3)

There is no pride in this statement. Yet, because of this statement and others Joseph Smith and the Church are often persecuted just as the prophets of old. "And ye shall be hated of all men for my name's sake: but he that endureth to the end shall be saved" (Matt. 10:22).

An angel said to Joseph Smith:

> . . . God had a work for me to do; and that my name should be had for good and evil among all nations, kindreds, and tongues, or that it should be both good and evil spoken of among all people (JS-H 1:33).

No doubt this prophecy was fulfilled.

Question 2

Was Joseph Smith known as a "money digger?"

Answer 2

Enemies of the Church latch on to anything they can to discredit the prophet Joseph Smith. The same question could have been asked about to a "49er" in California who went to find gold so he could feed his family. Would that person be a "money digger"? Or, would he just be a man with a job. Joseph Smith was twenty-one years old when he went to work for Josiah Stoal searching for silver. The prophet Joseph needed money to support his family. Those who fault him for being a hard worker would have also faulted Peter anciently for being a fisherman (Matt. 4:18). Joseph Smith would have spoke of himself like the Prophet Peter, "I myself also am a man" (Acts: 10:26).

JOSEPH SMITH PROPHECIES

(see PROPHECIES)

JERUSALEM

(see BIRTH OF CHRIST)

JUDGMENT

(see BAPTISM FOR THE DEAD; GOSPEL PREACHED TO THE DEAD; PUNISHMENT)

LAW OF MOSES

(see PRIESTHOOD)

LYING

Question 1

In the Book of Mormon, Ether 3:12, it states that God cannot lie. If this is true why does the Book of Abraham in the Pearl of Great Price have God telling Abraham to lie and say that his wife is his sister (Abr. 2:24)? Is this a contradiction between these two scriptures?

Answer 1

It is important to point out that the Bible records the same situation. Compare Hebrews 6:18 and Genesis 12:13. The other important point is that Abraham's words were *not* a lie. Genesis 20:12 states, "and yet indeed she is my sister." Of course if Abraham had not stated the fact that Sarah was his sister, he would have been killed.

MARRIAGE, CELESTIAL

(see also MARRIAGE, NECESSARY FOR CELES-
TIAL INHERITANCE)

Question 1

Did Jesus say that there would be no married people in
heaven? If so, why do Mormons believe they will be married in the next life?

Answer 1

No, Jesus did not say there would be no married
people in heaven. Let's take a look at the verses:

> The same day came to him the Sadducees, which
> say that there is no resurrection, and asked him,
>
> Saying, Master, Moses said, if a man die having no
> children, his brother shall marry his wife, and raise up
> seed unto his brother:
>
> Now there were with us seven brethren: and the
> first, when he had married a wife, deceased, and, having
> no issue, left his wife unto his brother:
>
> Likewise the second also, and the third, unto the
> seventh.
>
> And last of all the woman died also.
>
> Therefore *in the resurrection* whose wife shall she
> be of the seven? For they all had her.
>
> Jesus answered and said unto them, Ye do err, not
> knowing the scriptures, nor the power of God.
>
> For *in the resurrection* they neither marry, nor are
> given in marriage, but are as the angels of God in
> Heaven. (Matt. 22:23–30; italics added)

The scripture above is absolutely correct. No marriage
will be performed in the next life ("for in the resurrection
they neither marry, nor are given in marriage").

One with the proper authority must perform the sacred
ordinance of eternal marriage in a temple of the Lord, and it

must be performed *before* the resurrection. Also marriages performed "until death do us part" are not sealed and *will not be bound* in the next life. Those not sealed in a temple "are as the angels of God in Heaven." Mormons would have known this even without these verses in Matthew because of modern day revelation. That is why LDS Church does proxy marriages for our dead ancestors *on earth*. Truly the prophecy in Malachi 4:5–6 has come to pass "And he shall turn the heart of the fathers to the children, and the heart of the children to their fathers" (i.e. temple work, including eternal marriage, for our forefathers).

The verses in Matthew above discuss the Sadducees, who do not believe in the resurrection. They have come to the Savior to try and trap him and show that he is contradicting doctrines that he has previously taught. (Why bring up marriage unless he had previously taught about it?) They certainly were not asking him because they were sincerely wondering. They were reacting to what Christ had previously said. Thus, Christ had been teaching eternal marriage, which is also obvious in other scriptures.

> And he answered and said unto them, Have ye not read, that he which made them at the beginning made them male and female,
>
> And said, For this cause shall a man leave father and mother, and shall cleave to his wife: and they twain shall be one flesh?
>
> Wherefore they are no more twain, but one flesh. *What therefore God hath joined together, let not man put asunder.* (Matt. 19:4–6)

Other verses also reveal this sacred doctrine:

> I know that, whatsoever God doeth, It shall be forever. (Eccl. 3:14)

> Nevertheless neither is the man without the woman, neither the woman without the man, in the Lord. (1 Cor. 11:11)

> And the Lord God said, it is not good that the man should be alone. (Gen. 2:18)

> And I will give unto thee the keys of the kingdom of heaven: and whatsoever thou shalt bind on earth shall be bound in heaven: and whatsoever thou shalt loose on earth shall be loosed in heaven. (Matt. 16:19)

> For this cause shall a man leave his father and mother, and shall be joined unto his wife, and they two shall be one flesh" (Eph. 5:31–32)

We know there are also many other things that Christ did and taught that are not recorded (see John 21:25).

Reading the scriptures shows evidence that Adam and Eve were also married for time and eternity. (see Gen. 2:22–24).

With the restitution of all things the sealing power too was restored to the earth. If the couple remains worthy, the marriage sealed on earth is sealed in heaven.

MARRIAGE, NECESSARY FOR CELESTIAL INHERITANCE

(see also MARRIAGE, CELESTIAL)

Question 1

Do Mormons believe that for a person to gain salvation they have to be married? Does it state this in the Doctrine and Covenants?

Answer 1

No, you do not have to be married to gain salvation, but you do have to be married to inherit exaltation in the highest degree of the *Celestial* Kingdom. Let's take a look at the verse referred to in Doctrine and Covenants 132:18:

They cannot, therefore, inherit my glory; for my
house is a house of order, saith the Lord God.

Thus, you must be married in a temple with proper
authority to inherit the Celestial glory. The Creator himself
has said, "It is not good that man should be alone" (Gen.
2:18). Of course it is important to remember that righteous
individuals who have not had the opportunity to receive
temple marriage in this life will have the opportunity after
the second coming of Christ. This ordinance can be performed by proxies before and during the millennium, but
not after the final judgment.

Question 2

Why do Mormons believe you have to be married to
go to the Celestial glory when there is a verse in the Bible
that says some people should be eunuchs (castrated men)
for the kingdom of heaven's sake? Aren't there other verses
in the Bible that say not to get married?

Answer 2

Let's take a look at the verses referred to Matthew
19:12 (this verse is also used by Catholic priests to explain
a life of celibacy):

For there are some eunuchs, which were so born
from their mother's womb: and there are some Eunuchs,
which were made eunuchs of men: and there be
eunuchs, which have made themselves *eunuchs for the
kingdom of heaven's sake. He that is able to receive it
let him receive it.*

The Lord Jesus Christ often had Pharisees and others
before him trying to entrap him, and trying to prove to
others, that Christ was teaching doctrines not in harmony
with Moses' teachings and their law. Such was the case with
the doctrine of marriage. A look at Matthew 19 shows that
Jesus was teaching the importance of marriage and said,

"What therefore God hath joined together, let not man put asunder" (Matt. 19:6). The Pharisees disagreeing with the Savior said, "Why did Moses then command to give a writing of divorcement, and to put her away?"

In Matthew 19:7–8, the Savior answered:

> Moses because of the hardness of your hearts suffered you to put away your wives: but from the beginning it was not so.

The Saviors disciples were unsettled with his answer and asked: "If the case of the man be so with his wife, it is not good to marry" (Matt. 19:10). The Savior *corrected* them however and stated the verse above (Matt 19:8). The explanation of this verse is really quite simple. Jesus was simply explaining to his disciples that if a man marry a wife without conviction it would have been better for him to never get married.

Thus, it would be better for him to be a "eunuch for the kingdom of heaven's sake." This is because if he were to marry without conviction and later got divorced, he would be committing adultery (Matt. 19:9). It is better to be a eunuch, than to commit adultery. Getting married is the Lord's desire and has been from the beginning. "It is not good that man should be alone." The Lord does not want man to be alone in this life or in the next. The scriptures, as well as modern prophets have told us this.

Question 3

In the book of Corinthians does Paul tell others not to be married just as he was not married? In 1 Corinthians 7:8, it states:

> I say therefore to the unmarried and widows, It is good for them if they *abide even as I.* (italics added)

Answer 3

No, he does not, he does tell them to abide even as he, meaning to keep the commandments just as he does. Some have said that he referred to his status of not being married. Because he was addressing those not married, and he himself was a widower at the time he wrote the passage. This is an incorrect interpretation of the scriptures, for one thing Paul would never disagree with what Jesus has already said (see question 2).

Question 4

In 1 Corinthians 7:27, does Paul tell all the Saints not to get married or seek a wife?

> Art thou bound unto a wife? Seek not to be loosed.
> Art thou loosed from a wife? Seek not a wife. (1 Cor. 7:27)

Answer 4

No, he does not. In this verse, Paul is addressing only the missionaries. The fact he was only addressing missionaries is very obvious when you read 1 Corinthians 7:22: "For he that is called in the Lord being a servant."

It is the same today; missionaries are asked not to seek a wife while they are serving the Lord in a missionary capacity.

Question 5

Does 1 Corinthians 7:38 state that it is better not to be married than to be married? Let's take a look at the verse:

> So then he that giveth her in marriage doeth well;
> but *he that giveth her not in marriage doeth better.*
> (1 Cor. 7:38; italics added)

Answer 5

The answer to this question is the same answer as question 4 above. This verse is addressed to the missionaries only. Again, Paul would not say something different than God and Jesus taught (see Gen. 2:18; Matt. 19:3–8; D&C 49:15–16; etc.).

Question 6

How can marriage be required in order to enter the Celestial glory if Christ and some of the apostles were not married?

Answer 6

Nowhere in the scriptures does it state that Jesus and his apostles were not married. In fact, the evidence points to the fact that they were married. Let's take a look at the following scriptures showing this evidence:

> Have we not power to lead about a sister, a wife, as well as other apostles, and as the brethren of the Lord, and Cephas? (1 Cor. 9:5) (Paul speaking)

> Which knew me from the beginning, if they would testify, that after the most straitest sect of our religion I lived a Pharisee. (Acts 26:5) (Paul either a widower or divorced)

The "straitest sect," who was the Sanhedrin or highest court/ruling organization of that time, commanded that members be married at a young age.

> And when Jesus was come into Peter's house, *he saw his wife's mother* laid and sick of a fever" (Matt. 8:14; italics added) (Peter married).

> And there are also many *other things which Jesus did,* the which, if they should be written every one, I suppose that even the world itself could not contain the books that should be written. Amen" (John 21:25; italics added) (Jesus too could have been married).

Jesus was called "Master" and "Rabbi" (John 1:49; Matt. 17:24), both of these names identified people who were required by law to be married. Pharisees often accused Jesus of not obeying certain laws (Matt. 12:10; 17:24), but they never accused him of not obeying the law that required a Rabbi or Master to be married. This is because Jesus was in fact married.

Those who know the scriptures know that there was more than one Mary in Jesus' life. For instance, his mother Mary and Mary Magdalene. It is a possibility that Mary Magdalene was Jesus' wife. She certainly was with Jesus a lot and was even there with his mother Mary when Jesus died on the cross (John 19:25–26). She was at the burial (Matt. 27:61) at the tomb in the morning (Matt. 28:1), and Jesus appeared to her (John 20:14–18).

MARRIAGE AND PRIESTHOOD OFFICES

Question 1

Why are LDS deacons and elders not married, when in the New Testament it states they have to be married? Is this evidence that the Mormon Church is not the true Church and that their deacons and elders do not hold the priesthood at all?

Answer 1

Let's take a look at the verses:

Let the deacons be the husbands of one wife, ruling their children and their own houses well. (1 Tim. 3:12)

And ordain elders in every city, as I had appointed thee:

If any be blameless, the husbands of one wife, having faithful children. (Titus 1:5–6)

As a missionary in Arkansas, I remember times I would knock on a door to share the true gospel of Jesus Christ, only to be told to leave because my companion and I could not be elders because we were not married.

Just because deacons and elders had to be married at the time of Christ, does not mean the same rule holds true today. There have been many changes in certain regulations since the time of Christ. The following are just a few of the changes:

1. God commanded circumcision (Gen. 17:10:11), and later revoked it (Acts 15, Gal. 5:2-3).

2. Women at one time could not speak in Churches (1 Cor. 14:34–35), yet during other times they worked with Paul (Rom. 16:1–4). Some women were even prophetesses (Luke 2:36).

3. The law of Moses was in full force during Old Testament times and withdrawn during New Testament times (Matt. 5:17).

4. At one time, divorce was not allowed, and then later under certain circumstances it was permitted (Matt. 19:8–9).

5. Polygamy was commanded and later revoked.

6. The gospel was not initially brought to the gentiles (Matt. 10:5), but later it was commanded (see Matt. 28:19; Acts 10:1-48).

It is interesting that no one is confused by Paul's past instruction that "women keep silence in the Churches: for it is not permitted unto them to speak" (1 Cor. 14:34), or Paul's instruction to "greet all the brethren with an holy kiss" (1 Thes. 5:26). If we obeyed this instruction today you would not see anyone at Church. Although this instruction by Paul has some translation errors, the point is gospel principles are unchangeable, but change happens within the gospel under the direction of the Lord. Anciently marriage was required, but today the opportunity to hold certain priesthood offices is given to nonmarried, worthy brethren of appropriate age. How will those who close the door to missionaries answer the Savior in the next life?

When Peter was commanded to make a change and bring the gospel to the gentiles, he resisted at first, but being the obedient servant he was, he did what the lord asked (see Acts 10). Not having to be married to hold certain priesthood offices is a change that came under the direction of the Lord.

MISSOURI TEMPLE/ZION

(see PROPHESY)

MONEY DIGGING

(see JOSEPH SMITH)

MORMON

Question 1

Does the word *Mormon* mean *gates of hell* in Chinese?

Answer 1

Ask nearly any person who is fluent in the Chinese language this question and you are sure to get a laugh. The answer is really quite simple. When a relatively new English word is translated into Chinese, characters that have pronunciations similar to the English word are put together to sound like the original word, regardless of the characters' actual meaning. Each Chinese character is pronounced with only one syllable. Characters are put together to sound out one multisyllable English word. For example, the Chinese characters used to translate the English word for *disco* are pronounced *tee-se-go,* but the literal translation of those three characters means *kick dead dog.* When Mormonism was introduced to the Chinese people, they had an English word they had never heard of that needed characters. So the Chinese people took two characters that sounded like the word *Mormon.* Those characters were *mwo* and *men.* If translated literally, the character for *mwo* means to *encourage in study,* but it is used much more often to translate non-Chinese names such as Monoco, Morocco, Moses, and Mormon. The confusion and misrepresentation of the Chinese word for Mormon comes from the fact that the Chinese word for *devil* is *mwo wang,* which literally means *ghost king.* The *mwo* for *Mormon* and the *mwo* for *devil* are pronounced the same, but the character and meaning of the two words is completely different. The Chinese word representing the second syllable of *Mormon* is pronounced *men,* which literally means *door.* This character is used in the word that means *gate.* Consequently, there are those who teach in half-truths who bend the true translation of the word Mormon to mean things like *devil door,* or if they really stretch the truth, *Gates of Hell.* But again the characters are really completely different. Only those willing to lie and deceive can draw a different conclusion that Mormon means gates of hell. To show you that the characters are in fact different I have copied them below. You will see that in no way does one character look like the other. It is easy to see *Mormon* does not mean *gates of hell.* But once again this question shows how far enemies will go to deceive you.

Mormon	['mprm/&/n]	摩門教徒
Gate	[geit]	城門
Hell	[hel]	地獄

Joseph Smith told us the true meaning of the name *Mormon*; it literally means *more good.* (*The above information provided by Brett Bagley, Shelley, Idaho*).

MASONS

Question 1

Did Joseph Smith copy from Masonry?

Answer 1

Joseph Smith did not copy from Masonry. If Joseph had copied from Masonry, members of the Church, from the beginning, would have marked him a fraud. The Saints knew what was in Masonry and they knew what Joseph Smith brought forth. Had it merely been copied, they would have recognized it as forgery. Of course there is a reason that Masonry has existed from ancient dates. These ceremonies have existed for a long time and the originals are a part of God's plan. Of course, whenever something like Masonry or Christianity has existed for such a long time, precious truths can be lost and were lost along the way, only the LDS Church has all the truth. This is because of continuous revelation that other religions do not have. Joseph Fielding McConkie stated this on the subject:

> It is not inconceivable that the Prophet, sensing something about the ancient roots of Masonry, inquired of the Lord about it. In that sense it may have been one of the influences that prepared the way for the revelations that restored the ceremonies of the temple.

> The idea that the kind of faith and courage common to our pioneer forebears grew out of rituals copied from a fraternal organization is ludicrous. The experiences the Latter Day Saints have had in the temple have come too often and are too real for anyone to suppose that they stem from a borrowed ceremony. Similarly, the assurance that we will be endowed with power from on high does not lack for proof among our people.[51]

Joseph Smith did not copy Masonry, and he did not copy Christianity. What he did receive on the matter was revelation and restoration of Gods will. Joseph Smith knew much more than Masons. Mason rites are mere scattered clues to a bigger, more perfect representation. Heber C. Kimball said this:

> There is a similarity of priesthood in Masonry. Bro[ther] Joseph says Masonry was taken from priesthood but has become degenerated.[52]

Another evidence that suggests that today's LDS temple endowments were *restored* from *original ancient temple endowments* is to look at the resemblance between the early Christian *"rite of initiation"* for more information. It's suggested that research on the writings by Hugh Nibley be done on this subject.

MURDER (NO FORGIVENESS FOR MURDER IN THIS LIFE)

(see also BLOOD ATONEMENT)

Question 1

Mormons believe there is no forgiveness in this life or the life to come if a person commits murder. As stated in the Doctrine and Covenants:

> I speak unto the Church. Thou shalt not kill; and he that kills hall not have forgiveness in this world, nor in the world to come. (D&C 42:18)

If this scripture is true, why did Moses murder an Egyptian and later become a prophet of God? Isn't it obvious God forgave him to give him such a calling?

Answer 1

Let's take a look at the verse:

> And it came to pass in those days, when Moses was grown, that he went out unto his brethren, and looked on their burdens: and he spied an Egyptian

smiting an Hebrew, one of his brethren

And he looked this and that way, and when he saw that there was no man, he slew the Egyptian, and hid him in the sand. (Ex. 2:11–12)

The answer to this question is simple. If there is no law, there is no punishment. This is what the scriptures say about the subject:

And where there is no law given there is no punishment . . .

For the atonement satisfieth the demands of his justice upon all those who have not the law given to them. (2 Ne. 9:25–26)

Where no law is, there is no transgression. (Rom. 4:15)

Moses is the one who received the law; the Lord would *not* judge Moses by a law he had not yet received. It is important to realize the scripture above in Doctrine and Covenants 42 is written to the Church. It states, "*I speak to the Church.*" Those in the Church know the law, and will be judged by it.

Question 2

After Jesus died, there were many Israelites who believed and were baptized. Many believe that some of these Israelites were the ones who killed Jesus. If so, doesn't this prove that the Mormon belief of no forgiveness for murder is false?

Answer 2

Let's take a look at the verse:

Therefore *let all the house of Israel* know assuredly, that God hath made that same Jesus, whom *ye have crucified,* both Lord and Christ.

Now when they heard this they were pricked in their heart, and said unto Peter and to the rest of the apostles, men and brethren what shall we do?

> Then Peter said unto them Repent, and be baptized every one of you in the name of Jesus Christ for the remission of sins, and ye shall receive the gift of the Holy Ghost. (Acts 2:36–37; italics added)

The Israelites referred to were *not* the Pharisees who actually arranged with Judas to set the trap to have Jesus killed. Knowing that Christ had raised the dead did not change the Pharisees disbeliefs. Thus, when the scripture above says, "ye have crucified" it refers to Jesus being killed because of the disbelief of those of the house of Israel. For we know that not *all the house of Israel* killed Jesus. Yes, many watched and did nothing to stop the action, but again they were not the ones to set him up or kill him. In the book of Acts, it tells us that the Jews whose hands the blood of Christ were found were *not* given the invitation to repent and receive baptism. They were told they must wait until the return of Christ to have their sins blotted out, even though they had repented. Why must they wait? Because they were murderers, let's read the verse referred to.

> Repent ye therefore, and be converted, that your sins maybe blotted out, *when the times of refreshing shall come* from the presence of the Lord,
> And he shall send Jesus Christ, which before was preached unto you. (Acts 3:19–20; italics added).

In other words, their sins will not be blotted out *until* the time of refreshing or redemption. This time of redemption has reference to when Christ would return.

At that time, and that time only, will their sins be blotted out. Had it not been murder, they would not have had to wait. When it states in the verse that there sins would be blotted out, it is important to realize they are not forgiven in the sense that *Celestial* inheritance would be obtained (see "Murder").

Question 3

Does the Book of Mormon tell of a king who murdered and received forgiveness? If so, is this a discrepancy in Mormon doctrine?

Answer 3

Let's take a look at the verse:

"Now the servants of the king began to murmur, saying: Now the king will slay us, as he has our brethren because their flocks were scattered . . .

. . . Lamoni was under the power of God; he knew that the dark veil of unbelief was being cast away from his mind, and the light which did light up his mind, which was the light of the glory of God, which was a marvelous light of his goodness—yea, this light had infused such joy into his soul, the cloud of darkness having been dispelled, and that the light of everlasting life was lit up in his soul. (Alma 17:28; 19:6)

Just as with Moses, King Lamoni did not have the scriptures and did not know of the commandment "thou shalt not kill." So Lamoni too was not condemned for a law he had not received.

Question 4

Does the Book of Mormon document that a prophet named Nephi killed a man, and that the Lord told him to do it?

Answer 4

Let's take a look at the verse:

And it came to pass that I [Nephi] was constrained by the spirit that I should kill Laban; . . .

Therefore I did obey the voice of the spirit, and took Laban by the hair of the head, and I smote off his head with his own sword. (1 Ne. 4:10, 18)

Yes, Nephi slew the evil Laban, as commanded by the Lord. Had Nephi not killed Laban, his family would not have been able to obtain and keep the brass plates, which contained the scriptures of that time (the five books of Moses). Nephi's family would have traveled to the American continent with no scriptures. Without the scriptures, the entire nation would have perished in unbelief. The scriptures themselves document the reason for the death of Laban.

> Behold the Lord slayeth the wicked to bring forth his righteous purposes. It is better that one man should perish than that a nation should dwindle and perish in unbelief. (1 Ne. 4:13)

Thus, Nephi did *not* murder Laban. He did what the Lord commanded. Nephi was not a murderer, *just as those who slay others in war* are *not* murderers. Those who think that God would not tell Nephi to kill a man need only look at the scriptures. For example, in Joshua 6:21, the Lord provided a way for the walls of Jericho to fall. After the walls fell the Lord had all those in the city destroyed.

Let's take a look at the verse:

> And they utterly destroyed all that *was* in the city, both man and woman, young and old, and ox, and sheep, and ass, with the edge of the sword. (Josh. 6:21)

Nephi lived during the law of Moses. During this time if a person even gathered sticks on the Sabbath he was put to death.

Let's read the verse:

> And the LORD said unto Moses, The man shall be surely put to death: all the congregation shall stone him with stones without the camp. (Num. 15:35)

The Lord did not hesitate to have Nephi kill Laban and save a nation of people.

Question 5

What about King David, he murdered Uriah, yet the Lord loved him, and even considered him the apple of his eye?

Answer 5

Let's take a look at the verse:

> And he [David] wrote in the letter, saying, Set ye Uriah in the forefront of the hottest battle, and retire ye from him, that he may be smitten and die. (2 Sam. 11:15)

King David's circumstance is very different from those mentioned above. *He knew* the Ten Commandments. Thus, he knew that *murder* was wrong, but he still committed the sin. His situation is also probably the most enlightening—informing us what happens to a person who knows murder is wrong, yet commits the sin. The Lord loves David and you can imagine the sorrow the Lord felt when David committed the unforgivable sin of murder, and his chances of Celestial glory were lost.

To understand the answer to this question, some basic gospel knowledge must be understood. Many religions believe that after you die you either go to heaven or hell. This is not the case; the final judgment, which determines our final degree of glory, does not take place until *after* the resurrection. After death we either go to paradise or prison (Catholics call this wait before the final judgment purgatory). Those in prison are in a state of hell, but it only lasts until the final judgment, or until the "uttermost farthing" has been paid (Matt. 5:25–26). There are actually two states of hell in the hereafter; prison and outer darkness (Matt. 8:12). Prison is temporary and outer darkness is forever. When Christ was on the cross, he told the thief he would see him in paradise <u>not</u> heaven (Luke 23:43). Also, when Christ came to Mary he said, "touch me not" for he had not yet ascended and seen the father (John 20:17). After the second coming of Christ, the final judgment will occur and we will be assigned to one of three heavens—Celestial, Terrestrial, and Telestial (1 Cor. 15:35–42; "many mansions," John 14:2; "third heaven," 2 Cor. 12:2–5). Or if you deny the Holy Ghost, you will gain neither of the three heavens mentioned, but will be cast into "outer darkness" (Matt 5:25–26; Alma 40:13–14).

Now back to the question, what happens to those who murder and know that it is wrong? The apostle Peter said this about David being a murderer:

> For David is not ascended into the heavens. (Acts 2:34).

Yet, David was given a promise that his soul would not be "left in hell" (Acts 2:31).

Meaning he will not be left in prison, but will inherit the Telestial glory. *This same promise* is given to other murderers who have not denied the Holy Ghost. God is no respecter of persons (Rom. 2:11) he would not promise something to David that he would not promise to you or I, in the same circumstance. Thus, David will not be a son of perdition—he will not be in outer darkness. But 1 John 3:15 states "no murderer hath eternal life abiding in him." It is also obvious that David was not forgiven for this sin because committing it, the Lord would not allow David to built the temple (1 Chr. 17). The Lord waited until Solomon came into power to build it. If the Lord had forgiven David he would have let David do it. Another point revealing that David was clearly not forgiven for his sin is the fact that *another David* ("unto David") will be raised up in the last days to replace King David. As stated by Daniel H. Ludlow:

> The Lord gave several statements to his prophets anciently concerning a shepherd named David whom he would raise up in the last days to feed his flock. "And I the Lord will be their God, and my servant among them." (see Jer. 23:5; 30:9; 33:15–26; Ps. 89:3–4; Isa. 55:3–4; Ezek. 34:24; 37:22–25)

Prophets of this dispensation have also spoken and prophesied concerning the spiritual giant named David, who will come forth in the last days to be a blessing to gathered Judah.

> Just three months before his martyrdom, the Prophet Joseph Smith taught concerning this David: "The throne and kingdom of David is to be taken from him and given to another by the name of David in the last days, raised up out of his lineage."[53]

David, like all those who murder will not be left in hell but also will not inherit the Celestial glory.

Question 6

What about Paul (Saul)—he was called as an apostle. Didn't he participate in the murder of Stephen?

Answer 6

The scripture referred to is in Acts 7:58 (see also Acts 8:1).

Let's take a look at the verse:

> And cast him out of the city, and stoned him; and the witnesses laid down their clothes at a young man's feet, whose name was Saul.

Just because someone *supports* a wrongful death does *not* mean he or she "pulled the trigger," or even *arranged* for the trigger to be pulled. Obviously, the above scripture concerning Paul simply states the clothes were laid at the feet of Paul. *Nothing* is said about him actually throwing a stone. Thus, it appears Paul was a witness of the event, and not a murderer. It seems quite *obvious* that murder is not tolerated in the site of God. One example of this is in the book of Genesis when the Lord punished Cain when he murdered his brother Abel. God is "no respecter of persons" (Acts 10:34), he would not curse Cain and not Paul. Another example is Judas Iscariot. He arranged the betrayal and murder of Jesus. But he later "repented himself" (Matt. 27:3). Did it matter? Let's take a look at the verse:

> But woe to that man by whom the Son of man is betrayed! Good were it for that man if he had never been born. (Mark 14:21)

It is easy to see Paul was not a murderer.

Question 7

In the Book of Mormon, there is a verse telling the murdering Gentiles to repent. How can they repent if the LDS religion believes there is no forgiveness for murder?

Answer 7

Here is the verse referred to:

> Turn, all ye Gentiles, from your wicked ways; and *repent of your* evil doings, of your lying and deceiving, and of your whoredoms, and of your secret abominations and your idolatries, and of your *murders,* and your priest-crafts, and your envyings, and your strifes, and from all your wickedness and abominations, and come unto me. (3 Ne. 30:2)

The gentiles did not have the gospel. The Lord would not judge the gentiles by gospel commandments that they had not received (Luke 12:48). The gentiles did not even begin to hear about the commandments and other gospel principles until after Jesus was resurrected (Matt. 28:19–20). Furthermore, this verse refers to gentiles who took life in unrighteous *wars*. It does not refer to those who are murderers at heart. The Lord judges differently for those who kill in war.

FINAL COMMENTS ABOUT MURDER:

The Book of Mormon states this:

> Whosoever murdereth against the light and knowledge of God it is not easy for him to obtain forgiveness. (Alma 39:6)

This verse *appears* to contradict Doctrine and Covenants 42. As mentioned above, Doctrine and Covenants 42 is given specifically as a law *to the Church*. Thus, we see that not everyone who kills someone is condemned to the Telestial kingdom for eternity. "For unto whomsoever much is given, of him shall be much required" (Luke 12:48). Elder Bruce R. McConkie has stated:

> We do know that there are murders committed by Gentiles for which they at least can repent, be baptized, and receive a remission of their sins.[54]

In general, after the last farthing has been paid, those who murder will abide in the Telestial Glory and will not be left in hell. This is because murder, unlike a sin against the Holy Ghost, is not forgivable, but it is *pardonable*. However, the individual has lost their exaltation in the Celestial Kingdom.

PEARL OF GREAT PRICE

(see also SCRIPTURES)

Question 1

Is it true that there was a professor of Egyptology named Dee Jay Nelson who was given permission to translate the original ancient papyri for the Pearl of Great Price, and that professor Nelson's translation was different than Joseph Smith's?

Answer 1

The statement above is absolutely false. This question shows that Satan and his followers have no bounds to the amount of lies that have been and will be told in an effort to keep others from discovering the truth. However, the question also brings up an interesting proof. Even enemies of the

LDS Church cannot refute the know fact that Joseph Smith received ancient writings from the catacombs of Egypt. The LDS Church still has fragments of the papyri and they have been put on display for even the world's greatest scholars to evaluate. Dee Jay Nelson *claimed* to have received the original Papyri from the LDS Church and that he was commissioned by the Church to translate them. The LDS Church did not give permission to Nelson to translate any documents. Also it would be *impossible,* considering the LDS Church now has only fragments of the originals left.

Dee Jay Nelson was completely exposed in 1981 by Robert L. and Rosemary Brown in the book *They Lie in Wait to Deceive.*[55]

Fortunately the Lord, in his own due time, has exposed many of the deceivers like Nelson, Mark Hofmann, and others. Richard Lloyd Anderson has said this about those who persecute the LDS Church:

> A minority in the world believes in Jesus Christ, and the wrangling of Christians has certainly contributed to skepticism in the message and mission of the Master. Indeed, if the energy spent attacking other Christians had been seriously spent on uniting and teaching non-Christians, Christ's goal would have been much further along—"that the world may believe that thou hast sent me."[56]

POLYGAMY

Question 1

Why did the LDS Church practice polygamy for a time, and then during a period of persecution for this belief, changed the policy? If polygamy was commanded, isn't it true the Lord would continue the doctrine regardless of persecution?

Answer 1

An important point should be made before answering this question. It does not matter how much any person on this earth disagrees or dislikes the doctrine of polygamy. The fact is it is a doctrine from God. It has existed since the time of Adam and its evidence of being practiced is strewn throughout the scriptures. *Those who mock the doctrine of polygamy mock God.* Some of the greatest prophets of all time practiced polygamy. The following are only a few evidences in the scriptures of this God ordained principle: Genesis 16:3–4; 25:1–2; 29:23–35; 30:3–4; 8–9, 2 Chronicles 13:21, 2 Samuel 12:7–8.

Back to the question—would the Lord tell the saints to stop practicing polygamy because of persecution? The answer is *the Lord decided* to withdraw the doctrine of polygamy. It may have had something to do with the change in the law at that time which made the practice of polygamy against the law. The prophet Joseph Smith himself stated this in the twelfth article of faith.

> We believe in being subject to kings, presidents, rulers, and magistrates, in *obeying,* honoring, and sustaining *the law.* (italics added)

Thus, the saints obey the law as the Lord directs. There will be enemies of the Church who will say Daniel in the Lion's Den is an example of the law changing, but Daniel was willing to die so he would not disobey what God commanded. The answer to this is, so were the Saints. The members at that time would have been more than willing to give there lives to obey the Lord's command. The only reason they didn't is that they, like Daniel, were doing what *the Lord* commanded. In the Bible and Pearl of Great price we learn that God told Abraham not to tell the Egyptians he was married to Sarai (Sarah) (Gen. 12:13, Abr. 2:24). Was Abraham afraid of persecution? Did God not want Abraham to just do like Daniel did and stand up to the task? The answer is the same; Abraham did whatever God told him to do.

Members of the LDS Church are not afraid of persecution. They have certainly received enough of it. After moving to Salt Lake City they were so far away from the persecution there was definitely not enough to scare them into changing the doctrine. Wilford Woodruff gave "The Manifesto" in 1890 to "refrain from contracting any marriage forbidden by the law of the land." A year after giving the command to stop plural marriage President Woodruff said:

> The Lord showed me by vision and revelation exactly what would take place if we did not stop this practice.
>
> I know there are a good many men, and probably some leading men, in this Church who have been tried and felt as though President Woodruff had lost the Spirit of God and was about to apostatize. Now, I want you to understand that he has not lost the Spirit, nor is he about to apostatize. The Lord is with him, and with this people. He has told me exactly what to do, and what the result would be if we did not do it. . . . I want to say this: I should have let all the temples go out of our hands; I should have gone to prison myself, and let every other man go there, had not the God of heaven commanded me to do what I did do; and when the hour came that I was commanded to do that, it was all clear to me.[57]

As mentioned above, the law was changed because the Lord changed it.

Question 2

If the Lord did change the doctrine of polygamy because of persecution, are there other examples of this "giving in" by the Lord in the scriptures? If so, how does this relate to the following scripture?

> I know that, whatsoever God doeth, it shall be for ever: nothing can be put to it, nor any thing taken from it: and God doeth it, that men should fear before him. (Eccl. 3:14)

Answer 2

I don't think the words "giving in" are appropriate, but yes, the Lord has allowed decisions to be made that he did not necessarily desire. The example I am talking about is in the first book of Samuel. In this situation the Lord did *not* want the people to have a king. However, the people wanted one and would not listen to the prophet Samuel who brought the Lords words. The Lord told them to go ahead and have the king though he did not want them to. Let's take a look at the verses:

> Nevertheless the people refused to obey the voice of Samuel; and they said, Nay; but we will have a king over us; . . .
>
> And the Lord said to Samuel, Hearken unto their voice, and make them a king. And Samuel said unto the men of Israel, Go ye every man unto his city. (1 Sam. 8:19, 22)

Another example comparing polygamy to sometimes being practiced and sometimes not is to study the prophets. After Malachi, there were no prophets on earth for four hundred years. In other words, the Lord had polygamy for a while and then not, just as he had prophets for a while and then not. In the book of Genesis 17:8–10 the Lord commanded circumcision as an *"everlasting* covenant" But during New Testament times the command was changed (Acts 15, Gal. 5:2-3). The Lord put it best when he stated, "I the Lord, command and revoke, as seemeth me good; and all this to be answered upon the heads of the rebellious, saith the Lord (D&C 56:4).

Question 3

In the Book of Mormon, Jacob 2:27, it states there should be no plural marriage. Does this prove the Book of Mormon is false since it appears to contradict the known LDS belief that plural marriage is of God?

Answer 3

This proves that enemies of the Church will go to any extent to deceive, just as Satan, to turn others into following the wrong path. The answer is written, but of course those who persecute the Church never bother to point that out. In a nut shell the answer is this, *plural marriage is only authorized under the Lord's command, as has always been the case.* Even when polygamy was in its greatest numbers, only about three percent of the Church was allowed to practice it. No member of the Church has been able to just say, "I think I'll start practicing polygamy today" they had to have permission just as those recorded in the Book of Mormon. It just so happened that *during this period of the Book of Mormon* it was not allowed.

Let's take a look at the verses:

> Wherefore, my brethren, hear me, and hearken to the word of the Lord: For there shall not any man among you have save it be one wife; and concubines he shall have none. (Jacob 2:27)

> For if I will, saith the Lord of Hosts, raise up seed unto me, *I will command* my people; *otherwise* they shall hearken unto these things. (Jacob 2:30; italics added)

In other words, the Lord uses polygamy to "raise up seed" but *only* if He commands it. He did not command it here and in fact it was forbidden. This was also the case for David and his son Solomon. (Deut. 17:17)

Question 4

Is there a contradiction between Jacob 2:24 and Doctrine and Covenants 132:39?

Answer 4

No, there is not. In fact the Bible says the same thing. Let's take a look at the following verses:

> Behold, David and Solomon truly had many wives

and concubines, *which thing was abominable before me,* saith the Lord. (Jacob 2:24; italics added)

> *David's wives and concubines were given unto him of me, by the hand of Nathan,* my servant, and others of the prophets who had the keys of this power; and in none of these things did he sin against me save in the case of Uriah and his wife; and therefore he hath fallen from his exaltation. (D&C 132:39; italics added)

Both statements are absolutely correct. Solomon and David *initially* had wives and concubines given to them of the Lord.

God did *not* condemn Solomon and David for having the *wives that the Lord had given. But,* David married Bathsheba and Solomon married "strange women" that were not of the house of Israel (1 Kgs. 11:1). Let's read if the Lord was pleased with David Marrying Bathsheba.

> And when the mourning was past, David sent and fetched her to his house, and she became *his wife,* and bare him a son. *But the thing that David had done displeased the Lord.* (2 Sam. 11:27; italics added)

The Lord said it himself—"David also received many wives and concubines, and also Solomon . . . and in nothing did they sin save in those things which they received not of me" (D&C 132:38).

Thus, you can go to one area of the Bible and see where the lord was pleased with David and Solomon and gave permission for their wives, but you can go to another area of the Bible and prove the opposite. It is the same with the Book of Mormon and the Doctrine and Covenants. Polygamy is only okay if and when the Lord says it is okay, even for David and Solomon. "For if I will, saith the Lord of Hosts, raise up seed unto me, I will command my people; otherwise they shall hearken unto these things" (Jacob 2:30). The Lord is telling the Nephites in the book of Jacob that he will not tolerate them sinning like David and Solomon.

Question 5

Does the Doctrine and Covenants say that if you do not practice polygamy you cannot be saved in the Celestial Kingdom?

Answer 5

No it does not. Let's take a look at the verses:

> For behold, I reveal unto you a new and an everlasting covenant; and if ye abide not that covenant, then are ye damned; for *no one can reject this covenant and be permitted to enter into my glory.* (D&C 132:4; italics added)

> Go ye, therefore, and *do the works of Abraham;* enter ye into my law and ye shall be saved.
>
> But *if ye enter not into my law ye cannot receive the promise of my Father,* which he made unto Abraham" (D&C 132:32–33; italics added)

The covenant referred to is *eternal marriage,* not polygamy, and Mormons know that without eternal marriage you are damned. To be damned means to stop progression, just like water behind a dam.

The phrase above that says, "do the works of Abraham" again is *not* referring to polygamy. This same statement is recorded in John 8:39 and means good works.

PRIESTHOOD

(see also APOSTASY AND AUTHORITY)

Question 1

In the book of Hebrews, does it say that the Levitical priesthood would change and be done away with? If so, why does the LDS Church claim it is still on the earth?

Answer 1

Let's take a look at the verse:

> If therefore perfection were by the Levitical priest-
> hood, (for under it the people received the law,) what fur-
> ther need was there that another priest should rise after
> the order of Melchisedec, and not be called after the
> order of Aaron?
>
> For *the priesthood being changed,* there is made of
> necessity a change also of the law.
>
> For he of whom these things are spoken pertaineth
> to another tribe, of which no man gave attendance at the
> altar.
>
> For it is evident that our Lord sprang out of Juda;
> of which tribe Moses spake nothing concerning priest-
> hood. (Heb. 7:11–14; italics added)

In answer to the above scripture, the Aaronic or Levitical Priesthood was not done away with but, just as it states
above in Hebrews, it was changed. Why was it changed? To
answer this question it is important to understand the history of the Aaronic and Melchizedek Priesthood. From
Adam to Moses, every prophet has held the Melchizedek
Priesthood and in fact, the Aaronic Priesthood was not even
on the earth during that two and a half millenniums. When
Moses went up to the mount to get the Ten Commandments,
he was initially coming down with a higher law and the
Melchizedek Priesthood for the Israelites, but because of
the wickedness of the Israelites the higher law was taken
and they were given a lesser and more strict law. They were
given the Levitical Priesthood instead of the Melchizedek
Priesthood. The Aaronic Priesthood was not previously
needed as a separate priesthood, because the power of the
Levitical Priesthood was automatically embraced within the
Melchizedek Priesthood. In fact, Aaron and his sons held
the Melchizedek Priesthood when the Lord gave them the
Levitical Priesthood. The point being that the Aaronic or
Levitical Priesthood and the law of Moses were added

because of "transgressions" (Gal. 3:19).

Christ however, brought forth a higher law and the law of Moses was fulfilled. Because Christ fulfilled the law of carnal commandments there was a need for a "change" in the Levitical Priesthood. Again, it was a change and not an abolishment of the Levitical Priesthood. The *change* that occurred was the fact that the Melchizedek Priesthood was restored and things such as animal sacrifice (which the lesser priesthood administered) and other areas of the law of Moses were done away. It was *that function* of the Aaronic Priesthood that was discontinued or annulled. But other areas of the Aaronic Priesthood, such as administration of ordinances of the gospel, were not changed. Christ stated on the Mount, "Think not that I am come to destroy the law or the prophets: I am not come to destroy, but to fulfill" (Matt. 5:17). Hebrews 7:11–14 states that priesthood is necessary and that through it comes "perfection." It is very clear that the priesthood is not only necessary but also "everlasting," the Bible says:

> And thou shalt anoint them, as thou didst anoint their father, that they may minister unto me in the priest's office: for their anointing shall surely be an *everlasting priesthood throughout their generations.*

> Thus did Moses: according to all that the LORD commanded him, so did he. (Ex. 40:15–16; italics added)

> And he shall have it, and his seed after him, *even* the covenant of an *everlasting priesthood;* because he was zealous for his God, and made an atonement for the children of Israel. (Num. 25:13; italics added)

Question 2

Does the book of Hebrews state that the Aaronic priesthood would be annulled and thus taken from the earth?

Answer 2

No it does not. But it does refer to a "disannulling" of *the law* of sacrifice.

Let's take a look at the verse:

> For he that testifieth, Thou art a priest forever after the order of Melchisedec.
>
> For there is verily a *disannulling of the commandment* going before for the weakness and unprofitableness thereof.
>
> For the law made nothing perfect, but the bringing in of a better hope did; by the which we draw nigh unto God. (Heb. 7:17–19; italics added)

These verses are yet another way of saying the law of Moses would be done away with. The priesthood however, was not annulled and was used by Christ, the apostles, as well as worthy members today.

Question 3

In the book of Hebrews 7:24, it states that the priesthood is "unchangeable." Does this mean the priesthood cannot be transferred from one person to another?

Answer 3

Let's take a look at the verse:

> But this man, because he continueth ever, hath an unchangeable priesthood. (Heb. 7:24)

Does unchangeable mean not transferable? Christ held the Melchizedek priesthood, that is in fact *unchangeable* and always has been. Some enemies of the Church have tried to say unchangeable means not transferable. Obviously, if you traded every word that says "unchangeable" in the scriptures to "not transferable" the scriptures would not make sense. The priesthood *can* be transferred and must be transferred for others to be able to perform ordinances (see authority and questions that follow).

The priesthood can be given (transferred) as a gift, but it cannot be bought.

In the book of Acts is an example that *not* anyone who desires to receive the power of the priesthood can receive it. In this situation, Philip, who only held the Aaronic Priesthood, had taught some believers and baptized them. But Philip did not have the Melchizedek Priesthood, so he could not give the gift of the Holy Ghost. Lets take a look at the verses:

> Then Simon himself believed also: and when he was baptized, he continued with Philip, and wondered, beholding the miracles and signs which were done.
>
> Now when the apostles which were at Jerusalem heard that Samaria had received the word of God, they sent unto them Peter and John:
>
> Who, when they were come down, prayed for them, that they might receive the Holy Ghost:
>
> (For as yet he was fallen upon none of them: only they were baptized in the name of the Lord Jesus.)
>
> Then laid they their hands on them, and they received the Holy Ghost.
>
> And when Simon saw that through laying on of the apostles' hands the Holy Ghost was given, he offered them money,
>
> Saying, Give me also this power, that on whomsoever I lay hands, he may receive the Holy Ghost.
>
> But Peter said unto him, Thy money perish with thee, because thou hast thought that the gift of God may be purchased with money. (Acts 8:13–20)

Notice, Simon himself was a believer and had been baptized, yet he could not just assume that he had the priesthood or even buy it.

Question 4

The book of John states that anyone who receives Christ receives power. Does this mean priesthood is not necessary to do ordinances?

Answer 4

Let's take a look at the verse:

> But as many as received him, to them gave he power to become the sons of God, even to them that believe on his name. (John 1:12)

This verse says power *to become the sons of God*. This power is much different than actual priesthood authority (see APOSTASY AND AUTHORITY and questions below).

Question 5

In Hebrews 7:14 it states:

> For it is evident that our Lord sprang out of Juda; of which tribe Moses spake nothing concerning priesthood.

Does this mean that Christ did not hold or need the priesthood to do miracles?

Answer 5

No it does not. Let's take a look at evidences that Christ *did* in fact hold the Priesthood.

The higher priesthood was named after Melchizedek The reason it was named after him is because the man "Melchizedek was such a great High Priest" (D&C 107:2). Christ holds the Melchizedek Priesthood and in fact, the Savior is a High Priest in the priesthood just as Melchizedek. Here are some examples in scripture.

> Wherefore, holy brethren, partakers of the heavenly calling, consider the Apostle and High Priest of our profession, Christ Jesus. (Heb. 3:1)

> Seeing then that we have a great high priest, that is passed into the heavens, Jesus the son of God. (Heb. 4:14)

> So also Christ glorified not himself to be made a high priest; but he that said unto him, Thou art my Son, today I have begotten thee.

> As he saith also in another place, Thou art a priest forever after the order of Melchizedek. (Heb. 5:5–6)

> Wither the forerunner is for us entered, even Jesus made an high priest forever after the order of Melchizedek. (Heb. 6:20)

It is also obvious that Christ has a higher priesthood than John the Baptist because John could not bestow the Holy Ghost as Christ could. This is because *John only held the Aaronic Priesthood.*

> I indeed baptize you with water unto repentance: but he that cometh after me is mightier than I, whose shoes I am not worthy to bear: he shall baptize you with the Holy Ghost, and with fire. (Matt. 3:11)

If just anyone could have the priesthood and could perform whatever ordinances they wanted, John would have given the Holy Ghost himself. Only Jesus, and those with the higher priesthood like Peter, could perform it as discussed in Acts 8.

You must have the higher priesthood to give the gift of the Holy Ghost by the laying on of hands. It is very obvious that Jesus and the apostles had this priesthood.

Question 6

How did Christ get the Priesthood?

Answer 6

Even though Jesus was the Son of God, he did not just assume that he had the priesthood. He was *"called of God, a high priest after the order of Melchizedek"* (Heb. 5:10).

Question 7

Is there any evidence that the apostles held the priesthood?

Answer 7

The fact that the apostles hold the priesthood is an easy concept to show in the scriptures because there are instances where men tried to buy the apostles' priesthood authority without success (Acts 8:14–20 stated in question 3 above).

There are also instances where people tried priesthood ordinances on others, such as baptism or casting out devils, and because they did not truly have the priesthood, the ordinances had to be repeated or the devils could not be rebuked. Lets take a look at the above examples, and others.

The first example involves a group of people who were baptized by one who did not have the priesthood authority. The apostle Paul found those who had been "baptized" and questioned them about the baptism. Paul found out that someone had baptized these people and had not even told them about the Holy Ghost. John the Baptist always told the people that one would follow after him and give the Holy Ghost (Matt. 3:11). I'm sure this was Paul's first clue that they had not been baptized with the proper authority. Here is the passage and the answer to what Paul did about the situation.

> And it came to pass, that, while Apollos was at Corinth, Paul having passed through the upper coasts came to Ephesus: and finding certain disciples,
>
> He said unto them, Unto what then were ye baptized? And they said, unto Johns baptism.
>
> Then said Paul, John verily baptized with the baptism of repentance, saying unto the people, that they should believe on him which should come after him, that is, on Christ Jesus.
>
> When they heard this, they were baptized in the name of the Lord Jesus.
>
> And when Paul had laid his hands upon them; the Holy Ghost came on them; and they spake with tongues and prophesied. (Acts 19:1)

Thus, Paul *rebaptized* them with the proper *priesthood authority.* When the scripture above states "unto John's baptism," it is important to understand that this individual was doing the baptism like John (unto John), but *it was not John.* Think of how many people on this earth today have been baptized without proper authority. They too must be rebaptized by someone with the priesthood. If they have passed away, it must be done by proxy (see BAPTISM FOR THE DEAD).

The next example, again, sites a situation showing that not only did the Apostles have the priesthood but the priesthood authority is necessary to use the Lords name in many earthly situations. The scripture tells of the seven sons of a man named Sceva. They had seen Paul work miracles and they decided to give it a try themselves although they had not been given the priesthood.

Lets take a look at the verse that refers to what happened to these seven brothers.

> And God wrought special miracles by the hands of Paul:
>
> So that from his body were brought unto the sick handkerchiefs or aprons, and the diseases departed from them, and the evil spirits went out of them.
>
> Then certain of the vagabond Jews, exorcists, took upon them to call over them which had evil spirits the name of the Lord Jesus, saying, We adjure you by Jesus whom Paul preacheth.
>
> And there were seven sons of one Sceva, a Jew and chief of the priests, which did so.
>
> And the evil spirit answered and said, Jesus I know, and Paul I know; but who are ye?
>
> And the man in whom the evil spirit was leaped on them, and overcame them, and prevailed against them, so that they fled out of that house naked and wounded. (Acts 19:11)

It is obvious the apostles held the priesthood. It is also obvious that the priesthood was meant to continue and be transferred and that is why after Judas Iscariot died, Matthias was called (see Acts 1:15–26).

Question 8

How did the apostles get the priesthood?

Answer 8

Here are some scriptural references showing they were chosen just as Christ was chosen, and then *ordained.*

> Then said Jesus to them again, Peace be unto you: as my Father hath sent me, even so send I you. (John 20:21)

> Ye have not chosen me, but I have chosen you, and ordained you, that ye should go and bring forth fruit, and that your fruit should remain: that whatsoever ye shall ask of the Father in my name he may give it you. (John 15:16)

> And no man taketh this honour unto himself, but he that is called of God, as was Aaron. (Heb. 5:4)

> For every high priest taken from among men *is* *ordained* for men in things pertaining to God, that he may offer both gifts and sacrifices for sins. (Heb. 5:1; italics added)

To obtain the priesthood, you must be ordained. The scriptures clearly state this.

Question 9

In the Old Testament, only descendants of Aaron/Levi could have the Aaronic Priesthood (Ex. 28:43). How can members of the LDS Church hold the Aaronic Priesthood if they claim to be descendants of Ephraim or Manasseh?

Answer 9

Members of the LDS Church can hold the Aaronic Priesthood, even though they are not direct descendants of Aaron. The restoration of the Aaronic Priesthood is part of the restoration of all things prophesied in the scriptures.

> Whom the heaven must receive until the times of restitution of all things, which God hath spoken by the mouth of all his holy prophets since the world began. (Acts 3:21)

In the above scripture note that is states restitution of *all things*. The Aaronic and Melchizedek Priesthoods were both included in "all things." We have already seen that the Lord can change the manner in which things are done, such as the Law of Sacrifice, and the change in the priesthood (discussed in Heb. 7:12 above). There were many reasons the Levitical Priesthood initially was transferred by lineage. Later it was spread out among the people and was no longer confined exclusively to the chosen lineage. Reasons for this included:

- There were very few members of the tribe of Levi at the meridian of time, as well as in this dispensation.

- The Law of Sacrifice was discontinued, and Israel was no longer to exist as a separate nation.

As a result, the Lord authorized others who were not of the tribe of Levi, or through Aaron's lineage, the right to hold the Levitical Priesthood. (The descendants of Aaron will always have the right to the Levitical Priesthood.) The Levitical Priesthood is just *an appendage* to the higher Melchizedek Priesthood, thus from the beginning anyone holding the Melchizedek Priesthood could do *everything* a person with the Levitical Priesthood could do. An important point to remember is that Adam and his sons, as well as Abraham and others, did sacrifices and *they were not descendants of Aaron* because *Aaron was not even born yet.*

The Lord required sacrifices prior to the birth of Christ. Adam, the Nephites, the descendants of Aaron, were all to offer sacrifices. When sacrifices were still performed, priesthood authority was required. Adam, the Nephites, and the descendants of Aaron all held priesthood authority and thus, could perform the ordinance.

Concerning the eternal nature of the priesthood the scriptures state:

> Without father, without mother, without descent, having neither beginning of days, nor end of life; but made like unto the Son of God; abideth a priest continually. (Heb. 7:3)

Thus, the priesthood has always existed, and yes, it is still around today. The Melchizedek Priesthood has *no descent* (not based on lineage), *no beginning,* and *no end* without the priesthood—ordinances cannot be performed, and just as in ancient times, thanks to the restoration, the priesthood is on the earth today.

Question 10

Did the Nephites have the Priesthood?

Answer 10

Yes, but there was no *Aaronic* Priesthood among them. As mentioned above, none of the tribe of Levi was with the Nephites when they traveled to America. The Nephites held the *Melchizedek* priesthood and it was with this priesthood authority that they observed the law of Moses (Alma 13:6–18).

Any organization on the earth today performing ordinances, such as baptism, without *priesthood* authority are performing ordinances that are not binding in the hereafter. These and other ordinances will have to be redone by one with proper priesthood authority. The LDS Church is the *only* Church on the earth with this priesthood authority. Anyone who has not been baptized with this authority should be rebaptized, just as they were in Bible times (Acts 19:5). Those who ridicule the LDS Church for believing they are the only Church with this authority must also point their finger at Jesus, John the Baptist, and other disciples for believing the same thing.

PROPHECY

(see also BLOOD ATONEMENT; PROPHET; SAC- RIFICE; WITNESSES)

Question 1

In the book of Deuteronomy, does it state that if a per- son prophesies and it doesn't come to pass that that person is not a prophet? If so, are there things that Joseph Smith said would come to pass that did not?

Answer 1

Let's take a look at the verse:

> When a *prophet speaketh* in the name of the Lord, if the thing follow not, nor come to pass, that is the thing which the Lord hath not spoken, but *the prophet* hath spoken it presumptuously: thou shalt *not* be afraid of him. (Deut. 18:22; italics added)

This verse has confused many, both Mormons and members of other faiths. Note that this verse says absolutely nothing about a "false prophet." It does say however, if an actual prophet says something that does not come to pass, don't be afraid of him because it was merely presumed by the prophet, but not actually spoken by the Lord. The words of the scripture state, "the prophet hath spoken" and *not* "the false prophet hath spoken." A prophet can speak when it is not in the name of God. In other words, not all words spoken by prophets are from God. Remember even Peter denied Christ three times (John 13:38). If Joseph Smith had denied Christ three times, enemies of the Church would have been quick to ridicule. Let's take a look at some of the questions that have arisen about some of Joseph Smith's prophesies. Realize as the questions are discussed that most of the questions are misunderstood for one simple reason— the prophecy has not *yet* been fulfilled.

Joseph Smith, just as other prophets, often do not see their prophesies fulfilled until after they have died. For example, it would be easy to look at the prophesies of John the Revelator and state that he was a false prophet because they have not yet been fulfilled. Isaiah prophesied that a virgin would bear a son, the Lord Jesus Christ, but he never saw the prophesy fulfilled in his lifetime (Isa. 7:14). Joseph Smith also did not see all of his prophecies fulfilled in his lifetime.

Question 2

In the book of Doctrine and Covenants, did Joseph Smith prophesy that he would find gold and silver in a town called Salem and then it never happened?

Answer 2

Let's take a look at the verse:

> And it shall come to pass *in due time* that I will give this city into your hands, that you shall have power over it, insomuch that they shall not discover your secret parts; and its wealth pertaining to gold and silver shall be yours. (D&C 111:4; italics added)

Note that the verse above states "it shall come to pass in due time." The Lord's words certainly did *not* suggest the Church would receive this money in the immediate future. In fact it suggests they would not receive it while Joseph was in Salem. It is possible that even those with Joseph Smith hoped it would be sooner. In New Testament times, disciples expected prophecies to be fulfilled right away, though it was not what the Lord had in mind. For example, disciples thought the second coming of the Savior would be very soon because they knew it had been prophesied (Acts 1:11). They were corrected in a letter from the Apostle Paul and reminded that the apostasy (falling away) would come first. Let's take a look at the verse:

> Now we beseech you, brethren, by *the coming of our Lord Jesus Christ,* and by our gathering together unto him,
>
> That ye be not soon shaken in mind, or be troubled, neither by spirit, nor by word, nor by letter as from us, as that *the day of Christ is at hand.*
>
> Let no man deceive you by any means: *For that day shall not come except there come a falling away first,* and that man of sin be revealed, the son of perdition. (2 Thes. 2:1–3; italics added)

The situation in Salem is but another example of the fact Joseph Smith is a true prophet of God. No one except Joseph Smith knew he had received the revelation as stated in Doctrine and Covenants 111. If he was not a prophet and was thus fabricating the revelation, he would not have told anyone about it, or given it to the publisher to be printed. But Joseph Smith had nothing to hide, the revelation in Doctrine and Covenants 111 are the words of the Lord, not Joseph Smith. If Joseph was not a prophet, rather than telling others about his revelations, he would have kept them hidden until he could see if they were in fact going to come to pass, and then later reveal them and told what he had prophesied. Even if Joseph Smith spoke "presumptuously" (which he did not), it is important to remember, "thou shalt not be afraid of him" he is still a true prophet of God (Deut. 18:22).

It appears the Prophet Nathan referred to in the Old Testament, may have spoken "presumptuously," but he was still a true prophet of the Old Testament. In 2 Samuel 7:5–17, the Prophet Nathan prophesied that the Davidic

Empire would be established "forever," the house of Israel would stay in the Promised Land, and that they would "move no more." He also stated "neither shall the children of wickedness afflict them anymore." We all know this does not appear to be the case. The Davidic Empire was taken over, the Israelites were driven from the Promised Land and scattered, and wicked people definitely afflicted them. If Joseph Smith had made this prophesy he would have been called a false prophet. It is possible that the Prophet Nathan knew of a condition that he did not attach to his prophesy. It really doesn't matter because Nathan, like Joseph Smith is a true prophet of God. *This prophecy is not a hard prophesy to be fulfilled. Simple tithing fulfills this prophecy.* Members like Steve Young, Danny Ainge, Marriott, and yes, even the average Mormon, pay a lot in tithing every year. One member in Salem paying a lot of tithing fulfills this prophecy. Let us not be too critical of God's chosen prophets.

Question 3

In Doctrine and Covenants 84:4, did the prophet Joseph Smith Prophesy that a temple would be built yet it never was? Is this a false prophesy by Joseph Smith?

Answer 3

Let's take a look at the verse:

> Verily this is the word of the Lord, that the city New Jerusalem shall be built by the gathering of the saints, beginning at this place, even the place of the temple, which temple shall be reared in this generation. (D&C 84:4)

As mentioned above, timing is one of the most common "proofs" that enemies of the Church use to say that Joseph Smith was not a prophet. The Lord often uses phrases such as "not many years hence," "in this generation," or "the hour is nigh" to predict future events. The problem is mankind's time is not God's time. Timing is very difficult to interpret, even words like forever do not always mean forever. For example, in Exodus 12:14 concerning the feast of the Passover, it states:

> And this day shall be unto you for a memorial; and ye shall keep it a feast to the Lord *throughout all your generations;* ye shall keep it a feast by an ordinance *for ever.* (Ex. 12:14; italics added)

Again the Lord uses the word generation and notice that in this instance it refers to forever. Obviously, Christians do not celebrate the feast of the Passover. So how do we explain the words "throughout all your generations" and "forever" in this verse? It is important to try not to over interpret words like "generation" and "the hour is nigh" etc. too literally in the scriptures. Joseph F. Smith has explained the answer to the question in the following:

> The Feast of the Passover was fulfilled in that form in the crucifixion of Jesus Christ. The Passover was a law given to Israel which was to continue until Christ, and was to remind the children of Israel of the coming of Christ who would become the sacrificial Lamb. After he was crucified the law was changed by the Savior himself, and from that time forth the law of the sacrament was instituted. We now observe the law of the sacrament instead of the Passover because the Passover was consummated in full by the death of Jesus Christ. It was a custom looking forward to the coming of Christ and his crucifixion and the lamb symbolized his death.
>
> CHRIST INSTITUTED THE SACRAMENT
>
> Perhaps you know that Christ was crucified at the time of the Passover, and the night before he instituted the sacrament which may be said to constitute the continuation of the law.
>
> If you have a copy of John Taylor's *Mediation and Atonement,* you will find that he has made this matter perfectly clear.
>
> *The word forever used in the Old Testament does*

not necessarily mean to the end of time but to the end of
a period.[58]

If Joseph Smith had been the one to record Exodus 12:14 enemies would have called it a false prophecy. Now back to the original question of the prophesy in Doctrine and Covenants 84. The prophesy in Doctrine and Covenants 84 states a temple would be built in Missouri in this "generation." What is the definition of a generation? The word generation has many meanings including:

- A step in the line of decent from a relative
- One hundred years
- One hundred twenty years
- The time of our present dispensation
- An indefinite period of time.

The fact is the Lord often used the word generation in his speeches during New Testament times to refer to an indefinite period of time. For example, he said: "A wicked and adulterous generation seeketh after a sign" (Matt. 16:4). This statement by the Savior does not refer to a period of years, but to a period of iniquity. The reality is, the temple *will* be built in "this generation." In fact, the Church already owns the land.

Question 4

In the Doctrine and Covenants 97:19 it states:

> And the nations of the earth shall honor her, and shall say: Surely Zion is the city of our God, and surely *Zion cannot fall, neither be moved out of her place,* for God is there, and the hand of the Lord is there (D&C 97:19; italics added)

The Saints were driven from Missouri against their will? Isn't this evidence that Zion was "moved out of her place?" Is this a false prophesy?

Answer 4

The above prophesy is not a false prophesy. Anyone can go to any book of scripture and do what enemies of the church have done with the above verse. That is, take one verse as a final statement, without regard to context or the other verses. For example in the book of Jeremiah it states:

> Then *the LORD said* unto me, *The prophets proph-esy lies in my name:* I sent them not, neither have I com-manded them, neither spake unto them: they prophesy unto you a false vision and divination, and a thing of nought, and the deceit of their heart (Jer. 14:14; italics added)

If I wanted to do as enemies of the LDS Church do, I would use the above verse to say that all prophets prophesy lies. Do you see how easy it is? Well in the question above this is what has been done. The truth is, the Lord could eas-ily see that the saints would be forced out. During this time in Church history many saints were traveling to Missouri to inhabit the land. The Saints had too much pride and were bringing forth unacceptable fruit. The Lord gave them a warning.

> The ax is laid at the root of the trees; and every tree that bringeth not forth good fruit shall be hewn down and cast in to the fire. I, the Lord, Have spoken it. (D&C 97:7)

Even though the Lord gave the saints this warning they still refused to repent. The saints were told to start the temple first "Yea, let it be built speedily" (D&C 97:11), but they started other projects first. The Lord had given the above warning but he also gave them a conditional promise.

> And, now, behold, *if* Zion do these things she shall prosper, and spread herself and become very glorious, very great, and very terrible.
>
> And the nations of the earth shall honor her, and shall say: Surely Zion is the city of our God, and surely *Zion cannot fall, neither be moved out of her place,* for

God is there, and the hand of the Lord is there (D&C 97:18–19; italics added).

Of course, even with the above explanation, it is important to remember mankind still has freedom of choice. Events and ordinances are foreordained in this life but not predestined, for there is no such thing as predestination. It was Satan's plan to give mankind no choice of good or evil and thus, force mankind to do his will. But this plan was rejected and free agency was chosen. God knows us individually and knows how we will react in given situations. Nevertheless our path is chosen by each of us individually. If it were not so, there would be no point in us being tested on this earth, God would have just assigned us to our kingdoms. Thus there are many prophesies that are given with an "if" attached to it. For example, during ancient times the King and leader Jeroboam were given a prophesy by the Prophet Ahijah that his kingdom would be secure *if* he remained faithful to the Lords ways (1 Kgs. 11:38). Jeroboam did not remain faithful and thus, the prophecy never came to pass and the Assyrians overtook Jeroboam's kingdom. This did not mean Ahijah was not a prophet. President Joseph Fielding Smith has said this regarding the above question:

> Notwithstanding the fact that their enemies had come upon them but a few days before, and the Lord knew this fact, yet he promised the saints that his purposes would be accomplished if they would faithfully trust in him and abide in his word. In their weakness they were not prepared. The Lord impressed upon them that Zion was the pure in heart, and unless they were pure in heart, these blessings could not be accomplished. However, if they would be true, then Zion would rejoice while all the wicked should mourn. . . .
>
> The promise is also made that Zion shall escape if she will "observe to do all things whatsoever I have commanded her." (v. 25.) What a pity it is that we have not heeded this commandment: Heeding it is our safety, and while we may be preserved from many of the calamities,

yet the promise is made that if we observe not to do the things the Lord has commanded us, Zion—who should be the pure in heart—shall be visited with sore afflictions, pestilence, plague, sword, vengeance and devouring fire. Why will so many members of the Church refuse to heed this warning! We should have learned the lesson through the suffering of the past, many of us seemingly prefer to take life the hard way. Great blessings have been promised us, but the patience of the Lord is at an end, for he says: "Nevertheless, let it be read this once to her ears, that I, the Lord, have accepted of her offering; and if she sin no more none of these things shall come upon her," (v. 27.), but she would be blessed and multiplied in all her generations forever and ever. While in a measure this revelation applied to the inhabitants of Zion in the early days, yet it applies to us today, to Zion the land and also her inhabitants.[59]

Question 5

Is it true that the Prophet Joseph Smith said that "Zion" would be appointed in Missouri, but the Saints went to Salt Lake City instead?

Answer 5

Let's take a look at the verse:

And, behold, there is none other place appointed than that which I have appointed; neither shall there be any other place appointed than that which I have appointed, for the work of the gathering of my saints. (D&C 101:20)

Note that this verse says nothing about the all-important question of—*when*. Ask almost any member of the Church today, and he or she will tell you that the Church still plans on Zion, and the New Jerusalem (Rev. 3:12) spoken of in the scriptures being located in Missouri. As mentioned above, the Church already owns land in Missouri.

Zion will be located in Jackson County, Missouri. The

prophet Joseph Smith not only prophesied that this would occur, but also that the Saints would go west, and that transpired.[60] It just so happened they went west before they started Zion in Missouri. The saints at the time obviously thought Zion in Missouri would be first, or they would not have traveled to Missouri to inhabit the land. Freedom of choice determined their course. Because of the wickedness of the Missourians, and the pride of the saints, Zion in Missouri, and the building of the temple was put off to a later date. For the Lord said:

> Verily, verily, I say unto you, that when I give a commandment to any of the sons of men to do a work unto my name, and those sons of men go with all their might and with all they have to perform that work, and cease not their diligence, and their enemies come upon them and hinder them from performing that work, behold, it behooveth me to require that work no more at the hands of those sons of men, but to accept of their offerings. (D&C 124:49)

This was the case both anciently and today. The Lord has often given directions to prophets and apostles with no apparent reward, and at times even a poor outcome—again, because of free agency. For example, *apostles* were lead to areas to preach the gospel, *only to be cast out.*

> But when they persecute you in this city, flee ye into another. (Matt. 10:23)

The fact is the Lord may be sending the saints into these situations so that the wicked may be punished.

> For I have suffered them [enemies of the Church] thus far that they might fill up the measure of their iniquities, that their cup might be full. (D&C 103:3)

> Wherefore, behold, I send unto you prophets, and wise men, and scribes: and some of them ye shall kill and crucify; and some of them shall ye scourge in your synagogues, and persecute them from city to city:
>
> *That upon you may come all the righteous blood*

shed upon the earth, from the blood of righteous Abel unto the blood of Zacharias son of Barachias, whom ye slew between the temple and the altar.

Verily I say unto you, All these things shall come upon *this generation.*

O Jerusalem, Jerusalem, thou that *killest the prophets,* and stonest them *which are sent unto thee,* how often would I have gathered thy children together, even as a hen gathereth her chickens under her wings, *and ye would not.* (Matt. 23:35–37; italics added).

It is interesting that another true prophecy was predicted at this time.

But verily I say unto you, that I have decreed a decree which my people shall realize, inasmuch as they hearken from this very hour unto the counsel which I, the Lord their God, shall give unto them.

Behold they shall, for I have decreed it, begin to prevail against mine enemies from this very hour. (Matt. 23:35–37)

Obviously, this prophecy has been fulfilled just as stated, for since that time the saints have never again received the persecution that was received in Missouri, and there has been a steady triumph against all enemies of the Church.

If we ask the question, "why did the Lord send the saints to Missouri when all they did was receive persecution," we must also ask "why did the Lord send the House of Israel to Egypt only to become slaves?" (Gen. 46:3).

Question 6

Did the prophet Joseph Smith prophesy that the second coming of Christ would come before he was eighty-five years old?

Answer 6

No he did not. Let's take a look at the verse:

> I was once praying very earnestly to know the time
> of the coming of the Son of Man, when I heard a voice
> repeat the following:
>
> Joseph, my son, if thou livest until thou art eighty-
> five years old, thou shalt see the face of the Son of Man;
> therefore let this suffice, and trouble me no more on this
> matter.
>
> I was left thus, without being able to decide whether
> this coming referred to the beginning of the millennium
> or to some previous appearing, or whether I should die
> and thus see his face. (D&C 130:14–16)

The passage above concerning Joseph Smith's prophecies about the second coming of Christ are self explained
just by reading what the prophet wrote. The passage in Doctrine and Covenants 130, in fact told it like it happened.
Joseph was told *if* he lived until he was eighty-five, which
he did not, he would *see* Christ. Of course, Doctrine and
Covenants 130:16 above, tells us that Joseph Smith was not
claiming any prophecy on this matter.

Question 7

Is it documented in the *History of the Church* that
Joseph Smith prophesied that Christ's second coming would
be within fifty-six years?

Answer 7

No it does not. Let's take a look at the paragraph:

> It was the will of God that those who went to Zion,
> with a determination to lay down their lives, if necessary,
> should be ordained to the ministry, and go forth to prune
> the vineyard for the last time, or the coming of the Lord,
> which was nigh—even fifty six years should wind up the
> scene.[61]

The passage from *History of the Church* refers to
"Zion's Camp." Analysis of this passage shows an important
word—*or.* Either Zion's Camp be formed *or* Christ would

come. Obviously Zion's Camp was formed just as the Lord asked, so the "or" never happened. Another true prophecy. This particular prophecy just happened to be given with a condition. Another example of a revelation with a condition attached is recorded in Malachi 4:5–6.

> Behold, I will send you Elijah the prophet before the coming of the great and dreadful day of the Lord:
>
> And he shall turn the heart of the fathers to the children, and the heart of the children to their fathers, *lest I come and smite the earth with a curse.* (Mal. 4:5–6; italics added)

A look at this prophesy reveals that *if* Elijah did not come and do the specific job of turning *our hearts to our ancestors* (the fathers), the earth would be smitten with a curse. This is a huge conditional prophecy. This prophecy has been fulfilled. Do you know of any other religion that has anything near the genealogy/family history program than the LDS Church? Elijah did appear and set this up as recorded in Doctrine and Covenants 110:13–16.

There are certain times the Lord is so adamant about having something done that he gives a warning. Such was the case with Zion's camp. The Lord also gave a condition to Jonah. He told Jonah if Nineveh did not repent it would be destroyed. The city did repent and destruction was avoided. Thus, if the Lord tells you to do something, do it or consequences will follow.

Question 8

The prophet Joseph Smith said the following two prophesies:

> I prophesy in the name of the Lord God of Israel, unless the United States redress the wrongs committed upon the Saints in the state of Missouri and punish the crimes committed by her officers that in a few years *the government will be utterly overthrown and wasted,* and there will not be so much as a potsherd left, for their wicked-

ness in permitting the murder of men, women and children, and the wholesale plunder and extermination of thousands of her citizens to go unpunished, thereby perpetrating a foul and corroding blot upon the fair fame of this great republic, the very thought of which would have caused the highminded and patriotic framers of the Constitution of the United States to hide their faces with shame.[62]

> Therefore, let my servant *Joseph and his seed after him* have place in that house, from generation to generation, *forever* and ever, saith the Lord.

> And let the name of that house be called Nauvoo House; and let it be a delightful habitation for man, and a resting-place for the weary traveler, that he may contemplate the glory of Zion, and the glory of this, the corner-stone thereof. (D&C 124:59–60; italics added)

Isn't it true that both of these prophecies never happened? The government never was overthrown and the Nauvoo House no longer belongs to the Smith family.

Answer 8

Our time is not God's time. If Joseph Smith's prophecies are to be disregarded because of terms like "forever," "generation," or even "years," Bible prophesies must also be disregarded. There is absolutely no difference between God commanding that circumcision and the feast of the Passover be kept "forever" (Gen. 17:10–11, Ex. 12:14) and the Nauvoo house to belong to the Smith family "forever," or the government to be wasted in a number of "years." It is obvious that circumcision, (Acts 15) the feast of the Passover, and the Nauvoo house have not lasted forever. It is also obvious that the government has not *yet* fallen, but all of these prophecies are still true. Joseph Smith knew that no house can last forever but he wrote the prophecies he received just the way the Lord told him to.

Concerning Joseph Smith's prophecy of the overthrow of the U.S. government many prophets besides Joseph

Smith; have also prophesied that the United States Government will eventually fall. Gerald N. Lund has compiled the following information:

The Future Destiny of the United States

Joseph Smith was not the only one to testify of the coming destruction of this nation. Many of the apostles and prophets have also borne witness to this fulfillment of God's promises. Brigham Young told of hearing the Prophet speak of the coming destruction of the United States.

The whole government is gone; it is as weak as water. I heard Joseph Smith say nearly thirty years ago, "They shall have mobbings to their hearts' content, if they do not redress the wrongs of the Latter-day Saints." Mobs will not decrease but will increase until the whole government becomes a mob, and eventually it will be State against State, city against city, neighborhood against neighborhood, Methodists against Methodists, and so on.

In 1881, sixteen years after the close of the Civil War, President John Taylor said:

Do I not know that a nation like that in which we live, a nation which is blessed with the freest, the most enlightened and magnificent government in the world today, with privileges which would exalt people to heaven if they lived up to them-do I not know that if they do not live up to them, but violate them and trample them under their feet, and discard the sacred principles of liberty by which we ought to be governed-do I not know that their punishment will be commensurate with the enlightenment which they possess? I do. And I know I cannot help but know-that there are a great many more afflictions yet awaiting this nation.

President Wilford Woodruff was another who often spoke of the destruction that is to come upon the United States. In his history of the Church he wrote:

I warn future historians to give credence to my history; for my testimony is true, and the truth of its record will be manifest in the world to come. All the words of the Lord will be fulfilled upon the nations, which are written in this book. The American nation will be broken in pieces like a potter's vessel, and will be cast down to hell if it does not repent-and this, because of murders, whoredoms, wickedness and all manner of abominations, for the Lord has spoken it.

In 1880, in an address to the saints, he said:

I ask myself the question, "Can the American nation escape?" The answer comes, "No." Its destruction, as well as the destruction of the world is sure; just as sure as the Lord cut off and destroyed the two great and prosperous nations that once inhabited this continent of North and South America, because of their wickedness, so will He them destroy, and sooner or later they will reap the fruits of their own wicked acts, and be numbered among the past. . . .

There are changes awaiting us, they are even nigh at our very doors, and I know it by the visions of heaven; I know it by the administrations of angels, and I know it by the inspiration of heaven, that is given to all men who seek the Lord; and the hand of God will not stay these things. We have no time to lose. Elder Orson Pratt foretold the destruction and chaos yet coming upon the United States.

If it be asked, why is America thus to suffer? The answer is, because they have rejected the kingdom of God, and one of the greatest divine messages ever sent to man; because they have sanctioned the killing of the Saints, and the martyrdom of the Lord's Prophets, and have suffered his people to be driven from their midst, and have robbed them of their houses, and homes, and land, and millions of property, and have refused to redress their wrongs. For these great evils, they must suffer; the decrees of Jehovah have gone forth against them; the sword of the Lord has been unsheathed, and will fall

with pain upon their devoted heads. Their great and magnificent cities are to be cut off. New York, Boston,
Albany, and numerous other cities will be left desolate.
Party will be arrayed in deadly strife against party; State
against State; and the whole nation will be broken up; the
sanguinary weapons of the dreadful revolution will
devour the land. Then shall there be a fleeing from one
city to another, from one State to another, from one part
of the continent to another, seeking refuge, from the dev-
astations of bandits and armies; then shall their dead be
left unburied, and the fowls of heaven shall summer upon
them, and the beasts of the earth shall winter upon them.
Moreover, the Lord will visit them with the deadly pestilence which shall sweep away many millions by its rav-
ages; for their eyes shall fall from their sockets, and their
flesh from their bones, and their tongues shall be stayed
in their mouths, that they shall not be able to blaspheme
against their Maker. And it will come to pass, that the
heavens will withhold their rains and their fruitful fields
be turned into barrenness, and the waters of their rivers
will be dried up, and left in standing pools, and the fish
therein will die; and the Lord will send forth a grievous
plague to destroy the horses and cattle from the land.
Thus by the sword and by pestilence, and by famine, and
by the strong arm of the Almighty, shall the inhabitants
of that wicked nation be destroyed.[63]

It is also more than interesting that the congress during
the time of Joseph Smith's prophecy was almost entirely
dissolved within only a few short years. That's right, 94 percent of those congressman no longer had their jobs within a
few years. They had paid for their sin with their desired
employment.[64]

*The other important point that enemies of the LDS
Church do not want you to know* is that Joseph Smiths
prophesy written above, regarding the United States government, was not the only prophesy that the prophet gave at
that time. The person that Joseph was talking to while giving this prophesy was Judge Stephen A. Douglas. The
prophet Joseph prophesied:

Judge, you will aspire to the presidency of the United States; and if ever you turn your hand against me or the Latter-day Saints, you will feel the weight of the hand of the Almighty upon you; and you will live to see and know that I have testified the truth to you; for the conversation of this day will stick to you through life.[65]

This prophecy was written and even recorded in the newspaper before it occurred. Everything the prophet foretold occurred just as prophesied. Let's read the event:

Stephen A. Douglas, at the time of this prophecy, was a judge in Illinois, thirty years of age and not extensively known even in his own state. The remark by the Prophet that he would aspire to the presidency more than likely struck him at that time as being absurd. It could hardly be true that he had any such aspirations at that time. He was a man of exceptional ability, and in course of time became widely known, having served his state in Congress, and at the time when he aspired to the presidency was a United States senator representing the state of Illinois, and as such had acquired through his skill and keenness of intellect, an outstanding position among the leaders in the nation. At the time of this prophecy he was friendly with the Prophet and the Latter-day Saints. He had defended the Prophet in the courts and was as well informed in relation to the Latter-day Saints as any man in public life. It was only by the revelation from the Lord that the Prophet could make such a prediction, and its fulfillment stands out as one of the great prophecies coming from the lips of the Prophet Joseph Smith. . . .
On the 12th day of June, 1857, Mr. Douglas delivered a speech in his quest of the presidency, in the state house in Springfield, Illinois. In the course of his remarks he lent endorsement to the many falsehoods then current against the Church. He grouped his charges against the Church . . .

Then was printed the prophetic charge by Joseph Smith to Stephen A. Douglas which was delivered in the home of Mr. Douglas on the 18th day of May in the year 1843. The Prophet had declared that the words of that day should remain with Mr. Douglas all his life. When his attention was called to them through the publication in the *Deseret News*, it evidently was, to him, very disturbing. He was at the time of his speech the leading democratic candidate for the presidency. His nomination and election appeared to be secure. The hand of the Lord was laid upon him from the very hour when he turned traitor to Joseph Smith. The Democratic party which had won the election in the previous campaign by an overwhelming majority commenced to develop internal strife. . . .

Stephen A. Douglas *less than one year after the election died a broken and disappointed man at the age of 48. The Prophecy of Joseph Smith had been literally fulfilled.*[66]

Question 9

Did Joseph Smith prophecy that the LDS Church would practice the "United Order" and that it was an "everlasting" order? The Church is no longer under the United Order, is this a false prophecy?

Answer 9

Let's read the verse referred to:

Verily I say unto you, my friends, I give unto you counsel, and a commandment, concerning all the properties which belong to the order which I commanded to be organized and established, to be a united order, and an everlasting order for the benefit of my church, and for the salvation of men until I come. (D&C 104:1)

It was the Lord who gave the command to live by the United Order (the order of Enoch), but because of transgression the command was revoked. Orson Pratt said this:

The Lord established the United Order, or the Order of Enoch, when it had been demonstrated that the Saints were not able to practice the celestial law of consecration. This Order was to be permanent, but when the Saints also proved themselves unequal to its requirements, the Lord again released them, temporarily, and gave them the law of tithing.

Says one, "What, God revoke a commandment!" Yes, that is what He did in ancient times, and He is the same God yet. He did it for our good; for if that law had been in full force, this people would not have been in these mountains this day. Our selfishness and covetousness are so great that, as a people, we never would have complied with it. A few amongst us might have done so, but as a people we should have been overcome and ruined; but owing to that law being revoked, many of us will now, perhaps, be saved.[67]

Is it unusual that God would give an "everlasting" commandment like the United Order and soon after revoke it? The answer is no. If a person denies Joseph Smith as a prophet, because the United Order is no longer practiced, then by their own rule they must also deny the Bible and prophets like Moses. That's right, a similar situation happened in the Bible. When Moses went up to the Mount and received the ten commandments he was initially coming down with the higher law and the Melchizedek priesthood. But as he approached he saw the wickedness of the Israelites, Moses was so angry he broke the tablets. God did replace the tablets but the Israelites then received the "law of Moses" (Ex. 34:1–2 JST; Heb. 7:16–19; Gal. 3:19). You could ask, didn't God know the people weren't worthy? Why did God give a higher law with the Melchizedek priesthood and later change it to the law of Moses and the Aaronic or Levitical priesthood, and yet still later during New Testament times stop the law of Moses? A better question than all of these is, "should we question God?"

The point is this, *the priesthood, like the United Order is "everlasting,"* and was meant to continue *throughout all generations.* The Bible says this:

And thou shalt anoint them, as thou didst anoint their father, that they may minister unto me in the priest's office: for their anointing shall surely be an *everlasting priesthood throughout their generations.*

> Thus did Moses: according to all that the LORD commanded him, so did he. (Ex. 40:15–16; italics added)

> And he shall have it, and his seed after him, *even* the covenant of an *everlasting priesthood;* because he was zealous for his God, and made an atonement for the children of Israel. (Num. 25:13; italics added)

> If therefore perfection were by the Levitical priesthood, (for under it the people received the law,) what further need was there that another priest should rise after the order of Melchisedec, and not be called after the order of Aaron?

> For the priesthood being changed, there is made of necessity a change also of the law. (Heb. 7:11–12)

There has been a change in the priesthood, the law of Moses, and the United Order, yet all are everlasting. They were all setup to continue throughout all generations, yet during the dark ages there was no priesthood on the earth. It is obvious, the Lord has commanded and revoked as seemeth him good.

> Wherefore I, the Lord, command and revoke, as it seemeth me good; and all this to be answered upon the heads of the rebellious, saith the Lord. (D&C 56:4)

Joseph Fielding Smith points this out:

> This separation and dissolving of the former order came about also because of transgression and covetousness on the part of some.

> The Lord adds: "I give unto you this privilege, this once; and behold if you proceed to do the things which I have laid before you, according to my commandments, all these things are mine."[68]

The prophecy on the United Order is a true prophecy, there are numerous other examples stating that Gods time is not mans time. Words like everlasting, nigh at hand, forever, generation, etc., do not have the same meaning for God and man. The prophet Joel spoke of Christ's second coming as if it were "nigh at hand" yet we are still waiting for it:

> Alas for the day! for the day of the LORD *is at hand,* and as a destruction from the Almighty shall it come. (Joel 1:15; italics added)

> Blow ye the trumpet in Zion, and *sound an alarm* in my holy mountain: let all the inhabitants of the land tremble: for the day of the LORD cometh, for it is *nigh at hand.* (Joel 2:1; italics added)

If Joseph Smith had prophesied these verses enemies would have called him a false prophet. But the truth is, Joel was a prophet and so was Joseph Smith. Prayer can give you the answer that this is true.

COMMENTS ABOUT PROPHECY

Although Joseph Smith made no false prophesies it is important to remember that prophets are mortal men that do make mistakes. There are times recorded in the scriptures that prophets have stated things that were not the Lords words. In other words not every statement out of a prophet's mouth are the Lord's words even if given in the name of the Lord. For example, the prophet Jeremiah prophesied in the name of the Lord, to King Zedekiah that the king would "die in peace," but Zedekiah did not die in peace, in fact he had to witness his own son's deaths, his eyes were then put and he was bound in chains and put in prison until the day he died (Jer. 34:4–5; 52:10, 11).

To the wicked, such as those who look at prophecies in their own light, the Lord has said:

> Ye blind guides, which strain at a gnat, and swallow a camel. (Matt. 23:24)

Those who reject Joseph Smiths prophesies because of small insignificant points are straining at a gnat. Many of these same people believe they will be saved in heaven just by saying they believe in Jesus, thus they swallow a whole camel. Let us be careful, not to be like the Pharisees of old, and be too judgmental of God's chosen prophets. Joseph Smith had no false prophecies.

PROPHESIES ALREADY FULFILLED

All of the above are true prophesies, now let's take a look at *some* of the prophesies of Joseph Smith that have already been fulfilled.

Civil War Prophecy

> Verily, thus saith the Lord concerning the wars that will shortly come to pass, beginning at the rebellion of South Carolina, which will eventually terminate in the death and misery of many souls;

> And the time will come that war will be poured out upon all nations, beginning at this place.

> For behold, the Southern States shall be divided against the Northern States, and the Southern States will call on other nations, even the nation of Great Britain. . . .

> And it shall come to pass, after many days, slaves shall rise up against their masters, who shall be marshaled and disciplined for war. (D&C 87:1–4, given December 25, 1832, fulfilled 1861)

This would have been a bold prophecy without the Lord's help. The prophet Joseph Smith prophesied the Civil War nearly thirty years prior to its occurrence. Some enemies of the Church have tried to downgrade this by attempting to lie and say that it also foretold the second coming because in Doctrine and Covenants 130:12–13 it also stated that this war would occur before Christ's second coming. It is rather obvious to say Christ has not come, so of course it was before, just as the prophecy stated. The prophecy says nothing about it being dependent upon the Savior's return. Others have tried to say Joseph Smith could have guessed this prophesy would happen because it was speculated in the papers at the time Joseph Smith made the prophesy. All you have to do is read the detail of Joseph Smith's prophecy and it is easy to see that it was a true prophecy and not simple speculation.

Joseph Smith Prophesies His Own Death

"I am going like a lamb to the slaughter; but I am calm as a summer's morning; I have a conscience void of offense towards God, and towards all men. I SHALL DIE INNOCENT, AND IT SHALL YET BE SAID OF ME—HE WAS MURDERED IN COLD BLOOD." (D&C 135:4)

Joseph Smith Prophesied That Alcohol and Tobacco Are Harmful

Joseph Smith prophesied that wine and tobacco were harmful to the body in 1833, long before health professionals finally discovered it (D&C 89).

Joseph Smith Prophesies to Zion's Camp

Because of the continued disobedience to counsel, and rebellion on the part of some of the members of the camp, the Prophet said to them by prophecy, as he mounted a wagon wheel: "The Lord has revealed to me that a scourge would come upon the camp in consequence of the fractious and unruly spirit that appeared among them, and they would die like sheep with the rot; still, if they would repent and humble themselves before the Lord, the scourge, in a great measure might be turned away, but, as the Lord lives, the members of this camp will suffer for giving way to their unruly temper." This scourge did not come until the camp had practically finished its labors and had arrived in Clay County. As soon as the camp arrived on Rush Creek, Clay County, the cholera broke out among the members and continued for several days. The victims were stricken suddenly and so powerful was the disease that it was only a few minutes before those who were stricken were dead. About sixty-eight members were attacked and fourteen died.[69]

Many other prophesies, have been fulfilled, are being fulfilled, and will be fulfilled just as Joseph Smith said they would. Was Joseph Smith perfect? No, and neither were ancient prophets. As mentioned earlier, Peter denied Christ three times, and ancient apostles occasionally failed in their endeavors.

> And when they were come to the multitude, there came to him a certain man, kneeling down to him, and saying,
>
> Lord, have mercy on my son: for he is lunatick, and sore vexed: for ofttimes he falleth into the fire, and oft into the water.
>
> *And I brought him to thy disciples, and they could not cure him.* O faithless and perverse generation, how long shall I suffer you? Bring him hither to me.
>
> And Jesus rebuked the devil; and he departed out of him: and the child was cured from that very hour.
>
> Then came the disciples to Jesus apart, and said, Why could not we cast him out?
>
> And Jesus said unto them, Because of your unbelief . . .
>
> Howbeit this kind goeth not out but by prayer and fasting. (Matt. 17:14-21; italics added)

If Joseph Smith had failed to cast out this same devil, enemies of the Church would have accused him of being a false prophet, yet they do not accuse the prophets anciently. Of course prophets are generally not accepted in there own land (Luke 4:24).

PROPHETS
(see also PROPHECY)

Question 1

In the Bible (1 Cor. 13:8), does it say that revelation would cease? If this is true, why does the LDS Church claim to still receive revelation?

Answer 1

No it does not. Let's take a look at the verse:

Charity never faileth: but whether there be prophecies, they shall fail; whether there be tongues, they shall cease; whether there be knowledge, it shall vanish away. (1 Cor. 13:8; italics added)

Paul is using analogies comparing the perfect man to a mortal man. Of course prophesies will *eventually* fail when there is a *unity of the faith* (Eph. 4:11–13). If you read further in Corinthians, Paul explains his reasoning.

But *when that which is perfect is come,* then that which is in part shall be done away. (1 Cor. 13:10; italics added)

Paul even goes on to say that revelation now is like seeing through a glass darkly (a veil) but later it will be face to face (1 Cor. 13:12). He would not have stated this if there were no revelation.

Question 2

In the book of Hebrews 1:1–2, it states:

God, who at sundry times and in divers manners spake *in time past* unto the fathers by the prophets,

Hath in these last days spoken unto us *by his son.* (italics added)

If God spoke only in the past to his prophets, does this mean there was no prophets after Jesus?

Answer 2

This question shows a wrong interpretation of the scriptures. This verse is merely stating that there were no prophets for four hundred years from Malachi until Jesus. Nowhere in the verse does it say there would be no more prophets. The fact is the scriptures say we will have prophets until all faiths come into unity (Eph. 4:11–14). The book of Amos says, "Surely the Lord God will do nothing, but he revealeth his secret unto his servants the prophets" (Amos 3:7). There are many other verses stating there will be prophets. Peter was a prophet. Paul was a prophet and he came after Jesus. For instance, no one can look at Paul's words to Timothy in 2 Timothy 3:1–5 and say that Paul was not a prophet. Paul definitely foretold the future in these verses. Lets take a look at the verses:

> This know also, that in the last days perilous times shall come.
>
> For men shall be lovers of their own selves, covetous, boasters, proud, blasphemers, disobedient to parents, unthankful, unholy,
>
> Without natural affection, trucebreakers, false accusers, incontinent, fierce, despisers of those that are good,
>
> Traitors, heady, highminded, lovers of pleasures more than lovers of God;
>
> Having a form of godliness, but denying the power thereof: from such turn away.
>
> For of this sort are they which creep into houses, and lead captive silly women laden with sins, led away with divers lusts,
>
> Ever learning, and never able to come to the knowledge of the truth. (2 Tim. 3:1–7)

There is also a prophet on the earth today; the wise individual will listen to what he has to say just as if you were listening to Noah of old.

PUNISHMENT—ETERNAL OR TEMPORARY

Question 1

In the Doctrine and Covenants 19:6 and the book of Alma 42:16, it states that torment and punishment are *eternal*. *But* in the book "Doctrines of Salvation," it states torment has a release.

> A man may partake of endless torment, and when he has paid the penalty for his transgression, *he is released,* but the punishment remains and awaits the next culprit, and so on forever.[70]

Is this a discrepancy in Mormon doctrine? How can punishment be both "eternal" and "released" at the same time?

Answer 1

To understand the answer to this question some basic gospel knowledge must be understood. Many religions believe that after you die you either go to heaven or hell. This is not the case. The final judgment, which determines our final degree of salvation, does not take place until *after* the resurrection. After death, we either go to paradise or prison. (Catholics call this wait before the final judgment purgatory.) Those in prison are in a state of hell, but it only lasts until the final judgment, or until the "uttermost farthing" has been paid (Matt. 5:25–26). There are actually two states of hell in the hereafter; prison and outer darkness (1 Pet. 3:19; Matt. 8:12). Prison is *temporary* and outer darkness is *forever.* When Christ was on the cross, he told the thief he would see him in paradise *not* heaven (Luke 23:43). Also, when Christ came to Mary he said, "touch me not" for *he had not yet ascended and seen the father* (John 20:17). Thus, Christ would *not* have seen the thief in "*heaven*" and then came down to Mary and said I have not yet been to "*heaven.*" This is how it happened. Christ died and went to paradise. There he established a way for the gospel to be taught to those who have not had a chance to hear it (1 Pet. 3:18–19). When he came back down to earth, he saw Mary and said don't touch me until I see God the Father (John 20:17). He left, saw God, and later returned to earth to show the apostles his body. It was at that point he let someone touch his body (Luke 24:36–39). It is really not too confusing if you realize that Jesus just made a few trips.

After the second coming of Christ, *the final judgment* will occur and we will be assigned to one of three heavens— Celestial, Terrestrial, or Telestial (1 Cor. 15:35–42; "many mansions," John 14:2; "third heaven," 2 Cor. 12:2–5). *Or* if you deny the Holy Ghost, you will gain neither of the three heavens mentioned, but will be cast into "outer darkness" (Matt. 5:25–26; Alma 40:13–14).

Joseph Smith explains further:

> The same punishment always follows the same offense, according to the laws of God who is eternal and endless, hence it is called, endless punishment, and eternal punishment, because it is the punishment which God has fixed according to unchangeable law.[71]

This phrase more than explains the definition of endless punishment described. Another thing to remember is that when we discuss punishment, there are different punishments based on location. In other words, if you are in spirit prison, verses the Telestial Kingdom, verses outer darkness (with Satan) we are talking about different punishments. There is no discrepancy in Joseph F. Smith's words.

Question 2

Do Mormons believe that salvation will come to all? Mormon apostle, James E. Talmage wrote:

> The Extent of the Atonement is universal, applying alike to *all* descendants of Adam. *Even the unbeliever,* the heathen, and the child who dies before reaching the

years of discretion, all are redeemed by the Savior's self-sacrifice from the individual consequences of the fall.[72]

Does this mean that Mormons do not believe in hell?

Answer 2

The above statement does not say there is no condemnation for the wicked. It is simply saying that Christ's atonement is universally *available* to all. But the atonement only works if you use it. To use it you must repent of your sins. *All* who do this are "redeemed by the Savior's self-sacrifice." Even the unbeliever can repent and gain salvation. The Bible says the same thing:

> And being made perfect, he became the author of eternal salvation *unto all* them that obey him. (Heb. 5:9; italics added)

> But if we walk in the light, as he is in the light, we have fellowship one with another, and the blood of Jesus Christ his Son cleanseth us from all sin (1 Jn. 1:7).

RELIGIOUS REVIVAL

Question 1

Did Joseph Smith state that in his town there was a religious revival? Is it true that there never was one?

Answer 1

Actually history reveals it happened just as the prophet Joseph described it.

Here are the prophet's words.

> Some time in the second year after our removal to Manchester, there was in the place *where we lived* an unusual *excitement on the subject of religion.* It commenced with the Methodists, but soon *became general* among all the sects *in that region of country.* Indeed, *the*

whole district of country seemed affected by it, and great multitudes united themselves to the different religious parties, which created no small stir and division amongst the people, some crying, "Lo, here!" and others, "Lo, there!" Some were contending for the Methodist faith, some for the Presbyterian, and some for the Baptist.

For, notwithstanding the great love which the converts to the different faiths expressed at the time of their conversion, and the great zeal manifested by the respective clergy, who were active in getting up and promoting this extraordinary scene of religious feeling, in order to have everybody converted, as they were pleased to call it, let them join what sect they pleased; yet when the converts began to file off, some to one party and some to another, it was seen that the seemingly good feelings of both the priests and the converts were more pretended than real; for a scene of great confusion and bad feeling ensued—priest contending against priest, and convert against convert; so that all their good feelings one for another, if they ever had any, were entirely lost in a strife of words and a contest about opinions.

I was at this time in my fifteenth year. My father's family was proselyted to the Presbyterian faith, and four of them joined that Church, namely, my mother, Lucy; my brothers Hyrum and Samuel Harrison; and my sister Sophronia.

During this time of great excitement my mind was called up to serious reflection and great uneasiness; but though my feelings were deep and often poignant, still I kept myself aloof from all these parties, though I attended their several meetings as often as occasion would permit. In process of time my mind became somewhat partial to the Methodist sect, and I felt some desire to be united with them; but so great were the confusion and strife among the different denominations, that it was impossible for a person young as I was, and so unacquainted with men and things, to come to any certain conclusion who was right and who was wrong.

My mind at times was greatly excited, the cry and tumult were so great and incessant. The Presbyterians were most decided against the Baptists and Methodists, and used all the powers of both reason and sophistry to prove their errors, or, at least, to make the people think they were in error. On the other hand, the Baptists and Methodists in their turn were equally zealous in endeavoring to establish their own tenets and disprove all others.

In the midst of this war of words and tumult of opinions, I often said to myself: What is to be done? Who of all these parties are right; or, are they all wrong together? If any one of them be right, which is it, and how shall I know it?

While I was laboring under the extreme difficulties caused by the contests of these parties of religionists, I was one day reading the Epistle of James, first chapter and fifth verse, which reads: *If any of you lack wisdom, let him ask of God, that giveth to all men liberally, and upbraideth not; and it shall be given him.*

Never did any passage of scripture come with more power to the heart of man than this did at this time to mine. It seemed to enter with great force into every feeling of my heart. I reflected on it again and again, knowing that if any person needed wisdom from God, I did; for how to act I did not know, and unless I could get more wisdom than I then had, I would never know; for the teachers of religion of the different sects understood the same passages of scripture so differently as to destroy all confidence in settling the question by an appeal to the Bible.

At length I came to the conclusion that I must either remain in darkness and confusion, or else I must do as James directs, that is, ask of God. I at length came to the determination to "ask of God," concluding that if he gave wisdom to them that lacked wisdom, and would give liberally, and not upbraid, I might venture.

So, in accordance with this, my determination to ask of God, I retired to the woods to make the attempt. (JS—H 1:3–14; italics added in first verse)

Joseph said there was a religious excitement. It is easy to see that Joseph was not *just* talking about his town, or he would not have said "in that region of the country." Sure enough a look at history reveals that the prophet Joseph was indeed telling the truth. Research done by Milton V. Backman Jr. in his book *American Religions and the Rise of Mormonism* revealed that a Methodist camp meeting took place near Palmyra in 1820. Also in the "region of country," there were many revivals in western New York. In fact, there were at least six within twenty miles of where Joseph lived.[73]

REVELATION—MODERN DAY

(see also APOSTASY AND AUTHORITY; BOOK OF REVELATION)

Question 1

In John 19:30 it states:

> When Jesus therefore had received the vinegar, he said, it is finished: and he bowed his head and gave up the ghost. (John 19:30)

Does Christ state it is finished, meaning further revelation was finished?

Answer 1

Christ stating, "it is finished" refers to his life on earth and to his suffering for our sins. In fact, Christ later revealed himself to his apostles and promised to be with them always even unto the end (Mark 28:20).

Question 2

In the book of John it says all truth was given to the apostles. If all truth was given, is further truth through revelation needed?

Answer 2

The scripture states this:

> Howbeit when he, the Spirit of truth, is come, *he*
> *will guide you into all truth:* for he shall not speak of
> himself; but whatsoever he shall hear, that shall he speak,
> and he shall show you things to come. (John 16:13)

This verse plainly states that the apostles were given
all truth, but it was not the end of all truth. For instance,
Peter was given truth and revelation, and after him, other
apostles were also given revelation. John the Revelator is an
example of this for the book of Revelation was written *after*
Peter had died.

COMMENTS ABOUT REVELATION

Malachi prophesied that at Christ's second coming, the
savior would come to his temple. Why is this important to
revelation? Let's take a look at the verse:

> Behold, I will send my messenger and he shall pre-
> pare the way before me: and the Lord whom ye seek,
> shall suddenly *come so his temple,* even the messenger of
> the covenant, whom ye delight in: behold, he shall come,
> saith the Lord of hosts.
>
> But who may abide the day of his coming? And
> who shall stand when he appeareth? For he is like a
> refiner's fire, and like fullers' soap. (Mal. 3:1–3; italics
> added)

This prophecy refers to Jesus' second coming. Christ
did not come suddenly on his first visit and he did not come
to his temple. He did not purify the sons of Levi, but people
did abide his coming at that day. The words "who shall
stand" in the verse is a condition of retaliation on the
wicked. (He came the first time as a baby in a manger.) How
could he suddenly come to his temple, unless a temple was
built for him? We would only know to build the temple if
revelation told us to build it. It is interesting that very few
religions today even build temples, yet temples have always
been a part of the Lord's plan.

In the book of Malachi, the Lord gives a promise:

> I will send you Elija the Prophet before the coming
> of the great and dreadful day of the Lord. (Mal. 4:5–6)

This verse certainly signifies further knowledge and revelation would come from heaven.

SABBATH DAY

Question 1

Should the Sabbath Day be Saturday?

Answer 1

This question is answered superbly by LeGrand Richards.

The Sabbath Day

There has been considerable difference of opinion among Christians as to whether they should worship on the seventh day of the week (Saturday), the sabbath of the Jews, or the first day of the week (Sunday), the day upon which Christ arose from the tomb, called in Holy Writ, the Lord's day. It therefore seems proper that in the restoration of his Church in this dispensation, the Lord should express himself on this subject. He did so in a revelation to the Prophet Joseph Smith given in Zion, Jackson County, Missouri, August 7, 1831, from which we quote:

> "And that thou mayest more fully keep thyself unspotted from the world, thou shalt go to the house of prayer and offer up thy sacraments upon my holy day;
>
> For verily this is a day appointed unto you to rest from your labors, and to pay thy devotions unto the Most High;
>
> Nevertheless thy vows shall be offered up in righteousness on all days and at all times;

But remember that on this, the Lord's day, thou shalt offer thine oblations and thy sacraments unto the Most High, confessing thy sins unto thy brethren, and before the Lord" (D&C 59:9–12).

From this revelation, we learn that the Lord designates "the Lord's day" as "my holy day." Again, it is through the revelation of the Lord to his prophet of this dispensation that this truth is made plain, rather than through a study of ancient scriptures or of history. However, let us turn to the scriptures of old to learn that this revelation of the Lord in the reestablishment of his Church upon the earth in this dispensation in no way conflicts with instructions and revelations given by the Lord through his prophets of former days.

History of the Sabbath Day

Let us pursue a brief study of the history of the sabbath day:

"And on the seventh day God ended his work which he had made; and he rested on the seventh day from all his work which he had made.

And God blessed the seventh day, and sanctified it: because that in it he had rested from all his work which God created and made" (Gen. 2:2–3).

From this account it is clear that "God blessed the seventh day, and sanctified it: because that in it he had rested from all his work." But from a study of the scriptures it would appear that the first commandment given through any of the prophets that the people should observe this as a day of worship was that which was given through Moses about 2500 years after the creation. In Deuteronomy we learn why God gave the commandment to the children of Israel at that time:

"The Lord our God made a covenant with us in Horeb.

The Lord made not this covenant with our fathers, but with us, even us, who are all of us here alive this day . . .

Keep the sabbath day to sanctify it, as the Lord thy God hath commanded thee . . .

And remember that thou wast a servant in the land of Egypt, and that the Lord thy God brought thee out thence through a mighty hand and by a stretched out arm: therefore the Lord thy God commanded thee to keep the sabbath day" (Deut. 5:2–3, 12, 15).

From this scripture it is apparent that this was a new covenant the Lord made with Israel in Horeb; that he had not made this covenant with their fathers; that he made this covenant so that they might remember that they were servants in the land of Egypt; and that the Lord their God brought them out through a mighty hand and by a stretched-out arm, and therefore the Lord their God commanded them to keep the sabbath day.

This commandment to observe the sabbath day was incorporated in the law of Moses, as were also the sabbatic year and the forty-ninth and the fiftieth-year sabbath. Speaking of the law of Moses, the apostle Paul stated:

"Wherefore the law was our schoolmaster to bring us unto Christ, that we might be justified by faith" (Galatians 3:24).

If the law of Moses, therefore, were the schoolmaster to bring us unto Christ, it would seem perfectly reasonable to assume that when Christ came, there would be no further need of the schoolmaster.

Israel's Sabbath to Cease

When we understand that the law of Moses, including its sabbaths, was a schoolmaster to bring us unto Christ, we are better able to understand why the Lord permitted his prophet Hosea to declare that he would cause Israel's sabbaths to cease: "I will also cause all her mirth to cease, her feast days, her new moons, and her sabbaths, and all her solemn feasts" (Hosea 2:11).

Can we accept the scriptures as the word of God and question that this prophecy of Hosea should be fulfilled and that the Lord would truly cause Israel's sabbaths to cease? When Hosea's prophecy was fulfilled, the way was obviously opened for the introduction of a new sabbath.

A New Sabbath, the Lord's Day

The Savior understood that a change was to be made in the sabbath:

> "And he said unto them, The sabbath was made for man, and not man for the sabbath:
>
> Therefore the Son of man is Lord also of the sabbath (Mark 2:27–28).

Jesus did not come to break the law but to fulfill it. Thus, in him, the Jewish sabbath was fulfilled, as was the remainder of the law of Moses, which was the "schoolmaster to bring us unto Christ." Hence, when Christ came, he became also Lord of the sabbath. He himself declared that he came to fulfill the law: "Think not that I am come to destroy the law, or the prophets: I am not come to destroy, but to fulfil" (Matt. 5:17).

Since Jesus came to fulfill the law, why should some still want to retain it? Why should they not prefer to accept that which Jesus brought to take the place of the law, which includes the new sabbath, the first day of the week or the Lord's day (Sunday), the day upon which Jesus arose from the tomb? "The Lord's day" is the day he directed his saints in this dispensation to worship him (D&C 59:12).

John, the beloved disciple of the Lord, while banished upon the Isle of Patmos "for the word of God, and for the testimony of Jesus Christ," wrote: "I was in the Spirit on the Lord's day, and heard behind me a great voice, as of a trumpet" (Rev. 1:10).

Why should this day be called "the Lord's day," if it were not a sacred day? Remember, "the Son of man is Lord also of the sabbath."

Because the day on which the sabbath was observed was changed, the apostle Paul realized that the saints would be criticized, as they were for other practices to which the Jews objected: "Let no man therefore judge you in meat, or in drink, or in respect of an holy-day, or of the new moon, or of the sabbath days" (Col. 2:16).

This warning from the apostle Paul would have been entirely uncalled for were the saints worshipping on the Jewish sabbath, for the Jews then would have had no occasion to judge them on this matter.

The Saints Worshiped on the First Day of the Week

There is no record that the saints observed the Jewish sabbath as a day of worship following the resurrection of the Savior. The apostles did, however, meet with the Jews in their synagogues on their sabbath to teach them the gospel (see Acts 13:13–44; 17:1–2.)

The records are quite complete, however, in indicating that the saints often met to worship on the first day of the week (Sunday), the Lord's day, or the day that Jesus arose from the tomb:

Then the same day at evening, being the first day of the week, when the doors were shut where the disciples were assembled for fear of the Jews, came Jesus and stood in the midst, and saith unto them, Peace be unto you.

And after eight days again his disciples were within, and Thomas with them: then came Jesus, the doors being shut, and stood in the midst, and said, Peace be unto you. (John 20:19, 26.)

And upon the first day of the week, when the disciples came together to break bread, Paul preached unto them, ready to depart on the morrow; and continued his speech until midnight. (Acts 20:7.)

Now concerning the collection for the saints, as I have given order to the Churches of Galatia, even so do ye.

"Upon the first day of the week let every one of you lay by him in store, as God hath prospered him, that there be no gatherings when I come" (1 Cor. 16:1-2).

The following scripture is particularly significant, since the day of Pentecost was the day following the Jewish sabbath:

"And when the day of Pentecost was fully come, they were all with one accord in one place.

And suddenly there came a sound from heaven as of a rushing mighty wind, and it filled all the house where they were sitting.

And there appeared unto them cloven tongues like as of fire, and it sat upon each of them.

And they were all filled with the Holy Ghost, and began to speak with other tongues, as the Spirit gave them utterance" (Acts 2:1–4, Levi. 23:15–16).

What consistent explanation can be given for the fact that the saints met to worship on the first day of the week—Sunday, the Lord's day, the day upon which the Savior rose from the tomb—instead of on Saturday, the Jewish sabbath, except that the Lord did cause the Jewish sabbaths to cease, as the prophet Hosea declared he would? Jesus instituted a new sabbath, the Lord's day, thus becoming "Lord also of the sabbath."

Greek Bible Designates the First Day of the Week as a Sabbath

This conclusion is further sustained by the fact that the first day of the week (Sunday) is called a sabbath eight times in the original Greek Bible. Had the Bible, therefore, been correctly translated, much of the present confusion in this matter would have been eliminated. Why would the first day of the week (Sunday) be called a sabbath in the Bible if it were not a sabbath? And how did it become a sabbath other than as we have explained? "In the end of the sabbath, as it began to dawn toward the first day of the week . . ." (Matt. 28:1, In Greek, "sabbath" instead of "first day of the week").

This text may be confusing because of its reference

to two sabbaths, unless one keeps in mind the fact that the Christian sabbath (first day of the week) follows immediately the Jewish sabbath (seventh day of the week). Hence the reference to two sabbaths.

"And very early in the morning the first day of the week . . ." (Mark 16:2, In Greek, "sabbath" instead of "first day of the week").

"Now when Jesus was risen early the first day of the week . . ." (Mark 16:9, In Greek, "sabbath" instead of "first day of the week").

"Now upon the first day of the week . . ." (Luke 24:1, In Greek, "sabbath" instead of "first day of the week").

"The first day of the week . . ." (John 20:1, In Greek, "sabbath" instead of "first day of the week").

"Then the same day at evening, being the first day of the week . . ." (John 20:19, In Greek, "sabbath" instead of "first day of the week").

"And upon the first day of the week . . ." (Acts 20:7, In Greek, "sabbath" instead of "first day of the week").

"Upon the first day of the week . . ." (1 Cor. 16:2, In Greek, "sabbath" instead of "first day of the week").

From the foregoing, it should be clear that the writers of the New Testament fully understood that the first day of the week (Sunday) was a sabbath day, and that it was the day upon which the saints met to worship.

Early Christians Worshiped on the First Day of the Week

The early Church historians stated that the first day of the week, the day on which the Lord arose from the tomb, was held sacred by the Christians as a day of worship. This, together with the evidence we have already submitted, refutes the claims of some that the change from Saturday to Sunday was instituted by Constantine, Emperor of Rome:

It is indeed true, that Constantine's life was not such as the precepts of Christianity required; and it is also true that he remained a catechumen (unbaptized Christian) all his life, and was received to full membership in the Church, by baptism at Nicomedia only a few days before his death.

Footnote 25 . . . That Constantine, long before this time, A.D. 324, declared himself a Christian, and was acknowledged as such by the Churches, is certain. It is also true, he had for a long time performed the religious acts of an unbaptized Christian, that is, of a catechumen; for he attended public worship, fasted, prayed, observed the Christian Sabbath and the anniversaries of the martyrs, and watched on the vigils of Easter, etc. (*Mosheim's Church History*, Book 2, Century 4, Part 1, Chap. 1:8.)

The Christians of this century, in piety, assembled for the worship of God and for their advancement of the first day of the week, the day on which Christ reassumed his life; for that this day was set apart for religious worship by the apostles themselves, and that, after the example of the Church at Jerusalem, it was generally observed, we have unexceptionable testimony. *(Mosheim's Church History*, Book 1, Century 1, Part 2, Chap. 4:4.)

Those who were brought up in the ancient order of things, have come to the possession of a new hope, no longer observing the Sabbath (Jewish or seventh day), but living in the observance of the Lord's day (first day) on which also our life was sprung by him and his death. (Epistle to the Magnesians, 101 A.D., Chap. 9, *Ignatius*.)

On one day, the first day of the week, we assembled ourselves together. (*Barderaven*, A.D. 130.)

And on the day which is called Sunday, there is an assembly in the same place of all who live in cities, or in country districts; and the records of the Apostles, or the writings of the Prophets, are read as long as we have time. . . . Sunday is the day on which we all hold our common assembly, because it is the first day on which

God, when He changed the darkness and matter, made the world: and Jesus Christ our Savior, on the same day, rose from the dead. . . . (Justin Martyr, *Apologies*, 1:67 A.D. 140.)

He, in fulfilment of the precept according to the gospel, keeps the Lord's day. (*Clement of Alexandria*, Book 7, Chap. 12, A.D. 193.)

We neither accord with the Jews in their peculiarities in regard to food nor in their sacred days. (*Apologies*, Sec. 21, A.D. 200.)

We ourselves are accustomed to observe certain days, as for example, the Lord's day. (*Origen*, Book 3, Chap. 23, A.D. 201.)

But why is it, you ask, that we gather on the Lord's day to celebrate our solemnities? Because that was the way the Apostles also did. (*De Fuga* XIV:11, 141, 200 A.D.)

It will thus be seen that through the revelations of the Lord to the Prophet Joseph Smith in directing his saints of this dispensation to observe as a day of worship the Lord's day (Sunday), the first day of the week, he only confirmed his approval of the practice of the saints of former days, as fully sustained by Holy Writ and the early Church historians. If they had been in error in abandoning the seventh day (Saturday, the Jewish sabbath), in favor of the Lord's day (Sunday, the first day of the week), the Lord would surely have so indicated, for in restoring the gospel he did not hesitate to correct mistakes that had been made by alleged Church leaders through the ages.[74]

SACRAMENT

(see also WORD OF WISDOM)

Question 1

In Matthew 26:26–29, Jesus instituted the sacrament with bread and wine. So why does the LDS Church use water instead of wine? Do Mormons use water because they reject the blood of Christ?

Answer 1

When the Savior instituted the sacrament, he stated:

> "And he took *the cup,* and gave thanks, and gave it to them, saying, Drink ye all *of it.* (Matt. 26:27; italics added)

The Lord did *not* specify that *only* the "fruit of the vine" could be used in the sacrament. It is true that Jesus did have "fruit of the vine" when he instituted the sacrament. In the early days of the LDS Church, wine was used. Satan had mounted such persecution at that time, that enemies would try to poison the wine. The poison could not be detected in wine, but it could in water. The Lord revealed that water could be used instead of wine (D&C 27:1–2). Another important point is that if you were allergic to grapes, the Lord would not deny you to partake of the sacrament. The symbolism is what is important. It symbolizes the body and blood of Jesus that he freely gave as a ransom for us. The question if Mormons reject the blood of Christ is absolutely and entirely false. To reject the blood of Christ would be to reject his atonement. To reject his atonement would be to reject salvation in the Kingdom of God! Any person who says that Mormons reject the blood of Christ is a deceiver. Beware of that person. Each and every Sunday at a Mormon sacrament service a prayer is said for both the bread and water. The prayer for the water says this:

> O God, the Eternal Father, we ask thee in the name of thy Son, Jesus Christ, to bless and sanctify this water to the souls of all those who drink of it, that they may do it *in remembrance of the blood of thy Son,* which was *shed for them* that they may witness unto thee, O God, the Eternal Father, *that they do always remember him,* that they may have his Spirit to be with them. Amen. (Moro. 5:2; italics added)

SACRIFICE, ANIMAL

(see also BLOOD ATONEMENT; PROPHECY)

Question 1

In the *History of the Church* does it say that animal sacrifice will again be instituted in temples just as it was anciently?

Answer 1

Let's take a look at the paragraph:

> Sacrifices, as well as every ordinance belonging to the Priesthood, will, when the Temple of the Lord shall be built, and the sons of Levi be purified, be fully restored and attended to in all their powers, ramifications, and blessings. This ever did and ever will exist when the powers of the Melchizedek Priesthood are sufficiently manifest; else how can the restitution of all things spoken of by the holy Prophets be brought to pass? It is not to be understood that the law of Moses will be established again with all its rites and variety of ceremonies; this has never been spoken of by the Prophets; but those things which existed prior to Moses' day namely, sacrifice, will be continued.[75]

Animal sacrifice is another issue that is often misinterpreted. Of course during Moses' time animal sacrifice was performed as a similitude of God sacrificing his son Jesus Christ.

We know that after Christ's death animal sacrifice was ended. The question is, does the passage above prophesy that animal sacrifice would again be instituted in temples? The Prophet Joseph Fielding Smith has answered this question.

> We are living in the dispensation of the fullness of times into which *all things* are to be restored since the beginning. Even this earth is to be restored to the condition which prevailed before Adam's transgression. Now

in the nature of things, the law of sacrifice will have to be restored, or all things which were decreed by the Lord would not be restored. It will be necessary, therefore, for *the sons of Levi,* who offered the blood sacrifices anciently in Israel, to offer such a sacrifice again to round out and complete this ordinance in this dispensation. Sacrifice by the shedding of blood was instituted in the days of Adam and of necessity will have to be restored.

The sacrifice of animals will be done *to complete the restoration* when the temple spoken of is built; at the beginning of the millennium, or in the restoration, blood sacrifices will be performed *long enough to complete the fullness of the restoration* in this dispensation. Afterwards sacrifice will be of some other character.[76]

As prophesied in Acts 3:21, there will be a "restitution of all things." Although the timing of it will be limited, it still fulfills the prophecy.

Question 2

If animal sacrifice will be performed, how do members of the LDS Church describe the "last sacrifice" stated in the Book of Mormon, Alma 34:13? In other words, how can there be another sacrifice if they already described a *last one*?

Answer 2

Let's take a look at the verse:

Therefore, it is expedient that there should be a great and last sacrifice, and then shall there be, or it is expedient there should be, a stop to the shedding of blood; then shall the law of Moses be fulfilled; yea, it shall be all fulfilled, every jot and tittle, and none shall have passed away. (Alma 34:13)

The verse states there would be a "great and last sacrifice." This statement refers to *Christ's atonement* being great and last in regard to its spiritual relevance, eternalness, effect, and significance. Christ's atonement and sacrifice obviously is not an animal sacrifice. Certainly Christ's atonement will never be repeated, and since his great and last sacrifice, there has been a "stop to the shedding of blood." Even to this day and there will be no further sacrifice *until* the sons of Levi do again, offer a sacrifice unto the Lord (D&C 13). Likewise, modern day scripture reveals a different type of sacrifice to be done in the future, in the Independence, Jackson County, Missouri, temple by the sons of Moses and the sons of Aaron (D&C 84:31). It is not to be assumed that the law of Moses will be restored for there has never been a prophecy concerning this. Why then, in the restitution of all things, is sacrifice to be restored as recorded and prophesied in the Doctrine and Covenants? It may be that the purpose of this temporary restitution of blood sacrifice be performed as a remembrance of Christ's great and last sacrifice.[77]

It is not surprising that just sacrifice and not the entire law of Moses will be restored. Sacrifice was instituted with Adam; the law of Moses was instituted because of the Israelites failed to obey the higher law. To some, the thought of sacrifice being restored to the earth, even for a short time, seems gruesome and ancient, but the fact is that the sacrifice to be done in the future, as part of the restitution of all things, has been prophesied since ancient times. Only through modern day revelation do we know about the coming fulfillment of the ancient prediction that there would be such a sacrifice. Let's take a look at the Bible prophecy:

> And he shall sit as a refiner and purifier of silver: and he shall purify the sons of Levi, and purge them as gold and silver, that they may offer unto the Lord and offering in righteousness.
>
> Then shall the offering of Judah and Jerusalem be pleasant unto the LORD, as in the days of old, and as in former years. (Mal. 3:3–4).

It is obvious that nothing even close to this prophecy took place during Christ's time, and even to this day it remains to be fulfilled. When the Aaronic Priesthood was restored to the earth in 1829, Joseph Smith was informed that the Aaronic Priesthood "shall never be taken again from the earth, until the sons of Levi do offer again an offering unto the Lord in righteousness" (D&C 13). The offering spoken of will be made by the literal sons of Levi. This is clearly different than the offering by the adopted sons of Moses and Aaron, which involves temple and genealogical work that is spoken of in Doctrine and Covenants 84:31–32 and 128:24.

Question 3

In the Book of Mormon, Mosiah 2:3 states:

And they also took of the firstlings of their flocks, that they might offer sacrifice and burnt offerings according to the law of Moses.

Some have stated that "firstlings" were not used in the law of Moses for "burnt offerings" unless those of the tribe of Aaron handed them down. If this is the case how can those in the Book of Mormon claim to have done it.

Answer 3

As mentioned under the section "Priesthood," the Lord authorized others who were not of the tribe of Levi or through Aaron's lineage the right to hold the Levitical Priesthood. The Levitical Priesthood is only *an appendage* to the higher Melchizedek Priesthood, thus from the beginning anyone holding the Melchizedek Priesthood could do *everything* a person with the Levitical Priesthood could do. The Nephites in the Book of Mormon held the Melchizedek Priesthood. In Old Testament times the "firstlings" were given to the Aaronic priests. The Nephites had no Aaronic priests with them. But it is important to remember that Adam didn't either. Adam and his sons, as well as Abraham and others, did sacrifices and they were not descendants of

Aaron because obviously, *Aaron was not even born yet.* The Lord required these sacrifices prior to the birth of Christ. Adam, the Nephites, and the descendants of Aaron, were all to offer sacrifices. When sacrifices were still performed, priesthood authority was required to perform them. Adam, the Nephites, and the descendants of Aaron all held priesthood authority and thus could perform the ordinance. In short, the Nephites performed like Abel in the Old Testament.

> And Abel, he also brought of the firstlings of his flock and of the fat thereof. And the Lord had respect unto Abel and to his offering. (Gen. 4:4)

Concerning the eternal nature of the priesthood the scriptures state:

> Without father, without mother, without descent, having neither beginning of days, nor end of life; but made like unto the Son of God; abideth a priest continually. (Heb. 7:3)

Thus, the priesthood has always existed, and is still around today. The Melchizedek Priesthood has *no descent* (not based on lineage, no father, no mother), *no beginning* and *no end.* Without the priesthood, ordinances cannot be performed. It was with this priesthood authority that the Nephites did burnt offerings.

SATAN AND JESUS BROTHERS

Question 1

The LDS Church believes that Satan is a Son of God just as all mankind is (Acts 17:29). Many members of other faiths have a hard time believing this doctrine. After all, how could God make such a being? Is there any evidence that Satan is a brother to Jesus?

Answer 1

Yes, Satan is our brother, as is Hitler, Judas Iscariot, and others. I personally like to dwell on Jesus as my brother and not Satan, but it does not negate the fact that Satan too once lived with us in heaven, and is our brother. Let's take a look at this *very* evident fact in the scriptures.

> How art thou fallen *from heaven,* O Lucifer, *son of the morning!* How art thou cut down to the ground, which didst weaken the nations.
>
> For thou hast said in thine heart, I will ascend into heaven, I will exalt my throne above the stars of God: I will sit also upon the mount of the congregation, in the sides of the north:
>
> I will ascend above the heights of the clouds: I will be like the most high.
>
> Yet thou shalt be brought down to hell, to the sides of the pit. (Isa. 14:12–27; italics added)

Lucifer fell from heaven. To fall from heaven, you had to be in heaven. Why did he fall from heaven? He participated with God in developing the plan of salvation for all mankind, but he wanted the glory for himself. Jesus also was there and participated but he wanted to give the glory to God the Father. Jesus was chosen and Satan rebelled and took one third of the hosts of heaven with him. The one third that followed Satan is now on this earth tempting us and trying to lead us astray. The other two thirds are you and I and all the others that have been born and will be born on this earth.

> And he said unto them, I beheld Satan as lightning fall from heaven. (Luke 10:18–20)
>
> And there was war in heaven: Michael and his angels fought against the dragon; and the dragon fought and his angels
>
> And prevailed not; neither was their place found *any more* in heaven.
>
> And the great dragon *was cast out,* that old

serpent, called the Devil, and Satan, which deceiveth the whole world: he was cast out into the earth, and *his angels were cast out with him.* (Rev. 12:7–12; italics added)

To not be found "any more" in heaven means he was once in heaven.

For if God spared not the *angels that sinned,* but cast them down to hell, and delivered them unto chains of darkness, to be reserved unto judgment. (2 Pet. 2:4; italics added)

These angels were the one third of our brothers and sisters that followed Satan, and not Jesus.

And the angels which kept not their first estate, but left their own habitation, he hath reserved in everlasting chains under darkness unto the judgment of the great day. (Jude 6)

And unclean spirits, when they saw him, fell down before him, and cried, saying, Thou art the Son of God. (Mark 3:11–12)

These unclean spirits knew Jesus because they were with him in heaven before they were cast out with Satan. There is *not one* scripture in the Bible that says Satan is not Jesus' brother, yet there are numerous that say he is. This list does not include all the other wonderful verses in the Book of Mormon, Doctrine and Covenants, and Pearl of Great Price.

SAVED BY GRACE

(see WORKS)

SCRIPTURES

(see also BOOK OF MORMON; PEARL OF GREAT PRICE)

Question 1

Why are there copied chapters of Isaiah in the Book of Mormon (2 Ne. 11–25)? Did Joseph Smith copy them because he needed more writings in the Book of Mormon?

Answer 1

Joseph Smith did *not* copy Isaiah from the Bible. He did copy it from the gold plates.

Nearly the entire Book of Mormon was copied and abridged from other books, plates, scrolls, etc. *Nephi copied Isaiah* from the brass plates (2 Ne. 4:14–15), and the prophet Mormon compiled the Book of Mormon from these and many other writings. That is why it is called the Book of Mormon. It is named after the prophet that did the compiling and copying. No one questions the copying that came from *other documents* from ancient *America* because they don't have the original documents. But because we have the writings of the Bible, enemies claim Joseph Smith copied this portion. Again, the whole book was copied and compiled from other documents and placed into one book. Some of the writings from the Bible were part of this abridgment, why? Nephi said:

> And now I write some of the words of Isaiah, that whoso of *my people* shall see these words may lift up their hearts and rejoice for all men. Now these are the words, and ye may *liken them unto you and unto all me.* (2 Ne. 11:8; italics added)

Isaiah was talking to the people of Nephi. If you read the sections from Isaiah in the Book of Mormon, they are referring to the scattering and gathering of Israel. As Lehi and his family left Jerusalem, *they were being scattered* and driven out of Jerusalem. It gave great comfort to the Nephites to know that one day their descendants would again be gathered, just as Isaiah prophesied.

There is evidence in your own Bible that Joseph Smith did not copy Isaiah. If you turn to the Isaiah writings in the Bible you will see that those who translated Isaiah for our Bible accidentally forgot to write a line that Nephi did not forget. How do we know this? If you turn to the front of your King James Bible it says, "TRANSLATED OUT OF THE ORIGINAL TONGUES." In other words King James commissioned translators to take the original Greek and Hebrew documents and translate them into English. The original Greek and Hebrew documents still exist so we can compare the Greek, to the Hebrew, to the King James Version, and to the Book of Mormon. The comparison shows this:

- And upon all the ships of Tarshish (Isa. 2:16).
- Ships of the sea (Greek).
- Ships of Tarshish (Hebrew).
- And upon all the ships of the sea, and upon all the ships of Tarshish (2 Ne. 2:16).

These simple sentences irrefutably prove that Joseph Smith did not simply copy the writings of Isaiah out of the King James Bible. Joseph Smith did not have access to the Greek or Hebrew writings and even if he did he did not know the languages.

The Lord doesn't teach different doctrine based on location. Those in America needed these things revealed as well. There were a lot of Nephites, and Nephi knew one copy of the words of Isaiah was not enough for his people to read Isaiah's comforting words. By making an extra copy, it gave more of an opportunity for the people to read them. Of course this was not just Nephi's idea, many copies were made by others. In fact that is what monks did. They would just sit day after day and copy scripture. So if someone says that it looks like Isaiah was copied. Tell them it was, but it was Nephi who copied it, not Joseph Smith.

Question 2

Did Joseph Smith have the King James Version with him and refer to it when he translated the writings from Isaiah? If not, why is it written in King James English?

Answer 2

There is absolutely no evidence that Joseph Smith turned to the King James Version when he was translating Isaiah from the gold plates. Of course whether he did or not it makes no difference in any way, shape, or form. A comparison of Isaiah in the Bible and Isaiah in the Book of Mormon show some important insights in the Book of Mormon that were lost from the Old Testament version. Since the entire Book of Mormon is similar to King James English, the writings of Isaiah found, in the Book of Mormon, would naturally also be written in King James English. Enemies of the Church can use this question against the Church either way. If the writings were too different, they would claim the prophet Joseph didn't even know the scriptures. If they were too similar they can claim he copied it. In FARMS, review of books, they make an interesting analogy:

> An examination of the text suggests *not* that Joseph Smith deliberately used King James Bible wording, but that it was part of his vocabulary and therefore *naturally came to be used in the translation.* To illustrate, let's do a similar study of the first two paragraphs of Lincoln's Gettysburg Address.
>
> Gettysburg Address
> *Four score and seven years ago,*
>
> King James Bible
> four score and seven (1 Chron. 7:5)
>
> Gettysburg Address
> *our fathers brought forth*

King James Bible
their fathers, which brought forth (2 Chron. 7:22)

Gettysburg Address
*on this continent a new nation, conceived in Liberty
and dedicated to the proposition*

King James Bible
dedicated unto the (1 Chron. 18:11)

Gettysburg Address
that all men are created equal.

King James Bible
that all men (Job 37:7; John 1:7; 5:23)
that all men were (1 Cor. 7:7)
all men are (Ps. 116:11)
a man mine equal (Ps. 55:13)

Gettysburg Address
*Now we are engaged in a great civil war, testing
whether that nation*

King James Bible
if that nation (Jer. 18:8)

Gettysburg Address
*or any nation so conceived and so dedicated can long
endure. We are met on a great battlefield of that war. We
have come*

King James Bible
we would have come (1 Thes. 2:8)
we are come to (Matt. 2:2)

Gettysburg Address
to dedicate

King James Bible
to dedicate (2 Chron. 2:4)

Gettysburg Address
a portion of that field,

King James Bible
the portion of the field (2 Kings 9:25)
a portion of (Deut. 33:21)

Gettysburg Address
as a final resting place for those

King James Bible
a resting place for them (Num. 10:33)

Gettysburg Address
who here gave their lives

King James Bible
gave their life (Ps. 78:50)

Gettysburg Address
that that nation might live.

King James Bible
might live (Gen. 17:18; Deut. 4:42; Gal. 1:19; 1 John 4:9)

Gettysburg Address
It is altogether fitting and proper that we should do this.

King James Bible
that they should do (Neh. 5:12)
that ye should do that (2 Cor. 13:7)

Now, I don't believe for a moment that Abraham Lincoln was deliberately "plagiarizing" passages from the King James Bible, though it is clear that there are some very close parallels here. In fact, there are *many more* parallels by volume of text than the ones shown by the Tanners for Mosiah 1–6 and the KJV. To what, then, can we attribute Lincoln's use of these expressions that seem so clearly to be biblical? There are two obvious factors: (1) Both Lincoln and the King James translators spoke English. (2) *Lincoln, as a Bible-reading man, would have these expressions as part of his vocabulary.* What is important here is that the Bible words were used to describe *entirely different circumstances*, and yet were appropriate to those circumstances. I suggest that the same can be said of Book of Mormon passages that resemble the Bible. If, as I have suggested, Joseph Smith deliberately used the King James style so the Book of Mormon would sound like scripture, there is even more reason to find such parallels between the Book of Mormon and the Bible. *Using language and expressions also found in the King James Bible is* not *plagiarism.*[78]

In the English language there are often many meanings for the same word. Because of this translation can be quite a challenge. For example, If you were to translate a word like *heal* from reformed Egyptian to English, it is possible that the same Egyptian word Joseph recognized as heal could just as easily mean cure, make well, restore to health, mend, nurse back to health, repair, etc. Joseph could have had enough leeway to use his own style of English. Would it be any different if it were translated in "regular" English verses King James English? It appears to be up to the translator. This may also be the reason the French word *Adieu* is found in the Book of Mormon (Jacob 7:27; French words like *bruit* and Greek words like *Christian* are also found in the Bible). The other obvious possibility is that when Joseph was translating, God gave him the translation in King James English, because it was familiar to Joseph, you and I.

The Book of Mormon is in fact scripture, and it was translated by the gift and power of God. Those who want to find the strait and narrow path will abide by its teachings (Matt. 7:14).

Question 3

If the Lord knows the future, why would he command a repeat of scriptures (passages from Isaiah in the Book of Mormon) that would already be in print through Bible writing?

Answer 3

The Lord knew the information was important, so he commanded the writings. Remember this also happened with the Dead Sea scrolls. The Dead Sea scrolls repeat many of the same books of the Old Testament. The fact that the prophet Mormon compiled from other scrolls is not a secret. The prophet Mormon himself states this:

> Yea, a small record of that which hath taken place from the time that Lehi left Jerusalem, even down until the present time.
>
> Therefore I do make my record *from the accounts which have been given* by those who were before me, until the commencement of my day;

And I do make a record of the things which I have
seen with mine own eyes. (3 Ne. 5:15–17; italics added)

Question 3

Is it true that Joseph Smith used a Urim and Thummim
to translate the Book of Mormon? Doesn't the Bible speak
against using enchanters, witches, and divination (Deut.
18:9–14)?

Answer 3

The Urim and Thummim is not an enchanter or a
witch, etc. Calling the Urim and Thummim an enchanter is
like calling the white stone in Revelation 2:17 the same.

The words Urim and Thummim mean "lights and per-
fections" in Hebrew. This device is referred to in the Bible
many times. In fact in Leviticus 8:8, Moses himself used it.
In 1 Samuel 28:6, it tells us some ways the Lord gives
answers: "prophets, dreams, and the use of an Urim and
Thummim." The Urim and Thummim was the Lord's way of
helping the prophet Joseph translate the plates from
reformed Egyptian.

SYMBOLS

Question 1

On some Mormon temples there are symbols such as
suns, moons, and stars. Are these symbols Satanic or from
astrology cults?

Answer 1

The symbols on Mormon temples come from the Bible
and modern day revelation (D&C 76). This question reveals
just how desperate enemies of the Church are. They are *willing to deceive* to further the work of Satan. Those who

spread these lies will go to any length to try to mislead others. They will say the sun has a face, or the star has too many points, or the star has one bigger point, and so forth. The truth is, it was revealed to Joseph Smith that there is *not* just one heaven and one hell, but that there are three glories or degrees of heaven. These degrees or kingdoms of Heaven are compared to the sun, moon, and stars (see D&C 76). In the Bible, this was also revealed in the book of 1 Corinthians 15: 35–42. These verses compare the sun, moon, and stars to celestial and terrestrial glories.

> But some man will say *How are the dead raised up?* and with what body do they come?
>
> Thou fool, that which thou sowest is not quickened, except it die:
>
> And that which thou sowest, thou sowest not that body that shall be, but bare grain, it may chance of wheat, or of some other grain:
>
> But God giveth it a body as it hath pleased him, and to every seed his own body.
>
> *All flesh is not the same flesh:* but there is one kind of flesh of men, another flesh of beasts, another of fishes, and another of birds.
>
> There are also *celestial* bodies, and bodies *terrestrial:* but the glory of the celestial is one, and the glory of the terrestrial is another.
>
> There is one glory of the sun, and another glory of the moon, and another glory of the stars: for *one* star differeth from another star in glory.
>
> *So also is the resurrection of the dead.* It is sown in corruption; it is raised in incorruption. (1 Cor. 15:35–42; italics added)

Let's take a look at other scriptures revealing that there is more than one heaven. There are other verses referring to this fact not mentioned here.

> Such an one caught up to the third heaven. (2 Cor. 12:2–5)

In my Father's house are many mansions. (John 14:2)

Question 2

Mormons do not have crosses on their churches or temples. Is this because they do not believe in Jesus or his atonement?

Answer 2

Mormons *do* believe in Jesus and the atonement! Although Mormons do not have the same opinion of the use of crosses Mormons do *not* look down upon those who wear a cross as jewelry or display it on their Churches. We in the same respect hope others will not look down on us for not displaying crosses. There is a reason we don't. Bruce R. McConkie has said this:

> Because of its association with our Lord, the cross has come to have symbolic meanings for those who profess belief in his atoning blood. Paul *properly* used the cross of Christ to identify to the mind the whole doctrine of the atonement, reconciliation, and redemption (1 Cor. 1:17–18; Gal. 6:12–14; Eph. 2: 8–21; Philip. 2:5–9; 3:18; Col. 1:20; 2:14; Heb. 12:2).
>
> *In succeeding centuries,* the Churches which came into being *through an intermingling of pagan concepts* with the true apostolic Christianity developed the practice of using symbolic crosses in the architecture of their buildings and as jewelry attached to the robes of their priests. Frequently this practice of dwelling on the personal death struggle of our Lord has caused these Churches to put sculptured representations of Christ on their crosses, thus forming so called crucifixes. All this is inharmonious with the quiet spirit of worship and reverence that should attend a true Christian's remembrance of our Lord's sufferings and death. In fact, *the revealed symbolism* to bring these things to the attention of true worshipers *is found in the ordinance of the sacrament.*[79]

It was Christ's enemies that put him on the cross.

These enemies thought they had succeeded in destroying Christ and his gospel, but Christ overcame the cross and death and was resurrected. President Gordon B. Hinckley, reminded the saints, to never forget the excruciating suffering of Jesus, he then said this:

> For us the cross is a symbol of a dying Christ, while our message is a declaration of the living Christ.[80]

Many have said they like to dwell of Christ on the cross because that is where he atoned for our sins. Jesus' suffering on the cross was part of his atonement but the main portion of Christ's atonement was in the Garden of Gethsemane.

Marion G. Romney has said this about the atonement:

> "The pain he endured *in Gethsemane and on the cross* was sufficient to pay the penalty imposed by the demands of justice, sufficient to atone *for all the sins of all men* who ever had lived or ever would live in mortality upon the earth."
>
> The intensity of his suffering was beyond the ken of men. No mortal has ever understood it; none ever will, for it is beyond human comprehension. We do know, however, that it was of terrible intensity, for of Gethsemane Luke wrote:
>
> "He kneeled down, and prayed,
>
> Saying, Father, if thou be willing, remove this cup from me: nevertheless not my will, but thine, be done.
>
> And there appeared an angel unto him from heaven, strengthening him.
>
> And being in an agony he prayed more earnestly; and his sweat was as it were great drops of blood falling down to the ground" (Luke 22:41–44).

Speaking of that same suffering eighteen hundred years later, Jesus said to the Prophet Joseph Smith:

> "Which suffering caused myself, even God, the greatest of all, to tremble because of pain, and to bleed at

every pore, and to suffer both body and spirit—and would that I might not drink the bitter cup, and shrink—

Nevertheless, glory be to the Father, and I partook and finished my preparations unto the children of men" (D&C 19:18, 19).

This was the awful price demanded by the justice of God and paid by Jesus to put into effect the plan of mercy—that is, the gospel plan of redemption through which men may escape from spiritual death. In this manner Jesus literally bought us with his blood. Paul twice says, "Ye are bought with a price" (1 Cor. 6:20; 7:23), and Peter charges "false teachers" with "denying the Lord that bought them" (2 Pet. 2:1). His blood was drawn from him in blood sweat, the most torturous manner in which it could be spilt. From every beneficiary of the plan of redemption, Jesus merits everlasting praise, honor, and gratitude.

By his atonement, Jesus accomplished two things: (1) he overcame mortal death, and (2) he put into effect the plan of redemption from spiritual death.

By atoning for the fall of Adam, he overcame death and brought about the resurrection. As has already been pointed out, the benefits of this aspect of his atonement are extended to every creature to whom death came as a result of Adam's fall.[81]

The Christian cross was originally set forth as a *pagan* symbol from the Chaldeans and Egyptians. The cross seems to have first crept into the Christian Church in Egypt and Africa. Be assured that Jesus and the apostles did *not* wear a cross. The LDS Church is a restored Church. We believe and worship the same as Jesus and the apostles of old. Why did pagans bring forth the cross? Webster's dictionary tells us that the ancient heathens and pagans were polytheists and were regarded as idolaters. In other words it appears the cross originally came forth as an idol. Now I am not saying that other Christians who bear the cross are idol worshipers, but it does appear that pagans brought crosses forth as such and then many Christians adopted the symbol. As members of the restored Church of Jesus Christ, Mormons prefer not to wear a cross or have them on our churches, etc. Joseph Smith said this:

> We claim the privilege of worshiping Almighty God according to the dictates of our own conscience, and allow all men the same privilege, let them worship how, where, or what they may. (A of F 11)

TEMPLE IN MISSOURI

(see PROPHECY)

TEMPLES

Question 1

In the book of John 18:20 Christ said, "I spake openly to the world; I ever taught in the synagogue, and in the temple, whither the Jews always resort; and *in secret have I said nothing*" (italics added). If Jesus did nothing in secret at the temple, why do Mormons not let other religions into their temples? Is it a secret?

Answer 1

This question shows a misinterpretation of the scriptures. The true context of Jesus' words deal with the fact he was being questioned about his doctrine. His doctrine was not a secret, he preached it openly at the temple and essentially anywhere there were those of the house of Israel. The Mormon temples also are not a secret. If you want to go through one, all you have to do is attend at any new temple open house and walk through *before* it is dedicated. While on your tour, the guide will tell you about Mormon Doctrine. Doctrines taught in the temple are the doctrines taught in the scriptures. They include the creation of the world, the

Priesthood, the Garden of Eden, and the Kingdoms of Heaven. So why can't anyone walk in at anytime? There are many reasons; one is you must be worthy to enter this sacred structure that is much different than a Church house. Any sinner can walk into a Church house; in fact we encourage it, just as the Savior did. But the temple after its dedication is for worthy *saints only*. Even anciently not all Christians and Jews were permitted into the inner portion of the temple court. Why not let sinners and enemies in? The scriptures say it best:

> Give not that which is holy unto the dogs, neither cast ye your pearls before swine, lest they trample them under their feet, and turn again and rend you. (Matt. 7:6)

Mormon temples are not secret—they are sacred. Christ did not say there were no mysteries of the Kingdom of God. In fact, Christ and the apostles stated that there are mysteries. Christ said to his apostles:

> He answered and said unto them, Because it is given unto you to know the mysteries of the kingdom of heaven, but to them it is not given. (Matt. 13:11)

There have also been secrets:

He revealeth his secret unto his servants the prophets. (Amos 3:7)

the mystery, which was kept secret since the world began. (Rom. 16:26)

> I have yet many things to say unto you, but *ye cannot bear them now.* (John 16:12; italics added)

and heard *unspeakable words,* which it is *not lawful for a man to utter.* (2 Cor. 12:4; italics added)

It is true that secrets are eventually revealed, as well as mysteries. Though the temple is not a secret, its sacred ordinances await only those who are worthy members of the LDS Church.

Question 2

After Christ died the scriptures state:

> And behold the veil of the temple was rent in twain from the top to the bottom. (Matt. 27:51)

After the veil was rent in twain, were temples no longer needed because Christ had died and the law of Moses was fulfilled?

Answer 2

The veil being rent showed God's anger, not that temples were no longer needed. Temples have always and will always be apart of Christ's true gospel. With the apostasy, temples were taken from the earth for a time (see apostasy). After the Church was restored one of the first things the Lord did was reveal that temples should again be on the earth. Temples being restored were a part of the "restitution of all things" foretold by the prophets (Acts 3:21). Christ fulfilled the law of Moses while he was alive and yet temples were still important to Christ. In fact, the temple was so important to Christ that he drove the moneychangers out of it (John 2:15). There were times he went to the temple daily (Matt. 26:55).

There are several evidences that temples were not done away with after Christ's death. After Christ died, disciples were "continually in the temple, praising and blessing God" (Luke 24:53). Also if temples were no longer needed after Christ died, Paul would not have spoken of there importance:

> Do ye not know that they which minister about holy things live of the things of the temple? And they which wait at the altar are partakers with the altar. (1 Cor. 9:13)

John the Revelator saw the restoration of the gospel in Revelation chapter 7. He also saw that members would be dressed in white and "serve him day and night in his temple" (Rev. 7:15). Mormons today dress in white and serve in his temple. There is so much work to be done that there are temples that are open day and night.

Another evidence of the fact temples were planned for the future is recorded in Malachi. Speaking of Christ's second coming it states, "the Lord, whom ye seek shall suddenly come to his temple" (Mal. 3:1–2). Obviously, in order for Christ to come to his temple, there will have to be a temple.

TRANSLATION

(see SCRIPTURE)

TRINITY

(see GODHEAD)

URIM AND THUMMIM

(see SCRIPTURE)

WARS IN THE BOOK OF MORMON

Question 1

The Book of Mormon records many wars. Wars are obviously full of conflict and hatred. So why does the Book of Mormon speak of so many?

Answer 1

The Book of Mormon is a record of the Ancient inhabitants of the America's, and the Bible is a record of the Ancient Jerusalem area. The question above could just as easily be stated this way: Christ seemed to have a lot of enemies who hated him. Much of the Bible speaks of this, why is there so much conflict recorded in the Bible? The wars in the Book of Mormon have as much inner meaning as the parables recorded in the Bible.

The Bible states this about parables:

> Therefore speak I to them in parables: because they seeing see not; and hearing they hear not, neither do they understand.
>
> And in them is fulfilled the prophecy of Esaias, which saith, By hearing ye shall hear, and shall not understand; and seeing ye shall see, and shall not perceive:
>
> For this people's heart is waxed gross, and their ears are dull of hearing, and their eyes they have closed; lest at any time they should see with their eyes, and hear with their ears, and should understand with their heart, and should be converted, and I should heal them. (Matt. 13:13–15)

Christ's parables held deeper meaning. When reading the wars in the Book of Mormon I would caution the reader to not be like them of old. "Seeing see not; and hearing they hear not, neither do they understand" (Matt. 13:13).

I assure you the wars in the Book of Mormon were recorded for important reasons. Remember one of the reasons the Book of Mormon was written was for our day. There is much valuable information to be gained including substance of major spiritual importance, just as there is in Jesus' parables. You may ask what kind of information? The Book of Mormon tells us a great deal about what has happened and also about what is happening! Just watch the news and you will know what I am referring to. In the Book of Mormon wars show a cycle:

When the people of God are righteous, they prosper. When they prosper, they become proud and forget God, the source of their blessings. When they become proud and forget the Lord, they fight, quarrel, make war, and commit all manner of wickedness. This wickedness in turn leads to a disintegration and destruction of nations. These calamities bring the people to repentance, they turn to the Lord in righteousness, and the cycle begins again.[82]

Wars discuss people like you and I and the world today. The Book of Mormon gives us answers that governments and philosophers can't give. The prophet Mormon summarized it this way:

The Lord in his great infinite goodness doth bless and prosper those who put their trust in him.

Yea, and we may see at the very time when he doth prosper his people, yea, in the increase of their fields, their flocks and their herds, and in gold, and in silver, and in all manner of precious things of every kind and art; sparing their lives, and delivering them out of the hands of their enemies; softening the hearts of their enemies that they should not declare wars against them; yea, and in fine, doing all things for the welfare and happiness of his people; yea, then is the time that they do harden their hearts, and do forget the Lord their God, and do trample under their feet the Holy One—yea, and this because of their ease, and their exceedingly great prosperity. (Hel. 12:1–2)

The Book of Mormon is a volume of Holy Scripture that records God's dealings with the ancient inhabitants of the Americas. To leave out the wars is to leave out God's dealings with the people. The wars are a reality; they really happened and were recorded as such. To deny the wars would be like denying that Indians had bows and arrows and lived in teepees. I challenge you to look for the deeper meaning as you read the wars recorded in the Book of Mormon.

WITNESSES

(see also PROPHECY)

Question 1

Does the Doctrine and Covenants say there would only be three witnesses to the gold plates but really there were eleven? Is this a false prophecy?

Answer 1

The prophecy recorded in Doctrine and Covenants 5:11–15 speaks of three and only three that would actually be given power from a heavenly manifestation with an angelic visitation. The verses state this:

> And in addition to your testimony, the testimony of three of my servants, whom I shall call and ordain, unto whom I will show these things, and they shall go forth with my words that are given through you.
>
> Yea, they shall know of a surety that these things are true, for *from heaven* will I declare it unto them.
>
> I will give them power that they may behold and view these things as they are;
>
> And *to none else* will I grant *this power, to receive this same testimony* among this generation, in this the beginning of the rising up and the coming forth of my Church out of the wilderness—clear as the moon, and fair as the sun, and terrible as an army with banners.
>
> And the testimony of three witnesses will I send forth of my word. (D&C 5:11–15)

And it happened just like it was foretold. Only three witnesses were able to have this power and heavenly manifestation. There were other witnesses but they would only be able to look through the plates and testify to it. No one but the three would receive the "same testimony" of angelic visitation. This was even foretold in the Book of Mormon itself. (Ether 5:2–3; 2 Ne. 27:12–13).

WOMEN IN THE CHURCH

Question 1

Why would a woman want to join the LDS Church? Women cannot hold the priesthood. Are women given a second seat to men in the LDS Church?

Answer 1

The most important point I can make in answering this question is that I don't know why women have not been able to hold the priesthood during the time of Christ or now. The following explanation is one *possible* reason. Women have different responsibilities in the Church and at home. One reason for this difference is because *Adam and Eve* were each given *a curse* when they ate the forbidden fruit. You and I are not punished for Adam and Eve's transgression but because of the fall, you and I have to contend with the consequences of it. Adam was informed he had to work by the sweat of his face. And Eve was told, "I will greatly multiply thy sorrow and thy conception." Eve was given another order from God because, specifically, *she ate the fruit first.* God said, "thy desire shall be to thy husband and he shall rule over thee" (Gen. 3:16). Eve had taken the lead over Adam and instigated the eating of the fruit. Because of this, Eve was informed she would be subordinate to her husband *in righteousness.* In other words, this does *not* mean man is privileged to exercise unrighteous dominion over a woman. It did mean that man was to take the lead in establishing righteousness. Any woman after reading these lines may say their command is worse than man's command. Depending on who you were asking, you may get different answers on this question. And on the other hand maybe woman's command is worse because Eve ate the fruit first. The important point is because of the fall; men and women have different roles, neither has an inferior role. If God appeared to you right now and told you that what I am saying is true would you tell him you did not accept it? So back to the question, why would a woman want to join the LDS Church? It is the true Church set up just as Christ wanted it. In the LDS Church, woman stands next to man as a joint-inheritor to all that Christ has. This inheritance is for a man and woman as one.

> Nevertheless, neither is the man without the woman, neither the woman without the man, in the Lord.

> For as the woman is of the man, even so is the man also by the woman; but all thing of God. (1 Cor. 11:12–13)

WORD OF WISDOM

Question 1

The LDS Church believes alcohol is bad for the body and that you should not drink it. They call this and other guidelines the Word of Wisdom. Yet in the scriptures, there are numerous verses that refer to alcohol as being good for you. So why does the Church claim the Word of Wisdom as revelation? Here is the verse:

> Drink no longer water, but use a little wine for thy stomach's sake and thine often, infirmities. (1 Tim. 5:23)

Answer 1

The same apostle Paul stated:

> It is good neither to eat flesh, nor to drink wine. (Rom. 14:21)

So we would have to ask ourselves, is it okay or is it not okay? Part of the confusion comes because in the Bible wine meant everything from grape juice to an alcoholic beverage. It seems quite evident that during this time period of the Bible that fermented beverages were restricted. Also in the scripture above Timothy was sick (note even the

Lord's disciples got sick). It is possible that Paul was concerned about the water being contaminated. This seems obvious, because we have not been commanded to stop drinking water today. For Paul also said do not eat flesh (meat). Obviously, this verse has to be read in context. Timothy was sick and Paul was giving advice.

I am a physician and I can testify to you that fermented wine is bad for the body. Many, if not most, of America's health problems today stem from alcohol and tobacco. Some will say they have heard wine will lower cholesterol and you should drink one glass a day. I could just as easily say marijuana is calming to the nerves so smoke some every day. If you drink the alcohol you damage your liver etc. If you smoke the marijuana you damage your lungs. If you have high cholesterol and frazzled nerves see your doctor but don't trade one problem for another. The prophet Joseph Smith had a revelation stating that these substances and others like coffee and tea were bad for the body *years* before health professionals finally figured it out (see D&C 89). Tea and coffee have tannic acid in them. This is the same substance they have used to tan hides, and is toxic to the body.

The Lord has told us "our bodies are a temple."

> "If any man defile the temple of God, him shall God destroy; for the temple of God is holy, *which temple ye are.* (1 Cor. 3:17)

We have been warned; do not take harmful substances into our bodies. Alcohol destroys your body, as well as the fact it can destroy families.

Question 2

Mormons often claim the alcohol in the Bible was nonalcoholic but Noah got drunk. So isn't it obvious that alcoholic beverages are fine? Here are the verses:

> And Noah began to be an husbandman, and he planted a vineyard:

> And he drank of the wine, and *was drunken*. (Gen. 9:20–21; italics added)

Answer 2

During this period of time it was not against the Lord's command to drink fermented wine. As discussed in other areas of this book the Lord has said:

> Wherefore I, the Lord, command and revoke, as it seemeth me good; and all this to be answered upon the heads of the rebellious, saith the Lord. (D&C 56:4)

The Lord has shown numerous times throughout the scriptures that there are times he wants a particular issue to be in place and at other times He does not. Here are some examples:

- God commanded circumcision (Gen. 17:10:11) and later revoked it (Acts 15, Gal. 5:2-3).

- Women at one time could not speak in the Churches (1 Cor. 14:34–35). Yet, during other times they worked with Paul (Rom. 16:1–4). Some women were even prophetesses (Luke 2:36).

- The law of Moses was in full force during Old Testament times and withdrawn during New Testament times (Matt. 5:17).

- At one time divorce was not allowed then later under certain circumstances it was permitted (Matt. 19:8–9).

- Alcohol has been permitted at times and revoked at other times. Right now, it is not permitted (D&C 89).

Even during the beginning days of the LDS Church alcohol was permitted. In fact, when the Word of Wisdom was first given it was "not by commandment," but as a word of wisdom and "will of God" (D&C 89:2). Later, it was given as a commandment. Let's take a look at evidences, the

Lord has forbidden the use of alcohol or drunkenness.

> Drunkenness, revellings, and such like: of the which I tell you before, as I have also told you in time past, *that they which do such things shall not inherit the kingdom of God.* (Gal. 5:21; italics added)

> Do not drink wine or strong drink, thou, nor thy sons with thee. (Lev. 10:9)

> Wine is a mocker, strong drink is raging: and whosoever is deceived thereby is not wise. (Prov. 20:1)

> And be not drunk with wine, wherein is excess; but be filled with the Spirit. (Eph. 5:18)

Question 3

It is true that Joseph Smith prophesied that tobacco and alcohol were bad for the body years before the rest of mankind found out. But is it true that the only reason Joseph received this revelation is because Emma did not like cleaning up the mess left from tobacco, etc.? Doesn't this seem convenient?

Answer 3

The prophet Joseph Smith received the revelation on the Word of Wisdom from God. Nearly all revelation comes because of a question. For example, in Acts 15, Peter informed the Saints that circumcision was no longer required of the Lord. It would seem convenient that his revelation came at a time when there was a dispute over the question. But, on the other hand, a person would have to ask is there a better time to receive a revelation than when the question is at hand? Would it be better to receive a revelation long after the question needed answering? It is quite obvious that revelation often comes when the answer is needed most. Another clear point is that Joseph Smith received much more than just a restriction from tobacco. The prophet Joseph received the entire Lord's law of health.

Question 4

Jesus said:

> Not that which goeth into the mouth defileth a man; but that which cometh out of the mouth, this defileth a man.
>
> Do not ye yet understand, that whatsoever entereth in at the mouth goeth into the belly, and is cast out into the draught? (Matt. 15:11, 17)

Why do Mormon's believe in the restrictions of the Word of Wisdom if it is "not that which goeth into the mouth that difileth?"

Answer 4

The above question is another example of looking at the entire context of the situation, and not just a couple of verses. The true interpretation of these verses deal with the simple washing of hands. That's right, the scribes and Pharisees were persecuting Jesus for eating without washing his hands. Jesus responded by stating the above and added:

> For out of the heart proceed evil thoughts, murders, adulteries, fornications, thefts, false witness, blasphemies:
>
> These are the things which defile a man: but *to eat with unwashen hands defileth not a man.* (Matt. 15:19–20; italics added)

Do enemies of the LDS Church think it is okay to do heroin and crack cocaine based on the question above? It is clear that alcohol, tobacco, etc., is harmful to the body and the Lord does not want us taking these substances in to our bodies.

VIEW OF THE HEBREWS

(see BOOK OF MORMON)

WORKS

Does grace or works save man, or is it both? Many have debated this question. I do not understood why there is a debate. Comments like "once saved, always saved" and "once saved, you cannot fall from grace." It is *Satan* that wants you to believe that you can do anything you want, murder, commit adultery, steal, abuse your body even though it is a temple, beat your wife, abuse your kids, and the list goes on, but it is okay because you have been "saved." When the Catholic Church first heard of such a doctrine they called it "heresy," I don't know if this it the right word for it or not, but I agree that words relating to Satan's deceit would be appropriate. There is no doubt in my mind that it was Lucifer who put this thought in the minds of mankind. Many have tried to find an excuse for "saved individuals" who have committed grievous sins by saying they were not really saved to begin with. This excuse does not work. How can you say he didn't confess the name Jesus if the whole congregation heard the person do it? I realize some verses in the Bible are confusing on this issue, just as they are with trinity, etc. Let's take a look at some question regarding grace and works.

Question 1

Does Galatians 2:16 say that we are saved by faith, and not works?

Answer 1

Let's take a look at the verse:

> Knowing that a man is not justified by the *works of the law,* but by the faith of Jesus Christ, even we have believed in Jesus Christ, that we might be justified by the faith of Christ, and not by the works of the law: for by the works of the law shall no flesh be justified. (Gal. 2:16; italics added)

This verse is talking about the *works of the law of Moses*. Thus, this verse is absolutely correct at this point man was not justified by doing the works of the law of Moses. Faith in Jesus Christ is the way to salvation; of course if you have faith in Jesus Christ, you do his will. Specifically, you keep the commandments, are baptized, etc., or in other words have good works. Paul would not have said, "Work out your own salvation with fear and trembling" (Philip. 2:12). if all you had to do was say, "I believe in Jesus" (Gal. 3:21, 24; also refer to the law of Moses).

Question 2

In Romans 10:9 tells us that all we have to do is confess the name Jesus and we can be saved. Also in Ephesians 2:5–9 it states we are saved by grace not works, how can this be disputed? Let's take a look at the verses:

> That if thou shalt confess with thy mouth the Lord Jesus, and shalt believe in thine heart that God hath raised him from the dead, thou shalt be saved. (Rom. 10:9)

> Even when we were dead in sins, hath quickened us together with Christ, (*by grace ye are saved;*)
> And hath raised *us* up together, and made *us* sit together in heavenly places in Christ Jesus:
> That in the ages to come he might shew the exceeding riches of his grace in his kindness toward us through Christ Jesus.
> *For by grace are ye saved through faith;* and that not of yourselves: it is the gift of God:
> *Not of works,* lest any man should boast. (Eph. 2:5–9; italics added)

Answer 2

These verses are easily explained when we realize that some of Paul's writings are difficult to understand. Even the great prophet Peter recorded a warning about some of Paul's writings:

And account that the longsuffering of our Lord is salvation; even as our beloved brother *Paul* also according to the wisdom given unto him *hath written unto you;*

As *also in all his epistles, speaking in them of these things; in which are some things hard to be understood, which they that are unlearned and unstable wrest,* as they do also the other scriptures, *unto their own destruction.* (2 Pet. 3:15–16; italics added)

Knowing Paul's words are often hard to understand I would caution the reader not to be naïve enough to think all you have to do is confess the name Jesus and that you will be saved in heaven. If you believe this you are twisting the scriptures unto your own "destruction." Be assured Paul did not believe this false doctrine. Paul himself said this:

Be not deceived; God is not mocked: for whatsoever a man soweth, that shall he also reap.

For he that soweth to his flesh shall of the flesh reap corruption; but he that soweth to the Spirit shall of the Spirit reap life everlasting. (Gal. 6:7–8)

But after thy hardness and impenitent heart treasurest up unto thyself wrath against the day of wrath and revelation of the righteous *judgment of God;*

Who will render to every man according to his deeds:

To them who by patient continuance in well doing seek for glory and honour and immortality, eternal life:

But unto them that are contentious, and do not obey the truth, but obey unrighteousness, indignation and wrath,

Tribulation and anguish, upon every soul of man that doeth evil, of the Jew first, and also of the Gentile;

But *glory, honour, and peace, to every man that worketh good,* to the Jew first, and also to the Gentile:

For there is no respect of persons with God. (Rom. 2:5–11; italics added)

Why would Paul say "not of works" and in a different verse say we render according to our "deeds?" Paul's words are difficult to understand but not impossible. Let's see what LeGrand Richards said about it:

> "It is evident that none of our works or anything we can do can affect the grace of God, which is a free gift. But this does not alter the fact, as we have pointed out from the writings of Paul, that the "righteous judgment of God . . . will render to every man according to his deeds.
>
> What then is this grace Paul speaks of by which we are saved, being saved not of works, lest any man should boast?"

Grace represents what Jesus has done for us that we could not possibly have done for ourselves, among which are included:

1. He created this earth upon which we are privileged to live and gain experience (John 1:1–14).

2. He atoned for the transgression of our first parents, which brought death into the world, thus bringing to pass the resurrection from the grave, or the reuniting of our bodies and spirits in the resurrection (1 Cor. 15:22).

3. By giving us his everlasting gospel, "he became the author of eternal salvation unto all them that *obey* him" (Heb. 5:9).

4. All these glorious gifts, and many more that could be mentioned, come to us through his grace as free gifts and not of works, lest any man should boast (Eph. 2:8–9).

5. Nevertheless, to obtain these "graces," and the gift of eternal salvation, we must remember that this gift is only to "all them that obey him" (Heb. 5:9).

6. Paul's further thinking on this matter is conclusive: "Be not deceived; God is not mocked: for whatsoever a man soweth, that shall he also reap" (Gal. 6:7).

Take the farmer, as an illustration. No matter how much land he owns, he cannot expect to reap unless he sows. But when the farmer has prepared his land and sowed his seed, cultivated and irrigated the land, and harvested the crop, is he then entitled to all the credit? He did all the work and is entitled to reap as he has sowed, and the result of his effort will be his reward. But no matter how hard he may have worked, he could not have harvested his crop through his own effort, since there are other factors to be considered:

1. Who provided the fertile soil?
2. Who put the germ of life into the seeds he planted?
3. Who caused the sun to warm the soil, causing the seed to germinate and grow?
4. Who caused the rain to fall or the snows to fill the watersheds to give drink to his growing crops?

None of these things could the farmer have done or supplied for himself. They represent the free gift of grace, and yet the farmer will reap as he has sowed.

Paul's statement has been very much misunderstood, by both preachers and laity. Preachers have freely taught that salvation might be obtained as by the snap of the fingers, as one prominent minister expressed himself to the writer; that salvation comes through a lip confession of a belief in Christ, even though not accompanied by obedience to his commandments and works of righteousness. Such doctrine is obviously out of harmony with truth.

It was such interpretations of the scripture that Peter warned against when he said "which they that are unlearned and unstable wrest, as they do also the other scriptures, unto their own destruction" (2 Peter 3:16).

Many have thus been led astray and have contented themselves with a lip confession of faith, to their own destruction.

The enemy of all righteousness could not hope to succeed more effectively in thwarting the purposes of the Master and his gospel than to persuade men that all the blessings the Lord has prepared, through his grace, for his children can be obtained through their lip acknowledgment that he is the Christ. We have pointed out that those whose glory will be telestial, or like the stars, will be heirs of salvation. However, it should be kept in mind that the gospel of Jesus Christ is not given alone for man's salvation, but for his exaltation as well. This is what all lovers of truth should aspire to—the glory which has been.

Exaltation Dependent upon Good Works

This explanation of grace as a free gift of God that cannot be obtained through our works, as contrasted with obedience to the gospel, will help us to understand properly the following scriptures:

> "Not every one that saith unto me, Lord, Lord, shall enter into the kingdom of heaven; but he that doeth the will of my Father which is in heaven" (Matt. 7:21).

> "Therefore whosoever heareth these sayings of mine, and doeth them, I will liken him unto a wise man, which built his house upon a rock:

> And the rain descended, and the floods came, and the winds blew, and beat upon that house; and it fell not: for it was founded upon a rock.

> And every one that heareth these sayings of mine, and doeth them not, shall be likened unto a foolish man, which built his house upon the sand:

> And the rain descended, and the floods came, and the winds blew, and beat upon that house; and it fell: and great was the fall of it" (Matt. 7:24–27).

> "For the Son of man shall come in the glory of his Father with his angels; and then he shall reward every man according to his works (Matt. 16:27).

The apostle James understood the importance of being "doers of the word, and not hearers only":

"But be ye doers of the word, and not hearers only, deceiving your own selves" (James 1:22).

"What doth it profit, my brethren, though a man say he hath faith, and have not works? can faith save him?

If a brother or sister be naked, and destitute of daily food,

And one of you say unto them, Depart in peace, be ye warmed and filled; notwithstanding ye give them, not those things which are needful to the body; what doth it profit?

Even so faith, if it hath not works, is dead, being alone.

Yea, a man may say, Thou hast faith, and I have works: shew me thy faith without thy works, and I will shew thee my faith by my works.

Thou believest that there is one God; thou doest well: the devils also believe, and tremble.

But wilt thou know, O vain man, that faith without works is dead" (James 2:14–20)?

James makes it clear that to believe in God is not sufficient, for the devils do as much, and that "faith without works is dead." A farmer might just as well believe that he can harvest a crop without planting. Such faith is dead; it will not produce a harvest without works.

Consider Jesus' parable of the sower: "But other fell into good ground, and brought forth fruit, some an hundredfold, some sixtyfold, some thirtyfold" (Matt. 13:8).

Consider also this parable:

"For the kingdom of heaven is as a man travelling into a far country, who called his own servants, and delivered unto them his goods.

And unto one he gave five talents, to another two, and to another one; to every man according to his several ability; and straightway took his journey" (Matt. 25:14–15).

"When the man returned to conduct an accounting with his servants, the one who had received five talents had won another five, and the one who had received two talents had won other two. To each of these their lord said: "Well done, thou good and faithful servant: thou hast been faithful over a few things, I will make thee ruler over many things; enter thou into the joy of thy lord" (Matt. 25:21).

"But to him who had received one talent and hid it, the lord said:

Thou wicked and slothful servant, thou knewest that I reap where I sowed not, and gather where I have not strawed:

Thou oughtest therefore to have put my money to the exchangers, and then at my coming I should have received mine own with usury.

Take therefore the talent from him, and give it unto him which hath ten talents.

For unto every one that hath shall be given, and he shall have abundance: but from him that hath not shall be taken away even that which he hath.

And cast ye the unprofitable servant into outer darkness: there shall be weeping and gnashing of teeth" (Matt. 25:26–30).

How useless is one's faith without his works. What a glorious award awaits those who deal profitably with the talents they receive. How inconsistent is the thought that all who do good are rewarded alike, and all who do evil are punished alike. How difficult it would be to draw the line between the two groups. Hence, the need for "many mansions" in our Father's kingdom, where each will be rewarded according to his works.

Salvation Defined

The author was asked the following question by a minister of the gospel: "Can a man be saved before he dies, or must he die to be saved?"

The answer was, "If you will explain what you mean by being saved, I will try to answer your question."

It has been my experience that few Christians have any definite concept of salvation, other than to escape eternal burning, and this minister seemed totally at a loss to explain salvation. I explained that if we had not made ourselves worthy to come upon this earth before we were born, and if we had not taken upon ourselves bodies, we would have been cast out of heaven with Satan, since he took with him one-third of the spirits (Jude 6; Rev. 12:7–12, 12:4).

I pointed out that we may be saved every day that we live, for as we learn the laws of God and obey them, we free ourselves from the consequences of a broken law and entitle ourselves to the blessings predicated upon obedience to divine law. The following Latter Day Saints scriptures are quoted to point out this truth:

"There is a law, irrevocably decreed in heaven before the foundations of this world, upon which all blessings are predicated—

And when we obtain any blessing from God, it is by obedience to that law upon which it is predicated" (D&C 130:20–21).

"And unto every kingdom is given a law; and unto every law there are certain bounds also and conditions.

All beings who abide not in those conditions are not justified" (D&C 88:38–39).

"For all who will have a blessing at my hands shall abide the law which was appointed for that blessing, and the conditions thereof, as were instituted from before the foundation of the world" (D&C 132:5).

"It is impossible for a man to be saved in ignorance" (D&C 131:6). Thus one can see that, while "where no law is there is no transgression" (Rom. 4:15), it is also "impossible for a man to be saved in ignorance." Therefore, a man must know the law to be able to be rewarded for keeping it, and to be relieved of the consequences of a broken law, even though he may be forgiven for transgressing where no law has been given to him. Hence, as we continue our quest to know and understand the laws of God, and as we obey them, we increase the measure of our salvation or exaltation.

The author further explained to the minister that since we believe in eternal progression and that "a man is saved no faster than he gets knowledge" (*History of the Church*, vol. 4, p. 588), salvation to a Latter Day Saint is not an end but a process, since we shall never cease to gain knowledge.

The minister replied that he had never heard such a reasonable explanation. All this we have obtained through the revelations of the Lord to the Prophet Joseph Smith in this, the dispensation of the fullness of times.

All men are to receive "according to their works" (Rev. 20:12), which requires that suitable places shall be prepared for the souls of all men. Hence the statement of Jesus: "In my Father's house are many mansions" (John 14:2). The gospel of Jesus Christ provides a plan whereby men can not only be saved, but can also be exalted in the celestial kingdom, "in the day when God shall judge the secrets of men by Jesus Christ according to my gospel" (Rom. 2:16).[83]

Bruce R. McConkie also commented on Ephesians 2:5–9. Before reading his comments, let's again take a look at the verses:

"Even when we were dead in sins, hath quickened us together with Christ, (by grace ye are saved:)

And hath raised us up together, and made us sit together in heavenly places in Christ Jesus:

That in ages to come he might shew the exceeding riches of his grace in his kindness toward us through Christ Jesus.

For by grace are ye saved through faith; and that

not of yourselves: it is the gift of God:

Not of works, lest any many should boast" (Eph. 2:5–9).

When we were dead in sins "Before we joined the Church and were baptized for the remission of sins." **Hath quickened us together with Christ** "Hath made us new creatures of the Holy Ghost, so that we are now born again and have become alive in Christ." How else could salvation possibly come? Can man save himself? Can he resurrect himself? Can he create a celestial kingdom and decree his own admission thereto? Salvation must and does originate with God, and if man is to receive it, God must bestow it upon him, which bestowal is a manifestation of grace.

In heavenly places. In the celestial kingdom.

By grace are ye saved through faith "By grace are ye saved through faith in the Lord Jesus Christ, through repentance and baptism for the remission of sins, through receipt of the gift of the Holy Ghost, through keeping the commandments after baptism and thus enduring to the end." **And that not of yourselves** No man has power to save himself anymore than he has power to resurrect himself.

Not of works Salvation does not come by the works and performances of the law of Moses, nor by "circumcision," nor by "the law of commandments contained in ordinances" (Paul 11:15), nor does it come by any good works standing alone. No matter how righteous a man might be, no matter how great and extensive his good works, he could not save himself. Salvation is in Christ and comes through his atonement. God through Christ reconciles man to himself. But building on the atonement man must perform the works of righteousness to merit salvation, as verse 10 and the whole passage testify.

Good works Keeping the commandments after baptism. **God hath before ordained that we should walk in them** "God foreordained the saints to keep the commandments," a necessary requisite to the receipt of the foreordained promise of eternal life (Eph. 1:9–12).[84]

COMMENTS ABOUT WORKS AND GRACE

It is easy to understand that we are not saved by grace alone, just by looking at Judas Iscariot. He would have obviously confessed a belief in Jesus because he was one of his apostles. When Jesus told his apostles that one of them would betray him, he said this about Judas:

> But woe to that man by whom the Son of man is betrayed! Good were it for that man if he had never been born. (Mark 14:21)

If Judas were saved, the Lord would not have said this statement. Those who believe in deathbed repentance may say that the thief on the cross was saved because he repented at the last moment. Well this is not the case for even Judas Iscariot "repented himself."

> Then Judas, which had betrayed him, when he saw that he was condemned, repented himself, and brought again the thirty pieces of silver to the chief priests and elders. (Matt. 27:3).

Now let's read another verse regarding those who have obviously confessed Jesus' name.

> For it is impossible for *those who were once enlightened,* and have tasted of the heavenly gift, and were *made partakers of the Holy Ghost.*
>
> And *have tasted the good word* of God, and the powers of the world to come,
>
> *If they shall fall away,* to renew them again unto repentance; seeing they crucify to themselves the Son of God afresh, and put him to an open shame. (Heb. 6:4–6; italics added)

This verse is saying there has been people who have been enlightened and tasted of the heavenly gift and even partook of the Holy Ghost who have "fallen away." Obviously if they partook of the Holy Ghost, and were enlightened they had confessed the name Jesus. Yet as these verses state they can still fall away and thus not be saved.

> For if we sin willfully *after* that we have received the knowledge of the truth, there remaineth *no more sacrifice for sins.* (Heb. 10:26; italics added)

There is no such thing as being saved; except for a few the Lord himself has chosen and made their calling and election sure. We are saved by grace after all we can do (2 Ne. 25:23).

The book of Revelation states this:

> And I saw the dead, small and great, stand before God; and the books were opened: and another book was opened, which is the book of life: and the dead were judged out of those things which were written in the books, according to their works. (Rev. 20:12)

If all you had to do was say "I believe in Jesus" and you were saved the scriptures would say, "meandering is the gate and the path is wide, many will find it." But instead the scriptures say:

> Because strait is the gate, and narrow is the way, which leadeth unto life, and few there be that find it. (Matt. 7:14)

If you want to be one of the few, it is through the LDS Church. (Of course, "few" is relative tp the number of people who have lived on this earth. See Rev. 5:11; 7:9-10.)

Question 3

What about the thief on the cross, he was promised he would be with Jesus in Paradise and all he did was deathbed repentance?

Answer 3

Notice the Lord did not tell the thief he would see him in heaven. He told him he would see him in paradise. Many will ask, "Isn't paradise and heaven the same thing?" The answer is definitely not. You will recall when Jesus died his body lay in the tomb three days before he was resurrected. During this time, his spirit went to paradise, not heaven.

We know his spirit did not go to heaven because after the three days, he appeared and was seen by Mary. She went to hug him and Christ said, "Touch me not; for I am not yet ascended to my Father" (John 20:17). The Bible tells us where Christ went during the three-day wait until the resurrection. He went to the spirit world to prepare a way for the gospel to be preached to those who had died (1 Pet. 3:18–19; D&C 138:8, 20).

After Christ's resurrection, and after he had been to the Father he appeared to the Apostles in the upper room and showed him his resurrected body and the fact that he had risen. He also went to visit his "other sheep" (John 10:16) or other people. Of course Christ is the shepherd of all people, not just those in Jerusalem. After visiting the apostles, Christ went to America and visited the people there (3 Ne. 11–26). (This brings up a side note, which will only be discussed briefly.) Who was in America at this time? The answer is the American Indian. This brings up the question: how did the Indians get there? After all, we are all related through Adam, as well as Noah. The Book of Mormon tells us how the Indians got to America, as well as Christ's visit to them after he saw the apostles.

The American Indians even today have legends about a great white God who visited them and promised to return. The promise spoken of was the "second coming" of Christ. This promise of a return is the reason the Indians bowed down and worshiped Cortez when he visited America; they thought Christ had returned. The visit of Christ to America as well as the story of how the Indians or Lamanites got to America is recorded in the Book of Mormon. Of course Christ did not teach anything different to the American Indian than he did to his apostles and the people in Jerusalem. Thus, the teachings recorded in the Book of Mormon are just as important as the teachings in the Bible.

Now back to the thief on the cross. Joseph Fielding Smith stated this:

One of the most misunderstood biblical passages in Christian history has to do with this word *paradise*. To the thief on the cross Jesus said: "Verily I say unto thee, To day shalt thou be with me in paradise" (Luke 23:39–43). This account has spawned a host of incorrect perceptions of doctrine, which in turn have resulted in questionable practices on the part of Christians over the centuries, not the least of which is a type of "death-bed repentance," a notion that one can postpone his confession and repentance until the time just before death. Though we must never de-emphasize or denigrate the value of sincere repentance, no matter how late in one's earthly experience (Matt. 20:1–16)—for the word of the Lord is clear that "he that repents and does the commandments of the Lord shall be forgiven" (D&C 1:32)— confession and repentance coerced by the threat of death hardly prepare one's soul for a place hereafter among the sanctified.

In discoursing upon the subject, the Prophet Joseph Smith observed: "I will say something about the spirits in prison. There has been much said by modern divines about the words of Jesus (when on the cross) to the thief, saying, 'This day shalt thou be with me in paradise. 'King James' translators make it out to say paradise. But what is paradise? It is a modern word: it does not answer at all to the original word that Jesus made use of . . . There is nothing in the original word in Greek from which this was taken that signifies paradise; but it *was—This day thou shalt be with me in the world of spirits."* In confirming these truths, the Prophet said: "Hades, the Greek or Sheol, the Hebrew, these two significations mean a world of spirits. Hades, Sheol, paradise, spirits in prison, are all one: it is a world of spirits" (*Teachings,* pp. 309, 310). Not discounting in any way, therefore, any feelings of contrition that may have existed in the heart of the thief on the cross, Parley P. Pratt thus explained that this man went into the world of spirits "in a state of ignorance, and sin, being uncultivated, unimproved, and unprepared for salvation. He went there to be taught, and to complete that repentance, which in a dying moment he commenced on earth" *(JD* 1:9).

13–14. In a broad sense, the whole of the spirit

world—paradise and hell—is a "spirit prison," inasmuch as the spirits there, even the righteous, look upon the long absence of their spirits from their bodies as a bondage (D&C 45:17, 138:50, D&C 138:15, 16, 18). "I know it is a startling idea," President Brigham Young stated, "to say that the Prophet [Joseph Smith] and the persecutor of the Prophet, all go to prison together . . . But they have not got their bodies yet, consequently they are in prison" *(JD* 3:95; compare Moses 7:55–57). It is in this sense that Christ went and preached to the spirits in prison (1 Peter 3:18–20, 4:6). President Joseph F. Smith beheld in vision that the Savior went not in person to preach to the wicked in the postmortal spirit world, but rather that he organized his missionary force in that realm and commissioned the righteous to preach the gospel to the spirits who were in darkness and under the bondage of sin (D&C 138:20–22, 29–32). Christ went to the spirits in prison in the sense that he went to the spirit world.

Outer darkness, or hell, is made up of those who in mortality spurned the ways of righteousness, those who defied the word of truth, those who chose to walk in their own paths or in paths of disobedience. Joseph Smith pointed out, "The great misery of departed spirits in the world of spirits, where they go after death, is to know that they come short of the glory that others enjoy and that they might have enjoyed themselves, and they are their own accusers" *(Teachings,* pp. 310–11; compare p. 358). Thus hell or outer darkness is both a *place*—a part of the world of spirits where suffering and sorrow and appropriate preparation go on—and a *state*—a condition of the mind associated with remorseful realization.

The righteous, those who have received the ordinances of salvation and proven faithful to the attendant covenants, go into paradise at the time of their physical death. It would appear that all others, including the good and noble men and women of the earth who died without a knowledge of the gospel, enter into hell, outer darkness, or what is sometimes called (in a narrower sense than above—see Bruce R. McConkie, *Mormon Doctrine,* p. 755) spirit prison. This second division is not simply a place of suffering, but also a place of preparation and learning. Joseph Smith taught concerning the necessity of ordinances for entrance into paradise: "Every man that has been baptized and belongs to the, kingdom has a right to be baptized for those who have gone before; and *as soon as the law of the Gospel is obeyed here [the gospel ordinance] by their friends who act as proxy for them, the Lord has administrators there to set them free." (Teachings,* p. 367; D&C 138:58)[85]

Elder Bruce R. McConkie has written:

Before Christ bridged the gulf between paradise and hell—so that the righteous could mingle with the wicked and preach them the gospel—the wicked in hell were confined to locations which precluded them from contact with the righteous in paradise. . . . Now that the righteous spirits in paradise have been commissioned to carry the message of salvation to the wicked spirits in hell, there is a certain amount of mingling together of the good and bad spirits. Repentance opens the prison doors to the spirits in hell; it enables those bound with the chains of hell to free themselves from darkness, unbelief, ignorance, and sin. As rapidly as they can overcome these obstacles—gain light, believe truth, acquire intelligence, cast off sin, and break the chains of hell—they can leave the hell that imprisons them and dwell with the righteous in the peace of paradise.[86]

The Savior himself was asked: "Good Master, what good thing shall I do, that I may have eternal life" (Matt. 19:16)? The Lord *did not say* just confess with your mouth my name and you will be saved. What did Jesus say to him? He told him to have *good works and follow him.* These are the Savior's words:

but if thou wilt enter into life, *keep the commandments.*

He saith unto him, Which? Jesus said, Thou shalt do no murder, Thou shalt not commit adultery, Thou shalt not steal, Thou shalt not bear false witness,

Honour thy father and thy mother: and, Thou shalt love thy neighbour as thyself. (Matt. 19:17–19; italics added).

But even this was not enough. The Lord said we must follow him.

> Jesus said unto him, If thou wilt be perfect, go and sell that thou hast, and give to the poor, and thou shalt have treasure in heaven: and *come and follow me.* (Matt. 19:21; italics added)

In the book of Acts 14:22 it states, "We must through much tribulation enter into the kingdom of God." If all we had to do was say "I believe in Jesus" that would not be considered "much tribulation." It does not get any plainer than this.

ZION, IN MISSOURI

(see PROPHECY)

ZION'S CAMP

(see PROPHECY)

Conclusions and Comments

The Church of Jesus Christ of Latter Day Saints is Christ's Church on the earth. Lies directed at Christ's Church will not end at this time. I caution the reader to beware of lies and fabrications that arise. I dare say there is *not even one* anti-Mormon book, movie, or presentation that does not lie and stretch the truth. Lying is of the devil. So those who write lies or show movies of lies are of the devil. The scriptures say this:

> Let no corrupt communication proceed out of your mouth, but that which is good to the use of edifying, that it may minister grace unto the hearers. (Eph. 4:29)

So when you are presented with these lies ask yourself what would Jesus do if he were presented with such information. During the time I was writing this book I was looking for questions to put in it. I had a person come up to me and tell me he had some information he would like me to read "from the Church archives" in Salt Lake City. He told me the information proved the LDS Church is false. He asked if we could get together to discuss the information. I told him I would get back to him. I went to the temple and while in the Celestial room I prayed about it. I asked God if I should meet with this individual to get more information for my book. I had a distinct impression to turn to the scriptures that were sitting next to me. I opened the scriptures and the very first page and first section of scripture I turned to said this:

> Let no man deceive you with vain words: for because of these things cometh the wrath of God upon the children of disobedience
>
> Be not ye therefore partakers with them. . . .
>
> And have no fellowship with the unfruitful works of darkness, but rather reprove them. (Eph. 5:6–7, 11)

Needless to say, I did not meet with the individual to have a discussion. I know in my heart that the information presented would have been distortion and fabrication. Now that I look back I don't know why I even had to ask the Lord this question. It is common sense! You would not go to the Pharisees that set up Jesus' death and ask them for a discussion about Jesus. If you want to know about the Baptists go to the Baptists. If you want to know about the Mormons go to the Mormons. But I have to ask myself do I expect better treatment than Jesus himself received? The fact is the LDS persecution was foretold in the scriptures:

> I beheld, and the same horn made war with the saints, and prevailed against them.
>
> Until the Ancient of days came, and judgment was given to the saints of the most High; and the time came that he saints possessed the kingdom. (Dan. 7:21–22)

The Church of Jesus Christ of Latter Day Saints is Christ's Church! I exhort you to prepare for Christ's second coming like you have never prepared before! Let us do as the scriptures say:

> For behold, this life is the time for men to prepare to meet God; yea, behold the day of this life is the day for men to perform their labors.
>
> And now, as I said unto you before, as ye have had so many witnesses, therefore, I beseech of you that ye do not procrastinate the day of your repentance until the end; for after this day of life, which is given us to prepare for eternity, behold, if we do not improve our time while in this life, then cometh the night of darkness wherein there can be no labor performed.
>
> Ye cannot say, when ye are brought to that awful crisis, that I will repent, that I will return to my God. Nay, ye cannot say this; for that same spirit which doth possess your bodies at the time that ye go out of this life, that same spirit will have power to possess your body in that eternal world. (Alma 34:32–34)

APPENDIX A
A TRUE STORY

Now let me tell you a true story. The story starts with one man. This man was so great that nearly every religion on the earth today traces their roots to just him. This man is Abram or Abraham. God appeared to Abraham and gave him some promises. Thus, God made a covenant with Abraham. The promises given to Abraham were also given to his ancestors. These promises though given many years ago are important to you and I. This true story tells us God's plan it also gives us insight to the many religions on the earth today. Let's go through the story one step at a time:

> And when Abram was ninety years old and nine, *the LORD appeared to Abram,* and said unto him, I am the Almighty God; walk before me, and be thou perfect.
>
> And I will make *my covenant between me and thee,* and will *multiply thee exceedingly.*
>
> And Abram fell on his face: and God talked with him, saying,
>
> As for me, behold, my covenant is with thee, and thou shalt be a father of many nations.
>
> Neither shall thy name any more be called Abram, but thy name shall be Abraham; for a father of many nations have I made thee.
>
> And I will make thee *exceeding fruitful,* and *I will make nations of thee,* and *kings shall come out of thee.*
>
> And I will establish my covenant between me and thee and thy seed after thee in their generations for an everlasting covenant, to be *a God unto thee, and to thy seed after thee.*
>
> And *I will give unto thee,* and to thy seed after

> thee, the land wherein thou art a stranger, all the *land of Canaan,* for an everlasting possession; and I will be their God.
>
> And God said unto Abraham, Thou shalt keep my covenant therefore, thou, and thy seed after thee in their generations. (Gen. 17:1–9; italics added)

These were some pretty amazing promises considering Abraham was ninety-nine years old and childless! Abraham was told he would be *fruitful* or have children and be a father of many nations. Kings would come from his lineage, including Christ, etc.

Next in our true story Abraham had a son but his first son was from his second wife Hagar. The promises made to Abraham would *not* go through this son. In fact a very different future was foretold about this son, as told to Hagar:

> And the angel of the LORD said unto her, Behold, thou art with child, and shalt bear a son, and shalt call his name Ishmael; because the LORD hath heard thy affliction.
>
> And he will be a wild man; his hand will be against every man, and every man's hand against him; and he shall dwell in the presence of all his brethren. (Gen. 16:11–12)

Just watch the news and anyone can see this prophesy came to pass. The Islam nations are the ancestors of Abraham's first son.

Abraham then had a first-born son by his wife Sarah:

> And God said, Sarah thy wife shall bear thee a son indeed; and thou shalt call his name Isaac: and *I will establish my covenant with him* for an everlasting covenant, *and with his seed after him.* (Gen. 17:19; italics added)

Thus, the covenant went to Abraham's son Isaac. As we all know Abraham was tested and asked to sacrifice his son Isaac and Abraham passed the test (Gen. 22).

The Lord then had a plan for Isaac. He told Isaac not

to marry a Canaanite woman. Isaac was told this because the Canaanite's were descendants of Cane and had all been given a mark or curse of dark skin (Gen. 4:15–17). Let's take a look at the verse:

> And I will make thee swear by the LORD, the God of heaven, and the God of the earth, that thou shalt not take a wife unto my son of the daughters of the Canaanites, among whom I dwell:
>
> But thou shalt go unto my country, and to my kindred, and take a wife unto my son Isaac. (Gen. 24:3–4)

So Isaac married Rebekah and they had twins! Knowing this the promises went to the child who was born first. His name was Esau. Let's take a look at the verse:

> And when her days to be delivered were fulfilled, behold, *there were twins* in her womb.
>
> And *the first* came out red, all over like an hairy garment; and *they called his name Esau.*
>
> And *after that came his brother* out, and his hand took hold on Esau's heel; *and his name was called Jacob:* and Isaac was threescore years old when she bare them. (Gen. 25:24–26)

So Esau had the birthright but he despised it! The birthright then went to Jacob.

> And Jacob sod pottage: and Esau came from the field, and he was faint:
>
> And Esau said to Jacob, Feed me, I pray thee, with that same red pottage; for I am faint: therefore was his name called Edom.
>
> *And Jacob said, Sell me this day thy birthright.*
>
> And Esau said, Behold, I am at the point to die: and what profit shall this birthright do to me?
>
> And Jacob said, Swear to me this day; and he sware unto him: *and he sold his birthright unto Jacob.*
>
> Then Jacob gave Esau bread and pottage of lentiles; and he did eat and drink, and rose up, and went his way: *thus Esau despised his birthright.* (Gen. 25:29–34; italics added)

So now in our true story all these wonderful blessings given to Abraham were to go through the lineage of Jacob who had his name changed to Israel. Let's take a look at the verse:

> And God said unto him, Thy name is Jacob: thy name shall not be called any more Jacob, but Israel shall be thy name: and he called his name Israel.
>
> And God said unto him, I am God Almighty: be fruitful and multiply; a nation and a company of nations shall be of thee, and kings shall come out of thy loins;
>
> And *the land which I gave Abraham and Isaac, to thee I will give it,* and to thy seed after thee will I give the land. (Gen. 35:10–12; italics added)

So who is Jacob's first-born son that will now inherit the birthright promises? Jacob like Abraham had more than one wife through them he had twelve sons. His first son was named Reuben thus the promises went to him but Reuben like Esau lost it!

> Now the sons of *Reuben the firstborn of Israel,* (for he was the firstborn; *but,* forasmuch *as he defiled his father's bed, his birthright was given unto the sons of Joseph* the son of Israel: and the genealogy is not to be reckoned after the birthright.
>
> For Judah prevailed above his brethren, and of him came the chief ruler; but the birthright was Joseph's. (1 Chr. 5:1–2; italics added)

So Jacob/Israel had twelve sons. Everyone born to any of these twelve sons became "the House of Israel" And just as God said they were "fruitful." Thus there were a lot of them! *Jesus would only teach and work among the House of Israel* (Matt. 15:24). If you were not born to one of these twelve brothers you were considered a "gentile."

We all remember the story of Jacob/Israel's favorite son. His name was Joseph and Jacob gave him a coat of many colors. His brothers were jealous and sold him into Egypt (Gen. 37). But Joseph still had the birthright.

Before Jacob/Israel died he gathered his twelve sons and gave them all a blessing. What he said in these blessings is very important. This is what Judah or the Jews were told:

> *Judah,* thou art he whom thy brethren shall praise: thy hand shall be in the neck of thine enemies; *thy father's children shall bow down before thee.*
>
> *Judah is a lion's whelp:* from the prey, my son, thou art gone up: *he stooped down,* he couched as a lion, and as an old lion; *who shall rouse him up?*
>
> *The sceptre shall not depart from Judah,* nor a law-giver from between his feet, *until Shiloh come;* and unto him shall the gathering of the people be. (Gen. 49:8–10; italics added)

What does this blessing mean? Judah was praised by his brothers, and through Judah would come a King. ("Lion's whelp," a Lion is the king of the jungle) This King was Jesus Christ, a Jew. (Thy father's children shall bow down before thee) The "scepter" or staff of control did not depart from Judah until Christ/Shiloh came. Judah came to power when David was exalted to the throne. Verse 8 states, "he stooped down" and "who shall rouse him up?" This refers to Jesus he laid down his life, "No man taketh it from me; but I lay it down of myself, I have power to lay it down, and I have power to take it again" (John 10:18).

Now let's see what Joseph the holder of the birthright was told:

> Joseph is a fruitful bough, even a fruitful bough by a well; whose branches run over the wall:
>
> The archers have sorely grieved him, and shot at him, and hated him:
>
> But his bow abode in strength, and the arms of his hands were made strong by the hands of the mighty God of Jacob; (from thence is the shepherd, the stone of Israel:)
>
> Even by the God of thy father, who shall help thee; and by the Almighty, who shall bless thee with blessings of heaven above, blessings of the deep that lieth under, blessings of the breasts, and of the womb:

> The blessings of thy father have prevailed above the blessings of my progenitors unto the utmost bound of the everlasting hills: they shall be on the head of Joseph, and on the crown of the head of him that was separate from his brethren. (Gen. 49:22–26)

What does this blessing mean? It is really very easy to understand. If you look up "bough" in the dictionary it basically tells you it is a tree branch. This branch is referring to Joseph's family tree or ancestors. It is obvious his ancestors would be numerous or "fruitful" because that was part of the original blessing promised to Abraham. Joseph is told in this blessing that his ancestors would be by "a well." We all know that a well represents water. Joseph was told his ancestors would go over the wall of the well or in other words over the water! (Branches run over the wall.) Joseph's ancestors did in fact travel over the water in a ship and inherited the "utmost bound of the everlasting hills." Those who know geography know that to go across water and find everlasting hills you have to go a long way from the desert of the Jerusalem area. Joseph's ancestors did just this and got off their ship in South America! Pull out any map and follow the everlasting hills. They start at the top of Alaska and go south to the top of the Andes and extend to the bottom of South America. Joseph's land was further described in Deuteronomy:

> And of Joseph he said, *Blessed of the LORD be his land,* for the precious things of heaven, for the dew, and for the deep that coucheth beneath,
>
> And for the *precious fruits brought forth by the sun,* and for the precious things put forth by the moon,
>
> And for the chief things of the *ancient mountains,* and for the precious things of *the lasting hills,*
>
> And for the *precious things of the earth and fulness thereof,* and for the good will of him that dwelt in the bush: let the blessing come upon the head of Joseph, and upon the top of the head of him that was separated from his brethren. (Deut. 33:13–16; italics added)

The Book of Mormon is a record of the ancestors of Joseph while living in America/the everlasting hills. Within the first eleven pages of the Book of Mormon it is states:

> And it came to pass that my father, Lehi, also found upon the plates of brass a *genealogy of his fathers;* wherefore *he knew that he was a descendant of Joseph;* yea, even that Joseph who was the son of Jacob, who was sold into Egypt, and who was preserved by the hand of the Lord, that he might preserve his father, Jacob, and all his household from perishing with famine. (1 Ne. 5:14; italics added)

Thus the prophet Lehi was a descendant to Joseph and Lehi was the means by which the Lord would fulfill the promise given to Joseph. Lehi and his family traveled across the water to America:

> And it came to pass after we had all gone down into the ship, and had taken with us our provisions and things which had been commanded us, *we did put forth into the sea and were driven forth before the wind towards the promised land.* (1 Ne. 18:8; italics added)

The Old Testament prophet Ezekiel foretold that something very important regarding both Judah and Joseph. Ezekiel saw that a record (scroll or "stick") would be kept for both Judah and Joseph.

> The word of the LORD came again unto me, saying,
>
> Moreover, thou son of man, take thee *one stick, and write upon it, For Judah,* and for the children of Israel his companions: then take *another stick, and write upon it, For Joseph,* the stick of Ephraim, and for all the house of Israel his companions:
>
> And join them one to another into one stick; and they shall become one in thine hand.
>
> And when the children of thy people shall speak unto thee, saying, Wilt thou not shew us what thou meanest by these?
>
> Say unto them, Thus *saith the Lord GOD; Behold, I will take the stick of Joseph, which is in the hand of*

Ephraim, and the tribes of Israel his fellows, and will put them with him, even with the stick of Judah, and make them one stick, and they shall be one in mine hand.

And the sticks whereon thou writest shall be in thine hand before their eyes.

And say unto them, Thus saith the Lord GOD; Behold, I will take the children of Israel from among the heathen, whither they be gone, and will gather them on every side, and bring them into their own land. (Ezek. 37:15–21; italics added)

It happened just like Ezekiel foretold. There have been two records kept. One for Judah, known as the Bible, the other for Joseph, known as The Book of Mormon.

It was also foretold in the Book of Mormon:

Wherefore, *the fruit of thy loins shall write;* and the *fruit of the loins of Judah shall write;* and that which shall be written by the fruit of thy loins, and also that which shall be written by the fruit of the loins of Judah, *shall grow together;* unto the confounding of false doctrines and laying down of contentions, and establishing peace among the fruit of thy loins, and bringing them to the knowledge of their fathers in the latter days, and also to the knowledge of my covenants, saith the Lord. (2 Ne. 3:12; italics added)

The writings for the stick of Joseph contain the visitation of Jesus to the American Continent. Jesus himself said he would visit his "other sheep:"

And *other sheep I have,* which are not of this fold: them also I must bring, and *they shall hear my voice;* and there shall be one fold, and one shepherd. (John 10:16; italics added)

The Book of Mormon records the fulfillment of this prophecy! Jesus did show himself to the people of Nephi and they did here his voice (3 Ne.11–26). It states specifically in 3 Nephi:

And verily I say unto you, that ye are they of whom I said: Other sheep I have which are not of this fold; them also I must bring, and they shall hear my voice; and there shall be one fold, and one shepherd.

And they understood me not, for they supposed it had been the Gentiles; for they understood not that the Gentiles should be converted through their preaching.

And they understood me not that I said they shall hear my voice; and they understood me not that the Gentiles should not at any time hear my voice—that I should not manifest myself unto them save it were by the Holy Ghost.

But behold, ye have both heard my voice, and seen me; and ye are my sheep, and ye are numbered among those whom the Father hath given me. (3 Ne. 15:21–24)

If we did not have the Book of Mormon many of the Bible scriptures would make no sense! How do people explain verses above like Genesis 49, Ezekiel 37, Isaiah 29, and others without the Book of Mormon? The answer is you can't! The Book of Mormon proves the Bible is true (D&C 20:11).

ARE YOU OF THE HOUSE OF ISRAEL? The scriptures say this:

For ye are all the children of God by faith in Christ Jesus.

For *as many of you as have been baptized* into Christ have put on Christ.

There is neither Jew nor Greek, there is neither bond nor free, there is neither male nor female: for ye are all one in Christ Jesus.

And if ye *be* Christ's, then are ye Abraham's seed, and heirs according to the promise. (Gal. 3:26–29; italics added)

If baptized by the proper authority, *you are adopted* into Abraham's family and are heirs according to the promise! If you are not already baptized into the Church of

Jesus Christ of Latter Day Saints I invite you to seek out the missionaries. But don't wait until it is too late.

When I was a boy there was a dam that broke near my hometown. Concerning the dam, Boyd K. Packer pointed this out:

- The Teton Dam broke in 1976.
- Seven thousand people were warned.
- Six people died, of the six:
- Three went back for material possessions.
- Two did not believe the dam had broke until it was too late.
- One was too close to the dam when it broke and he could not get to safety in time.

NOTHING is as important as your salvation and exaltation in the Kingdom of God. If you wait until the doors to the ark are closed you can't get on. Now is the time, I invite you to pray and ask God our Heavenly Father if the Church of Jesus Christ of Latter Day Saints is the one true Church on the earth. I witness to you that it is.

Appendix B
Comments About
the Book of Mormon

Critics of the LDS Church have essentially attempted to make a set of rules concerning the Book of Mormon. For example they say the Book of Mormon is false if it says there was horses in America, etc. But critics like the Tanners and others are not in charge of making the rules. Unfortunately they are gambling with their own salvation by making a list of such petty rules. God and his Son Jesus Christ have made the rules. The Book of Mormon is here for you yourself to read and decide. The Lord is not to be blamed for any imperfections found in the Book of Mormon. The Book of Mormon preface, presumably written by Moroni himself, states,

> "And now, if there are faults they are the mistakes of men; wherefore, condemn not the things of God, that ye may be found spotless at the judgment-seat of Christ."

Following are evidences that the Book of Mormon and the LDS Church are true. Except for some of the headings the majority of what follows I have not written. I have simply compiled the information from different sources. At the end of each authors writing I have written the source it was taken from.

The Bat Creek Inscription

In 1889 the Smithsonian Institution excavated a hitherto undisturbed burial mound at Bat Creek,

Tennessee. This mound disclosed nine skeletons. Directly under the head of one of these skeletons, they found several artifacts, including what appeared to be two copper bracelets, several small pieces of polished wood, and a stone bearing an inscription. In 1971 Cyrus Gordon showed that the script found on the stone was paleo-Hebrew and could be translated "For Judah."

The evidence for the inscription shows: (1) The Hebrew inscription was found in a hitherto undisturbed burial mound that was not opened until the Smithsonian Institution opened it in 1889. (2) The inscription can be read as paleo-Hebrew and is similar to other examples dating to the period of the Second Temple. (3) Wood fragments from the tomb yielded a Carbon-14 date between A.D. 32 and A.D. 769, making it not only pre-Christian but pre-Viking as well. (4) Brass bracelets from the tomb were tested and found to contain a percentage of lead comparable with a form of Roman brass produced only between 45 B.C. and A.D. 100. (5) Based on the above evidence, it is most reasonable to view the inscription as genuine, pre-Columbian, and pre-Viking. "The battle cry of the die-hards," observes Cyrus Gordon, "was that no authentic pre-Columbian example of an Old World script or language has been excavated on American soil; and until such a one is discovered by bona fide archaeologists, the diffusionists do not have a leg to stand on." The apparent authenticity and pre-Columbian nature of the Bat Creek inscription changes this situation significantly because "it does show that an Atlantic crossing was made ca. A.D. 100 and consequently it can no longer be said that no authentic pre-Columbian text in an Old World script or language has ever been found in the Western Hemisphere." Accordingly,

We shall have to re-examine the other inscriptions and artifacts found in America, that are possibly of Old World origin. Some are doubtless fakes, but others will turn out to be genuine. Each case will have to be re-evaluated on its own merits. But, here and now, we know that trans-Atlantic crossings were not only possible before Columbus and the Vikings, but did actually take place and we can prove a specific crossing in Imperial Roman times.

Based on research by Matthew G. Wells and John W. Welch, May 1991. [87]

Concrete Evidence for the Book of Mormon

The people who went forth became exceedingly expert in the working of cement. (Hel. 3:7)

Helaman 3:7–11 reports that Nephite dissenters moved from the land of Zarahemla into the land northward and began building with cement. "The people . . . who went forth became exceedingly expert in the working of cement; therefore they did build houses of cement," "all manner of their buildings," and many cities "both of wood and of cement." The Book of Mormon dates this significant technological advance to the year 46 B.C.

Recent research shows that cement was in fact extensively used in Mesoamerica beginning largely at this time. One of the most notable uses of cement is in the temple complex at Teotihuacan, north of present-day Mexico City. According to David S. Hyman, the structural use of cement appears suddenly in the archaeological record. Its earliest sample "is a fully developed product." The cement floor slabs at this site "were remarkably high in structural quality." Although exposed to the elements for nearly two thousand years, they still "exceed many present-day building code requirements."

After its discovery, cement was used at many sites in the Valley of Mexico and in the Maya regions of southern Mexico, Guatemala, and Honduras. It was used in the construction of buildings at such sites as Cerro de Texcotzingo, Tula, Palenque, Tikal, Copan, Uxmal, and Chichen Itza. Further, the use of cement "is a Maya habit, *absent* from non-Maya examples of corbelled vaulting from the south-eastern United States to southern South America."

Mesoamerican cement was almost exclusively lime cement. The limestone was purified on a "cylindrical pile of timber, which requires a vast amount of labor to cut and considerable skill to construct in such a way that combustion of the stone and wood is complete and a minimum of impurities remains in the product." The fact that very little carbon is found in this cement "attests to the ability of these ancient peoples."

John Sorenson further noted the expert sophistication in the use of cement at El Tajin, east of Mexico City, after Book of Mormon times. Cement roofs covered areas of seventy-five square meters! "Sometimes the builders filled a room with stones and mud, smoothed the surface on top to receive the concrete, then removed the interior fill when the [slab] on top had dried."

The presence of expert cement technology in pre-Hispanic Mesoamerica is a remarkable archaeological fact, inviting much further research. Cement seems to take on significant roles in Mesoamerican architecture close to the time when the Book of Mormon says this development occurred. It is also a significant factor in locating the Book of Mormon lands of Zarahemla and Desolation, for Zarahemla must be south of areas where cement was used as early as the middle first century B.C. Until samples of cement are found outside of the southwest areas of North America, one may reasonably assume that Book of Mormon lands were not far south of the sites where ancient cement is found.[88]

Proof in a Word

In the Book of Mormon it states:

And it came to pass that Ishmael died, and was buried in the place which was called Nahom. (1 Ne. 16:34).

Concerning this word "Nahom" FARMS states,

Lehi's Desert Journey

In a previous article, I that the recent discovery of an ancient place name, *Nehem,* poses difficulties for the Tanners since they would like to dismiss the Book of Mormon and particularly 1 Nephi as a shallow forgery, lacking any significant historical information. Work by recent Latter Day Saint scholars such as Ross Christensen and Warren and Michaela Aston has established that in fact a site with that rare name existed in what is now northern Yemen, at a point where the ancient trade routes would turn eastward. The Tanners' recent rebuttal fails to come to grips with the evidence provided by the Astons. "Actually, there are two different locations which Mormon scholars have set forth as the 'place which was called Nahom.' Nehhm is *over 350 miles* from Al Qunfudhah!" (p. 181). This point, as the Tanners must surely know, is completely irrelevant since Lynn and Hope Hilton's research, to which they refer, was done before the Christensen article or the Astons' more complete analysis. The Hiltons were unaware at the time they did their research that there was in fact a place name from the root *NîM along the western Arabian trade route. In the absence of such evidence, they simply suggested Al Qunfudhah as a possible location. Obviously, the Hiltons' earlier views must now be superseded by more recent data. Shortly after the Hiltons published their articles, Ross Christensen reported that in 1763 Carsten Niebuhr had published a map of Arabia showing a place called "Nehhm," which Christensen suggested might be equated with the Book of Mormon site. This place name finds confirmation in numerous other maps published since then. Warren and Michaela Aston have demonstrated that this place name is very rare, occurring only once in the entire Arabian Peninsula.

According to the Tanners, "only three of the five letters in Nehhm agree with the spelling Nahom. The second letter in Nehhm is *e* rather than *a* , and the fourth letter is *h* instead of *o*. The variant spellings of Nehem, Nehm, Nihm, Nahm and Naham, do not really help to solve the problem" (p. 183). But the Tanners' criticism is not valid since, in Semitic languages such as Hebrew or Arabic, it is the *consonants* and not the vowels that have lexical value. The vowels have nothing to do with the meaning of the root. Thus it makes little difference whether the name is spelled *Nehem, Nehm, Nihm, Nahm*, or *Naham*—the root is the same.

The Tanners believe "it would have been very easy for Joseph Smith to write a story about a trip through

Arabia" (p. 183). Any old map, they reason, would show the would-be forger that if he followed the eastern shore of the Red Sea this would lead him in a south-southeasterly direction. The Tanners simply assume that such a choice would be inevitable, but why choose that direction anyway? Lehi might also go north or east or west across the Mediterranean. If he had a map, a writer might have chosen to send Lehi's family along a south-south-easterly direction, but it was certainly not the only choice. "The only other important thing Joseph Smith would have to know," the Tanners assert, "is that although Arabia contains a great deal of barren land, there was a more fertile land in the southern portion of the country" (p. 183). As I have already explained, no American geographical sources published before 1830 mention the site Nahom, although we now know that it is an authentic ancient place name, which occurs only once in the entire region, and that in a location consistent with Nephi's description. Joseph Smith could *not* have learned about Nahom from early nineteenth-century sources.

Suppose for a minute that Joseph might have had access to the works of Jedidiah Morse, as the Tanners suggest. If that were so, he might pick up on the idea of a fertile area somewhere in the south, but he would place that region along the southeastern shore of the Red Sea: "*Arabia Felix*, or the Fruitful Arabia, situated on *the eastern shore of the Red Sea*, and *Arabia Deserta*, or the Desert Arabia, occupying the rest of the country between the Arabian and Persian gulfs." Other geographies would have been equally superficial and misleading: "Arabia Felix, or the Happy Arabia, in the *south-western* extremity, *towards the shores of the Red Sea." In* order to reach the Bountiful region Lehi would have to go east from Nahom, not south, as Morse would lead one to believe. Nahom, the southernmost location mentioned in Nephi's account, is never said to be a fruitful or happy place, but a place of death and mourning at which Lehi's family almost perishes from hunger (1 Ne. 16:39). This does not sound like the Arabia Felix of nineteenth-century geographies.

Even if we were to suppose that Joseph might have

learned of a bountiful region on the southeastern shores of the Arabian Peninsula, the Book of Mormon goes further by specifying various characteristics of that region.

1. Bountiful is "nearly eastward" from a place which was called *Nahom* (1 Nephi 17:1).

2. The text implies that the terrain and water sources from Nahom eastward permitted reasonable access from the interior deserts to the coast (1 Nephi 17:1–3).

3. Bountiful was a fertile region (1 Nephi 17:5–6).

4. It was a coastal location (1 Nephi 17:5–6).

5. Fruit and wild honey and possibly other food sources were available (1 Nephi 17:5–6; 18:6).

6. The availability of natural fruit (1 Nephi 17:5–6; 18:6) and the bountiful nature of the region suggest the availability of fresh water at this location.

7. Timber was available that could be used to construct a ship (1 Nephi 18:1).

8. A mountain was nearby (1 Nephi 17:7; 18:3).

9. Substantial cliffs, from which Nephi's brothers might attempt to throw him into the sea, are near the ocean (1 Nephi 17:48).

10. Sources of flint (1 Nephi 17:11) and ore (1 Nephi 17:9–10) were available in the region.

11. Suitable wind and ocean currents were available to carry the vessel out into the ocean (1 Nephi 18:8–9).

Nephi provides some very specific information on Lehi's journey, which exceeds what could have been known from nineteenth-century sources antedating the Book of Mormon. The Astons have demonstrated that (1) the Wadi Sayq on the southeastern coast of Oman meets all the textual criteria for the Old World Bountiful, (2) it is the only site in that region which does, and (3) that fertile location is "nearly eastward" from an attested site called Nahom just as Nephi says it was. These characteristics surpass the information available

in even the most informed geography books and
gazetteers of Joseph Smith's day.[89]

FARMS further states,

Book of Mormon Names

In a past review I chided the Tanners for failure to
address some of the scholarship relating to Book of Mormon names. I find it most significant that many of the
names frequently appear in a context that clearly reflects
their Old World usage, and I cited several examples I felt
were significant. The Tanners, apparently unable to
address this issue in a coherent fashion, have simply
ignored what I said there (pp. 139–41). In any case, here
are several additional examples, discovered by other
scholars, which are not easily explainable under the
assumption that the Book of Mormon is a shallow forgery.

Jershon. The Book of Mormon name *Jershon* can
be traced to a Hebrew root meaning "to inherit." In the
Book of Mormon we read "Behold, we will give up the
land of Jershon, which is on the east by the sea . . . and
this land of *Jershon* is the land which we will give unto
our brethren for an *inheritance*" (Alma 27:22).

Sheum. "And we began to till the ground, yea, even
with all manner of seeds, with seeds of corn, and of
wheat, and of barley, and with neas, and with *sheum*"
(Mosiah 9:9). *Sheum* is a perfectly good Akkadian cereal
name (*Áe<*) dating to the third millennium b.c., which
in ancient Assyria referred to wheat, but in other regions
of the Near East could be applied to other grains. Since
the Book of Mormon passage mentions sheum in addition to wheat and barley, this suggests that Book of Mormon people who came from the Old World probably
applied this term to some species of New World grain.
This raises an interesting question for the Tanners, who
would simply dismiss the Book of Mormon as a shallow
forgery by Joseph Smith. Incidentally, the term *sheum* is
not found in early nineteenth-century sources because
Akkadian could not be read until 1857, twenty-seven
years after the Book of Mormon was published and

thirteen years after the death of the Prophet. So if Joseph Smith really made this name up, how did he just happen to choose this peculiar term *sheum* and just happen to use it in an agricultural context? I find it easier to believe that this is an indication of the antiquity of the Book of Mormon record.

Shilum. Alma 11:5–19 describes various monetary units that the Nephites used at one point in their history. Alma 11:16 in our current edition of the Book of Mormon records that one of these units was a "shiblum." However, both the 1830 edition of the Book of Mormon and the printer's manuscript indicate that this originally read *shilum*. Significantly, *shilum* is a perfectly good Hebrew word, meaning literally "retribution . . . a fee: recompense, reward." That makes excellent sense in a monetary context.

Nahom. Nephi recorded, "And it came to pass that Ishmael *died*, and was buried in the place which was called *Nahom*. And it came to pass that the daughters of Ishmael did *mourn* exceedingly, because of the loss of their father" (1 Ne. 16:34–5). Biblical scholars suggest that the root *NîM means to "comfort" or "console." In some forms the word "comes simply to mean 'suffer emotional pain'. The sense 'be comforted' is retained in contexts of mourning for the dead." Damrosch notes that all references to the root *NîM in the Hebrew Bible are associated with death. "In family settings, it is applied in instances involving death of an immediate family member (parent, sibling, or child); in national settings, it has to do with the survival or impending extermination of an entire people. At heart, *naúam* means 'to mourn,' to come to terms with a death; these usages are usually translated . . . by the verb 'to comfort,' as when Jacob's children try to comfort their father after the reported death of Joseph." The events in 1 Ne. 16:34–5 fit this context quite well since we are told that Ishmael, a close family member, died and his daughters mourned and murmured.

Alan Goff has written an important article on the meaning of the root *NîM as it relates to 1 Ne. 16:34–9. Goff was apparently the first to note that the significance of this term may go beyond the obvious context of mourning for the dead. Nephi related:

"And Laman said unto Lemuel and also unto the sons of Ishmael: Behold let us slay our father, and also our brother Nephi . . . And it came to pass that the Lord was with us, yea, even the voice of the Lord came and did speak many words unto them, and did chasten them exceedingly; and after they were chastened by the voice of the Lord they did turn away their anger, and did repent of their sins, insomuch that the Lord did bless us again with food, that we did not perish (1 Nephi 16:37, 39).

According to one scholar, the root *NïM can also be "extended to describe the release of emotional tension involved in performing a declared action (executing wrath), or retracting a declared action (such as sin, punishment or blessing)."Damrosch notes that the Hebrew term *naúam* is sometimes applied to contexts involving "cases of regret or change of heart," frequently when the repenter is meditating murder. "Repentance" [or change of heart] then involves either the decision to kill, or conversely, the decision to stop killing. The term can then be used in quite ignoble circumstances, as when Esau comforts himself for the loss of his birthright by deciding to kill Jacob (Gen. 27:42), but usually it is God who repents, either negatively or positively; negatively, by deciding to destroy his people; positively, by commuting a sentence of destruction.

Again, this explanation clearly fits the context of 1 Ne. 16:34–9, where Laman and Lemuel and the sons of Ishmael contemplate the murder of their father Lehi and their brother Nephi, the Lord is angry with them, and after being chastened by the Lord they turn away their anger and repent of their sins. The Lord also apparently turns away his wrath and does not destroy them with hunger. It is interesting, furthermore, that while they had up until this time been traveling southward (1 Ne. 16:13), they now *turn* and travel eastward (1 Nephi 17:1), (Jerald and Sandra Tanner. Answering Mormon Scholars: a Response To Criticism Raised by Mormon Defenders. [Matthew Roper], *FARMS Review of Books, vol. 9, no. 1, 1997*).

MULEK a son of Bible King Zedekiah recorded in the Book of Mormon

The Babylonians forced Zedekiah to witness the execution of his captured sons, had his eyes put out, and took him in bronze fetters to Babylon (see 2 Kings 25:4–7; 2 Chron. 36:13).

According to the Book of Mormon, that was not the end of the matter. One son named Mulek escaped (see Omni 1:15–16; Hel. 8:21), even though the details remain shadowy. Since he landed first at the land of Desolation on the east coast (see Alma 22:30–31; Hel. 6:10), he probably journeyed to Mesoamerica via the Mediterranean, Atlantic Ocean, and Caribbean, perhaps with Phoenician help.

The first clue of the existence and escape of Mulek, son of Zedekiah, can be found in 2 Kings 25:1–10, which reports that Nebuchadnezzar and "*all* his host" scattered "*all* the men" and "*all* [the king's] army" and burnt "*all* the houses of Jerusalem," and with "*all* the army" they destroyed the walls. In the midst of all this, however, 2 Kings 25:7 omits the word *all* when it reports only that "the sons" of Zedekiah were killed, leaving open the question whether all of his sons were slain.

Biblical scholars have recently had interesting things to say about a person named *Malchiah*. Jeremiah 38:6 speaks of a "dungeon of Malchiah the son of Hammelech . . . in the court of the prison." But the Hebrew name here, *MalkiYahu ben-hamMelek,* should be translated "MalkiYahu, son of the king," the Hebrew word *melek* meaning "king."

Was this MalkiYahu a son of King Zedekiah? Several factors indicate that he was. For one thing, the title "son of the king" was used throughout the ancient Near East to refer to actual sons of kings who served as high officers of imperial administration. The same is certainly true of the Bible, in which kings' sons ran prisons (see 1 Kings 22:26–27; Jerem. 36:26; 38:6) or performed other official functions (see 2 Kings 15:5; 2 Chron. 28:7). Moreover, in view of the fact that the name MalkiYahu has been found on two ostraca from Arad (in southern Judah), the late head of the Department of

Archaeology at Tel Aviv University, Yohanan Aharoni, said that "Malkiyahu is a common name and was even borne by a contemporary son of king Zedekiah."

But was this MalkiYahu the same person as Mulek? Study of these names tells us he may very well be. In the case of Baruch, scribe of Jeremiah, for example, the long form of his name, BerekYahu, has been discovered on a seal impression by Nahman Avigad of the Hebrew University in Jerusalem. The full name has been shortened in Jeremiah's record to Baruch.

In view of this shortening, as in many other biblical names, there is no reason why a short form such as Mulek might not be possible. Indeed, the archaic Hebrew *qutl*-form could account for it, and *mulk* actually appears in Ugaritic and Phoenician, meaning "royal, princely-sacrifice; tophet-vow" (= Punic *molk*/Hebrew *molek* [see Lev. 18:21; 2 Kings 16:3]; child-sacrifice [see Acts 7:43]), and in Arabic meaning "reign, sovereignty, dominion" (Amorite *Muluk* = Akkadian and Eblaite *Malik*). One might, incidentally, be led to compare this with Mayan *Muluc,* the red-Bacab of the East, whom David H. Kelley correlates with "blood" and "devourer of children."

A prominent non-Mormon ancient Near Eastern specialist declared recently of the Book of Mormon naming "Mulek" as a son of Zedekiah, "If Joseph Smith came up with that one, he did pretty good!" He added that the vowels in the name could be accounted for as the Phoenician style of pronunciation. He found himself in general agreement that "MalkiYahu, son of the King" might very well be a son of King Zedekiah, and that the short-form of the name could indeed be *Mulek.*

Based on research primarily by Robert F. Smith, February 1984 and supplemented by Benjamin Urrutia in *Insights,* February 1985. For the latest statements about Mulek and the Mulekites, see the entry on Mulekites by Curtis Wright in Macmillan's Encyclopedia of Mormonism (1991) and the article by John L. Sorenson, "The Mulekites," *BYU Studies* 30 (Summer 1990):6–22.[90]

Chiasmus in the Book of Mormon

We now turn to the question of *chiasmus in the Book of Mormon.* The first chapter of the book claims that it was written in "the language of the Egyptians" but according to "the learning of the Jews" (1 Nephi 1:2); that is, it was written with Egyptian characters and elements but in Hebraic style. If the Book of Mormon truly is a direct translation of a text formulated in accordance with ancient Hebrew learning, chiasmus might well be present as an integral part of its literary style. If so, an understanding of chiasmus should be helpful in interpreting and understanding the design of the total book.

If chiasmus can be convincingly identified in the Book of Mormon, it will testify of the book's ancient origin. No one in America, let alone in western New York, fully understood chiasmus in 1830. Joseph Smith had been dead ten full years before John Forbes's book was published in Scotland. Even many prominent Bible scholars today know little about chiastic forms beyond the name and a few passages where they might to found. *The possibility of Joseph Smith's noticing the form accidentally is also remote, since most biblical passages containing inverted word orders have been rearranged into natural word orders in the King James translation. Even had he known of the form, he would still have had the overwhelming task of written original, artistic chiastic sentences. Try writing a sonnet of a multi-termed chiasm yourself: your appreciation of these forms will turn to awe.* If the Book of Mormon is found to contain true chiastic forms in an ancient style, then is not the book's own repeated claim to be the product of an ancient culture veritated substantiated?

An understanding of chiasmus will also greatly enhance interpretation of Book of Mormon scriptures. If the another authors of the Book of Mormon consciously set particular elements parallel to each other, then these elements must be considered together in order to be fully understood in their complete context. Moreover, the thoughts which appear at the center of a chiastic passage must always be given special attention, and any antithetical ideas introduced at the turning point must be contrasted with their properly corresponding ideas.

Knowledge of chiasmus will clarify questions of structure with shorter passages and of unity within whole books. For example, why Nephi divided his writings into two books instead of leaving them all in one, will be explained in chiasmus. Stylistic devices, especially the frequent repetition which have often been seen as ignorant and redundant, will be appreciated in the light in which they originally shone.[91]

A Stone Is Found

Dr. Stirling also found in southwestern Mexico at Izapa a stone covered with carvings which have been interpreted by Dr. M. Wells Jakeman of Brigham Young University as a representation of Lehi's dream of the "Tree of Life," recorded in 1 Nephi 8:1–38. To quote Dr. Jakeman:

> the resemblance of this sculpture to the Book of Mormon account cannot be accidenta.l . . . It practically establishes an historical connection . . . between the ancient Central American priests responsible for the sculpture and the Lehi people of the Book of Mormon! Indeed, the accurate and detailed knowledge of Lehi's vision . . . displayed by these priests in this sculpture, can be explained only by their identification as an actual group of the Lehi people. (M. Wells Jakeman, "An Unusual Tree of Life Sculpture from Ancient Central America" Bulletin of University Archaeological Society (March, 1953), pp. 26–49).[92]

The Name Nephi

Elder George Reynolds traces this celebrated name to an Egyptian root. He says:

> "Its roots are Egyptian; its meaning, good excellent, benevolent. . . . One of the names given to this god [Osiris], expressive of his attributes, was Nephi, or Dnephi, . . . and the chief city dedicated to him was

called N–ph, translated into Hebrew as Noph, in which form it appears in Hosea, Isaiah, and Jeremiah. Its modern English name is Memphis."[93]

The Name Moroni

This is, as is well known, the name of the last of the Book of Mormon prophets, who finished the records of his father, Mormon, added his own abridgment of the plates of the Jaredites, and deposited the completed volume in the Hill, Cumorah, about A.D. 421 (Morm. 8:14; Moro. 10:2), in the same hill, where Mormon had deposited the original plates entrusted to his care, from which he had compiled his briefer history (Morm. 6:6).

Moroni was also the name of the great Nephite general who was the first to proclaim the American continents the *Land of Liberty,* or, as we should say, "The Land of the Free" (Alma 46:11–17).

There was a City of Moroni on the East Sea, "on the south by the line of the possessions of the Lamanites" (Alma 50:13) and a Land of Moroni, "on the borders by the sea shore" (Alma 51:22; 62:25).

The word is Semitic. At the beginning of our era it had found its way into the Syriac spoken in Palestine, and was so generally understood that Paul used it in his first letter to the Corinthians (16:22), although that document was written in Greek, when he says: "If any man love not the Lord Jesus Christ, let him be Anathema Maranatha."

These words, *Maranatha,* have puzzled commentators, and various interpretations have been suggested, such as "In the coming of our Lord"; or, "Our Lord has come"; or, "Our Lord will come." Some read the word as two words, Marana tha, which would mean, "Come, Lord," and which is the very prayer that closes the Revelation by John, *erchou, Kyvie Iesou.* (Rev. 22:20.) It was, in all probability, a conventionalized expression of pious sentiment, something similar to the old, "Peace be with thee," or our own "adieu," or "goodbye," which, if spelled out, would, of course, be, "God be with you." But all agree that *Marana,* or as the word is transliterated in the Book of Mormon *Moroni* means "Our Lord." We have also, in the Book of Mormon, a longer form of the same word, *Moronihah,* which I take to mean, "Jehovah is my Lord," which gives us a meaning almost identical with that of the name *El-i-jah,* "Jehovah is my God."

This name, *Marana,* or *Moroni,* has been preserved in the name *Maranon,* which is the name by which the mighty Amazon River is known when it first begins its course towards the ocean.

In the valley of the Maranon remains of cyclopean buildings have been found, proving that the region was inhabited in prehistoric times. In 1840 a remarkable sculptured stone was found there, now known as the Chavin Stone, from the locality where it was discovered. It is 25 feet long by 2 feet 4 inches, and represents either some mighty ruler or some divine personage, standing under a number of rays, each ending in a serpent head, reminding one of an Egyptian pharaoh under the so-called Aten rays.

Dr. Brinton gives the name of a *Morona* tribe of Indians among the Zaparo linguistic stock, in the upper Amazon Valley.

On the east coast there is also a river named after the great prophet. The *Maroni* River flows from the Tumakurak range and forms the frontier line between French and Dutch Guiana, and, after a course of about 380 miles, reaches the Atlantic.

The name Moroni is found even in Peruvian literature. The Peruvians had a drama, called *Apu Ollantay,* composed about the year 1470, long before the arrival of the Spaniards, and first committed to writing in 1770. Sir Clements Markham has published an elegant translation of it. Von Tschudi, in his work on the Quicha language, also gives it in full.

The first act is supposed to depict something that happened at the end of the 14th century of our era. The other two acts cover the first ten or twelve years of the 15th century. The hero is the great chief Ollanta, and the story is about his love for Cusi Coyllur, a daughter of the proud Inca Pachacutec at a time when such a venture might have cost the lives of both. The first scene of the third act of this drama is laid in a street in Cuzo called *Pampa Moroni.*

We know not how far back this name as a street name in Cuzco goes. Montesinos says the fifth king, Inti Capac Yupanqui, divided Cuzco into two districts, Upper and Lower, and divided the first into streets to which he gave names. If it was this Inca who gave the street or square referred to, the name of Moroni, that name must have been so well known in Indian tradition, in the first half of the fifth century A.D., as to suggest the propriety of naming a public place in the "holy city" of the Peruvians in his honor.[94]

The Name Manti

In the Book of Mormon this word occurs as the name of the hill upon which Nehor, the murderer, was executed (Alma 1:15). It was also the name of a Nephite soldier (Alma 2:22), and there was a Land of Manti, on the head waters of the river Sidon (Alma 16:6–7) and a city of the same name (Alma 57:22).

The name is very ancient. It is mentioned in the earliest Egyptian inscriptions as the name of an Asiatic people, probably the same as the Hyksos, or Shepherds, or, perhaps, rather a tribe of that people.

In this country there was at one time, in South America, the Manta Indians, on the coast north of the Gulf of Guayaquil. In Stanford's *Compendium of Geography and Travel,* the Mantas are referred to as an extinct Quito race of ten tribes. There was also a city of Manti and a district of the same name, as in the Book of Mormon.[95]

The Name Lehi is in the Bible

In the Hebrew this word is *Lechi,* the "ch" being practically the same as our "h." In Palestine a hilly district in Judea, near Jerusalem, was known as *Lehi.* (Judg. 15:19) Samson, after his battle with the Philistines, threw away his unique weapon, the jawbone of an ass, and called the place of combat *Ramath-Lehi,* "the Hill of Lehi." Then he was thirsty, and the Lord, in answer to his prayer, opened a crevice in the hill, and "there came water thereout." So he called the spring, *En-hakkore,* "the spring of him that called" (in answer to prayer), "which," we read, "is in Lehi unto this day." This incident is recalled by the name of the father of Nephi.

In the Lenape language the word is *lechau,* which is identical with the Hebrew *lechi.* In the Indian tongue it means a "fork of a river," and that may well have been suggested by the form of a jawbone of a donkey.

T. A. Joyce mentions an Indian tribe in Colombia, located to the north of the Chibchas, which he calls the *Laches,* a name which seems to be identical with the Hebrew *Lechi* and the Book of Mormon *Lehi.*

In North America there are several places named *Lehigh.* The Lehigh River in Pennsylvania, which flows into the Delaware at Easton, Northampton Co., is well known. The one-hundred mile channel through which it winds its way is called Lehigh Valley, and there is a good sized county having the same name.

We have noticed that the name is known far away in the Hawaiian Islands. In the November 1921 issue of *The Paradise of the Pacific,* a magazine published in Honolulu, the statement occurs that the ancient name for *Diamond Head,* a prominent volcanic mountain, was *Leahi.* This is but a very slight variation in spelling, from the name, as it is given in the Book of Mormon.[96]

The Name Liahona

This interesting word is Hebrew with an Egyptian ending. It is the name which Lehi gave to the ball or director he found outside his tent the very day he began his long journey through the "wilderness," after his little company had rested for some time in the Valley of Lemuel (1 Nephi 16:10; Alma 37:88).

L is a Hebrew preposition meaning "to," and sometimes used to express the possessive case. *Iah* is a Hebrew abbreviated form of "Jehovah," common in Hebrew names. *On* is the Hebrew name of the Egyptian

"City of the Sun," also known as Memphis and Heliopolis. *L-iah-on* means, therefore, literally, "To God is Light"; or, "of God is Light." That is to say, God gives light, as does the Sun. The final a reminds us that the Egyptian form of the Hebrew name On is *Annu,* and that seems to be the form Lehi used.

Lehi had just received the divine command to begin his perilous journey. The question uppermost in his mind, after having received that call, must have been how to find the way. That must have been quite a problem. But he arose early in the morning, determined to carry out the command given. Undoubtedly he had prayed all night for light and guidance. And now, standing in the opening of the tent, perhaps as the first rays of the sun broke through the morning mists, his attention is attracted by a metal ball "of curious workmanship." He picks it up and examines it. And then, as he realizes that it is the guide for which he had been praying, he exclaims in ecstacy, *L-iah-on-a!* Which is as much as to say, This is God's light; it has come from him! And that became the name of the curious instrument. This was not a compass. It was a miraculously formed instrument which served both as compass and octant.

Now, the fact is that this manner of giving names was an ancient Semitic custom. Hagar, when her son Was perishing in the wilderness and she beheld the angel by the life-giving spring, exclaimed, *Beer-lachai-roi!* which means, literally, "Well, to live, to see." That is to *say,* "the well of him that liveth and seeth me," for that was the thought that came to her mind. (Gen. 16:13, 14.) And that became the name of the well. In the same way, Abraham called the place where he had offered Isaac on the altar, *Jehovah-jireh,* "the Lord will provide"; because the Lord did provide for himself a ram instead of Isaac, as Abraham had assured his son the Lord would do (Gen. 27:7–14). And that became the name of the Mount "to this day."

Lehi gave the metal ball a name commemorative of one of the great experiences of his life, just as these Old Testament worthies had done. And, furthermore, he gave it a name that no one but a devout Hebrew influenced by Egyptian culture would have thought of. Is that not the strongest possible evidence of the truth of the historic part of the Book of Mormon?[97]

The Name Laban

Laban was the name of a prominent resident of Jerusalem, a contemporary of Lehi, and the owner of certain brass plates containing historical and genealogical data of the greatest importance (1 Nephi 3:5).

Laman, the name of the eldest son of Lehi (1 Ne. 2:5), and also of a king mentioned in Mosiah 7:21, is the same name as Laban. *Lamoni* is formed from this word by the addition of the suffix "i."

The word is Hebrew and means "white." Several forms of it are found in the Old Testament, such as "Laban," the father-in-law of Jacob; "lebanah," the "moon," because of its whiteness; "Libnah," a place name (Num. 33:20). "Libni the name of a person (Ex. 6:17). "Lebanon the well-known name of a mountain, and "Libnites," as the descendants of Libni were called (Num. 3:21).

Nor is the word confined to the Semitic group of languages. Compare the Greek "alphos" and "Olympos"; also the Latin "albus," from which we have a number of words, such as "albino," "Albion," "Albany," "album," the latter being originally white tablets for writing. Some derive even "Alps" from the same root, while others claim that this name is from a Gaelic source meaning "height."

It would, indeed, be a surprise if we should not find that word, so common in the Old World anciently, in use among the prehistoric Indians. But it seems to have been just as common on this side of the world.

Dr. Brinton tells us that the Yamcos Indians on the Maranon are also called Llameos, Lamas, and Lamistas. In the Lama linguistic stock he places the *Alabonos,* the *Nahuapos,* and the *Napeanos.* In *A-labono* we can easily recognize *Labon,* and in *Nahuapos* and *Napeanos* we seem to have the name of Nephi preserved, just as we have the name of *Laban,* or *Laman,* preserved in *Lamas* and *Lamistas.* Near Truxillo, in South America, there are also the *Lamanos* or *Lamistas,* of the Quichua linguistic stock.

According to Reclus, quoted by Dr. Cyrus Thomas, there is, or was, a tribe of Indians, of the Ulva stock, near Blewfields, called *Lamans.* The Blewfields River was also called the *Lama* River. Dr. Brinton does not classify the Lamans, but he mentions the *Ramas* as living on a small island in the Blewfield Lagoon, and the Lamans and the Ramas may be the same name, since "l" and "r" interchange in all languages.

In Yucatan we have the ancient city of *Labna,* which name certainly seems to be the same as *Laban.*

We are aware of the fact that *Lab-na* is said to mean "old house." But that does not say that the root of the word is not the same as the Hebrew "white." For white is often a sign of old age.

The word *Laban* means the same in the Indian, as in the Old World languages. In the Lenape, Rafinesque says, *Lapan-ibi* means "white water." *Lumonaki,* according to the same authority, "white land." This word is also spelled *abnaki,* with the initial "l" dropped. Dr. Brinton says the Algonquins used to call their eastern kindred *Abnakis,* "our white ancestors," an expression which, since [l]*abn* means "white," would be the same as "our Lamanite ancestors"; *aki,* however, means "land," and "white land" is, therefore, a better translation.

Charles Christian Ravn, the Danish scholar, is authority for the statement that the Indians whom the Icelanders met when exploring the North American coast in the early part of the Eleventh Century, had a tradition concerning a country called, in Icelandic, *Hvitramanna-land,* "White-men's-land." That would be identically the same name as *Lumon-aki,* or the land of Laman. Conjecture has located *Hvitramannaland* along the Chesapeake Bay, mending down into the Carolinas, and peopled it with "white" colonists, but it is more probable that it is the *Lumonaki* of the Algon.[98]

Truths Revealed and Prophecies Fulfilled in This Dispensation by LeGrand Richards

To provide a brief summation, we will mention some of the great truths upon which the Lord has shed his divine light through the instrumentality of the Prophet Joseph Smith:

1. The true personality of God
2. Man's true relationship to God
3. The proper foundation of the gospel
   a. Faith in the Lord Jesus Christ
   b. Repentance
   c. Baptism by immersion for the remission of sins
   d. Laying on of hands for the gift of the Holy Ghost
4. An understanding of the difference between the Aaronic and Melchizedek Priesthoods (Heb. 7:11–12)
5. An understanding of the different offices in these two priesthoods; the duties of each, the number required to form a quorum, etc.
6. The proper organization of the Church and its purpose
7. The correct name that the Church of Jesus Christ should bear
8. That the followers of Christ's Church were and should be called "saints"
9. Where we came from and that we lived before we were born
10. Why we are here upon the earth
11. The three degrees of glory and what one must do to prepare for celestial glory
12. Who are to come forth in the first resurrection, and that the rest of the dead are not to come forth until the end of the thousand years, which will be the great judgment day
13. That obedience to the ordinances of the gospel is so necessary that the perfect plan of God

provides for a vicarious work of the living for the dead, for the benefit of those to whom the gospel has not been preached or who have not accepted it in this life

14. That the gospel is being preached to the dead, and for what purpose

15. That the millennium of one thousand years has been provided to complete this work, without which the final judgment day should come at the beginning and not the end thereof

16. That the condition and time of one's life here upon the earth is as much the result of a life previously lived as the life to come will be the result of how we live and what we do in this life

17. That the Church established by Christ in the meridian of time should fall into an apostate condition, of which fact both the ancient prophets and the apostles of the Master freely bore witness

18. That the prophets of the Old Testament and the apostles of the New Testament predicted a complete restoration of "all things which God hath spoken by the mouth of all his holy prophets, since the world began" (Acts 3:21), rather than a reformation to correct the false teachings of the Churches

19. The meaning and fulfillment of the following prophecies:

    a. "And I saw another angel fly in the midst of heaven, having the everlasting gospel to preach unto them that dwell on the earth, and to every nation, and kindred, and tongue, and people, "Saying with a loud voice, Fear God, and give glory to him; for the hour of his judgment is come: and worship him that made heaven, and earth, and the sea, and the fountains of waters" (Rev. 14:6–7).

    b. "And he shall send Jesus Christ, "Whom the heaven must receive until the times of restitution of all things, which God hath spoken by the mouth of all his holy prophets since the world began" (Acts 3:20–21).

c. "Behold, I will send my messenger, and he shall prepare the way before me: and the Lord, whom ye seek, shall suddenly come to his temple, even the messenger of the covenant, whom ye delight in: behold, he shall come, saith the Lord of hosts" (Mal. 3:1).

d. "Wherefore the Lord said, Forasmuch as this people draw near me with their mouth, and with their lips do honour me, but have removed their heart far from me, and their fear toward me is taught by the precept of men: "Therefore, behold, I will proceed to do a marvellous work among this people, even a marvellous work and a wonder: for the wisdom of their wise men shall perish, and the understanding of their prudent men shall be hid" (Isa. 29:13–14).

e. "And in the days of these kings shall the God of heaven set up a kingdom, which shall never be destroyed: and the kingdom shall not be left to other people, but it shall break in pieces and consume all these kingdoms, and it shall stand for ever" (Dan. 2:44).

20. That Elijah has been sent back to this earth, and for what purpose (Mal. 4:5–6)

21. Why there has been such a marvelous change in the world with respect to genealogical record keeping, genealogical organizations, societies, libraries, and research work

22. That marriage, according to the scriptures, was intended to be eternal

23. That the family unit is to endure beyond the grave

24. Why temples are erected unto the Most High,

and for what purpose they are used

25. Where the temple is that Isaiah saw that should be built in the tops of the mountains in the last days (Isa. 2:2–3)

26. That in case of sickness, we should call the elders of the Church to anoint the sick with oil (James 5:14–16)

27. The command of God to Ezekiel that two sticks (or records) should be kept, one of Judah and his companions and one of Joseph and his companions, and these two records are (Eze. 37:15–19)

28. What people should speak out of the ground with a voice that hath a familiar spirit (Isa. 29:1–4, 2 Nephi 25:7–8, 26:15–17)

29. What the "sealed book" is to which Isaiah refers (Isa. 29:11–12; 2 Nephi 27:5–26)

30. To what people Jesus referred when he said, "Other sheep I have which are not of this fold" (John 10:16; 3 Nephi 15:11–12)

31. The promises made to Joseph by his father Jacob, and by Moses, when he was promised a *new land* in "the *utmost* bounds of the everlasting hills" (Gen. 49:22–26; Deut. 33:13–18), and where that *new land and the everlasting hills* are to which they referred

32. When and how the cities that are being excavated in Central and South America came to be buried in the depths of the earth (3 Nephi 8)

33. Where the civilized people who once inhabited the land of America came from and who they were, as evidenced by their great cities and buildings being excavated

34. That there were to be two gathering places, not one, in the last days—one for Judah at Jerusalem and one for Israel or the seed of Joseph, in America (Ether 13)

35. The difference between Judah's blessing and Joseph's blessing as pertaining to priesthood

(Heb. 7:4; 1 Chron. 5:1–2)

36. That Israel, or the seed of Joseph, should be gathered in the last days to that portion of America designated as wilderness or desert in the mountains and requiring irrigation (Jerem. 31:6–13; Isa. 2:2–3, 35, 41:18–23, 43:18–21)

37. The calling of a patriarch, or evangelist, as he is often called (Gen. 49; Deut. 33; Acts 2:29, 7:8–9; Heb. 7:4; D&C 124:91–93)

38. That Jesus did not baptize little children, nor did any of his apostles, but "he took them up in his arms, put his hands upon them, and blessed them" (Mark 10:16)

39. What the Urim and Thummim are, and what they were used for by the prophets of old, and what became of them (1 Sam. 28:6; Ezra 2:62–63; Lev. 8:8; Deut. 33:8; Exo. 28:30; Num. 27:21)

40. That the Lord's plan of financing his kingdom on the earth is the law of tithing

41. That the Word of Wisdom was given as a revelation by the Lord for the temporal salvation of his people in the latter days, and that it was ahead of science in declaring things which are not good for the body

42. That The Church of Jesus Christ of Latter Day Saints maintains a missionary system as instituted by the Savior, whereby the missionaries labor without compensation for their services.[99]

A Marvelous Work and a Wonder

Joseph Smith, or any other man, could not have obtained all this information by reading the Bible or studying all the books that have ever been written. It came from God. It is exactly what Isaiah promised the Lord would do when conditions upon the earth should become as Joseph Smith found them when he went into the woods to pray for light as to which of all the Churches he should join.

Consider again the promise of the Lord through Isaiah:

"Wherefore the Lord said, Forasmuch as this people draw near me with their mouth, and with their lips do honour me, but have removed their heart far from me, and their fear toward me is taught by the precept of men:

Therefore, behold, I will proceed to do a *marvellous work* among this people, even *a marvellous work and a wonder*: for the wisdom of their wise men shall perish, and the understanding of their prudent men shall be hid" (Isa. 29:13-14).

It truly is a marvelous work and a wonder. Can you conceive of anything that could be more marvelous or more wonderful?

In the face of it all, the wisdom of wise men does perish. The world has no satisfactory explanation. In the Church Historian's Office in Salt Lake City are more than 20,000 volumes, large and small, each of which says something about the Prophet Joseph Smith. There are also some 2,000 pamphlets on the subject. Many of these publications represent attempts on the part of non-Mormon writers to explain the conundrum of Joseph Smith and the work he established, but all without avail. All these writings have been accumulated since the birth of Joseph Smith in 1805. In contrast, in the more than two centuries that have elapsed since the birth of George Washington, it is reported, there are only some 3,000 volumes written about him on file in the Library of Congress.

Well did Isaiah predict: "For the wisdom of their wise men shall perish, and the understanding of their prudent men shall be hid" (Isa. 29:14).

How could this prediction possibly be more literally fulfilled than in the case of Joseph Smith and the work the Lord established through him?

We emphasized a statement published in the *New York Herald*, which we quoted in this chapter: "Joseph Smith is creating a spiritual system, combined with morals and industry that may change the destiny of the race." This statement was made in 1842, and at this writing, more than a century and a half later, it is evident, from the present accomplishments of the Church founded under his leadership, that this prognostication is sure to achieve a complete fulfillment.[100]

MORMON MIRACLES
(GOD IS WATCHING OVER
HIS SAINTS)

Crickets and Seagulls

B. H. Roberts

The pioneers when entering the valley, it will be remembered, noted that in the foothills there were great numbers of large, black crickets, which then excited but a passing remark. Now, however, in this month of May, [1848], they came swarming from the foothills literally by millions, and descended upon the new-made fields of grain. They devoured all before them as they came to it. Their appetite never abated. They were cutting and grinding day and night, leaving the fields bare and brown behind them. There seemed to be no end to their numbers. They could not fly; their only means of locomotion was by clumsily hopping a scant foot at a time—hence, once in the fields, the difficulty of getting them out; and they came in myriads, increasing daily. Holes were dug; and for the radius of a rod the pests were surrounded by women and children, and driven into them and buried— bushels of them at a time; and this was repeated again and again; but what was the use? This method seemed not to affect the numbers of the pests. Then the men plowed ditches around the wheat fields, turned in the water, and drove the black vermin into the running streams and thus carried them from the fields and destroyed them by hundreds of thousands—all to no purpose; as many as ever seemed to remain, and more were daily swarming from the hills. Fire was tried, but to no better purpose. Man's ingenuity was baffled. He might as well try to sweep back the rising tide of the ocean with a broom as prevail against these swarming pests by the methods tried. Insignificant, these inch or inch and a half long insects separately, but in millions, terrible. The incident illustrates the formidableness of mere numbers. Since the days of Egypt's curse of locusts there was probably nothing like it. The failure to destroy these pests spelled famine to these first settlers of Salt Lake Valley. It meant starvation to the companies of thousands of women and children then en route across the plains. Small wonder if the hearts of the colonists failed them. They looked at one another in helpless astonishment. They were beaten. That is something awful for strong men to admit, especially when beaten by units so insignificant. Meantime the ceaseless gnawing of the ruthless and insatiable invader went on. The brown patches of the wheat fields grew larger. Soon all would be bare and brown, and hope of food and life would disappear with the recently green wheat fields.

Then the miraculous happened. I say it deliberately, the miraculous happened, as men commonly view the miraculous. There was heard the shrill, half-scream, half-plaintive cry of some hovering over the wheat fields. Presently they alight and begin devouring the crickets. Others come—thousands of them—from over the lake. The upper feathers of the gull's wings are tinted with a delicate grey, and some of the flight feathers, primaries, to be exact, are marked with black, but the prevailing color is white; and as they came upon the new wheat fields, stretched upward and then gracefully folded their wings and began devouring the devourers, to the cricket-vexed colonists they seemed like white-winged angels of deliverance—these gulls. They were tireless in their destructive—nay, their saving work. It was noted that when they were glutted with crickets they would go to the streams, drink, vomit, and return again to the slaughter. And so it continued, day after day, until the plague was stayed, and the crops of the pioneers saved.[101]

"The Quails Descend"

Thomas Bullock

On the 9th of October several wagons with oxen having been sent by the Twelve to fetch the poor Saints away, were drawn out in a line on the river banks ready to start. But hark! what is that? See! the quails descend. They alight close by our little camp of twelve wagons, run past each wagon tongue, when they arise, fly around the camp three times, descend and again run the gauntlet past each wagon. See! the sick knock them down with sticks and the little children catch them alive with their hands! Some are cooked for breakfast.

While my family were seated on the wagon tongue and ground, having a washtub for a table, behold they come again! One descends upon our tea-board in the midst of our cups, while we were actually around the table eating our breakfast, which a little boy eight years old catches alive with his hands. They rise again, the flocks increase in number, seldom going seven rods from our camp, continually flying around the camp, sometimes under the wagons, sometimes over, and even into the wagons where the poor, sick Saints are lying in bed; thus having a direct manifestation from the Most High that although we are driven by men He has not forsaken us, but that His eyes are continually over us for good. At noon, having caught alive about fifty and killed about fifty more, the captain gave orders not to kill any more, as it was a direct manifestation and visitation from the Lord. In the afternoon hundreds were flying at a time. When our camp started at three p.m. there could not have been less then five hundred, some said there were fifteen hundred, flying around the camp.

Thus am I a witness to this visitation. Some Gentiles who were at the camp marveled greatly. Even passengers on a steamboat going down the river looked with astonishment.

James A. Little, *From Kirtland to Salt Lake City* (Salt Lake City: James A. Little, 1890), pp. 74-75.[102]

"The Angels of God Were There"

David O. McKay

A teacher, conducting a class, said it was unwise ever to attempt, even to permit [the Martin handcart company] to come across the plains under such conditions.

[According to a class member] some sharp criticism of the Church and its leaders was being indulged in for permitting any company of converts to venture across the plains with no more supplies or protection than a handcart caravan afforded.

An old man in the corner sat silent and listened as long as he could stand it, then he arose and said things that no person who heard him will ever forget. His face was white with emotion, yet he spoke calmly, deliberately, but with great earnestness and sincerity.

In substance [he] said, "I ask you to stop this criticism. You are discussing a matter you know nothing about. Cold historic facts mean nothing here, for they give no proper interpretation of the questions involved. Mistake to send the Handcart Company out so late in the season? Yes. But I was in that company and my wife was in it and Sister Nellie Unthank whom you have cited was there, too. We suffered beyond anything you can imagine and many died of exposure and starvation, but did you ever hear a survivor of that company utter a word of criticism? Not one of that company ever apostatized or left the Church, because everyone of us came through with the absolute knowledge that God lives for we became acquainted with him in our extremities.

"I have pulled my handcart when I was so weak and weary from illness and lack of food that I could hardly put one foot ahead of the other. I have looked ahead and seen a patch of sand or a hill slope and I have said, I can go only that far and there I must give up, for I cannot pull the load through it. . . . I have gone on to that sand and when I reached it, the cart began pushing me. I have looked back many times to see who was pushing my cart, but my eyes saw no one. I knew then that the angels of God were there.

"Was I sorry that I chose to come by handcart? No. Neither then nor any minute of my life since. The price we paid to become acquainted with God was a privilege to pay, and I am thankful that I was privileged to come in the Martin Handcart Company."

Relief Society Magazine, January 1948, p. 8.[103]

The Storm Kept Back the Mob

Joseph Smith

This night we camped on an elevated piece of land between Little Fishing and Big Fishing rivers, which streams were formed by seven small streams or branches.

As we halted and were making preparations for the night, five men armed with guns rode into our camp, and told us we should "see hell before morning;" and their accompanying oaths partook of all the malice of demons. They told us that sixty men were coming from Richmond, Ray county, and seventy more from Clay county, to join the Jackson county mob, who had sworn our utter destruction.

During this day, the Jackson county mob, to the number of about two hundred, made arrangements to cross the Missouri river, above the mouth of Fishing river, at Williams' ferry, into Clay county, and be ready to meet the Richmond mob near Fishing river ford for our utter destruction; but after the first scow load of about forty had been set over the river, the scow in returning was met by a squall, and had great difficulty in reaching the Jackson side by dark.

When these five men were in our camp, swearing vengeance, the wind, thunder, and rising cloud indicated an approaching storm, and in a short time after they left the rain and hail began to fall. The storm was tremendous; wind and rain, hail and thunder met them in great wrath, and soon softened their direful courage, and frustrated all their designs to "kill Joe Smith and his army." Instead of continuing a cannonading which they commenced when the sun was about one hour high, they crawled under wagons, into hollow trees, and filled one old shanty, till the storm was over, when their ammunition was soaked, and the forty in Clay county were extremely anxious in the morning to return to Jackson, having experienced the pitiless pelting of the storm all night. . . .

Very little hail fell in our camp, but from half a mile to a mile around, the stones or lumps of ice cut down the crops of corn and vegetation generally, even cutting limbs from trees, while the trees, themselves were twisted into withes by the wind. The lightning flashed incessantly, which caused it to be so light in our camp through the night, that we could discern the most minute objects; and the roaring of the thunder was tremendous. The earth trembled and quaked, the rain fell in torrents, and, united, it seemed as if the mandate of vengeance had gone forth from the God of battles, to protect His servants from the destruction of their enemies, for the hail fell on them and not on us, and we suffered no harm, except the blowing down of some of our tents, and getting wet; while our enemies had holes made in their hats, and otherwise received damage, even the breaking of their rifle stocks, and the fleeing of their horses through fear and pain.

Many of my little band sheltered in an old meetinghouse through this night, and in the morning the water in Big Fishing river was about forty feet deep, where, the previous evening, it was no more than to our ankles, and our enemies swore that the water rose thirty feet in thirty minutes in the Little Fishing river. They reported that one of their men was killed by lightning, and that another had his hand torn off by his horse drawing his hand between the logs of a corn crib while he was holding him on the inside. They declared that if that was the way God fought for the Mormons, they might as well go about their business.

Joseph Smith, *History of The Church of Jesus Christ of Latter-day Saints,* 7 vols., 2d ed. rev., edited by B. H. Roberts (Salt Lake City: The Church of Jesus Christ of Latter-day Saints, 1932–51), 2:103-5.[104]

Nauvoo Temple and God's Tornado

In September, 1846, the Nauvoo Temple was in possession of the mob; and the people whose energy and substance, whose sweat and blood had been spent in its rearing, were driven into the wilderness or slain. For two years the once hallowed structure stood as an abandoned building; then on November 19, 1848, it fell a prey to the wanton act of an incendiary. After the conflagration, only blackened walls remained where once had stood so stately a sanctuary. *Strange to say, an attempt was made by the Icarians, a local organization, to rebuild on the ruins, the professed intent being to provide for a school; but while the work was in its early stages a tornado demolished the greater part of the walls. This occurred on May 27, 1850.* What remained of the temple has been taken away as souvenirs or used as building material for other structures. Stones of the Temple have been carried into most of the states of the Union and beyond the seas, but upon the site where once stood the House of the Lord not one stone is left upon another. Before the demolition of the Nauvoo Temple was complete, the Latter-day Saints had established themselves in the vales of Utah, and were already preparing to build another and a greater sanctuary to the name and service of their God.[105]

This tornado damaged very few structures in Nauvoo besides the temple. The Saints feel God sent this tornado because his temple was being desecrated.

Mississippi River Froze so the Saints Could Cross

Now, my brethren and sisters, I know whereof I speak with reference to these matters, for I have come down through every atom of it, at least from the expulsion from the city of Nauvoo; in February, 1846, I stood upon the bank of the river and saw President Young and the Twelve apostles, and as many of the people of Nauvoo as had teams or could possibly migrate, cross the Mississippi river on the ice. The river froze within a day or two, because of heavy frost, which enabled them to cross as they did, and thus the first real marvel and manifestation of the mercy and the power of God was manifest, in making a roadway across the Mississippi a mile wide at that place by which our people could go on their journey to the West. I saw them go. My brother was with them, and I wondered if I would ever see him again. We remained there in Nauvoo until September, 1846, when the city was besieged, at the mouth of the cannon and musket, and my mother and her family were compelled to take all that they could move out of the house—their bedding, their clothing, the little food they possessed, leaving the furniture and everything else standing in the house, and fled across the river, where we camped without tent or shelter until the war was over. The city was conquered, and the poor people that were left there were compelled to seek shelter somewhere else. From that moment on, I have been in the conflict. I have seen it and experienced it all the way through; and I am satisfied with my experience.[106]

There are many more Mormon miracles. I refer the reader to *Best-Loved Stories of the LDS People.*

NOTES

1. Harold B. Lee, in *Conference Report,* October 1950, 129.

2. Orson F. Whitney, *Life of Heber C. Kimball,* collector's ed. (Salt Lake City: Bookcraft, 1992), 446, 449–50.

3. Harold B. Lee, *The Teachings of Harold B. Lee*, edited by Clyde J. Williams [SLC: Bookcraft, 1996], 304.

4. George Q. Cannon, *Collected Discourses*, vol. 1: p. 1, February 24, 1889.

5. Neal A. Maxwell, "For I Will Lead You Along," *Ensign* May 1988, Vol. 18, p. 5.

6. *The Teachings of Harold B. Lee,* 355.

7. Whitney, *Life of Heber C. Kimball,* 322.

8. Elder C. Dunn, "Before I Build a Wall," *Ensign*, May 1991, Vol. 21.

9. Brigham Young, *Journal of Discourses,* 26 vols. [London: Latter-day Saints' Book Depot, 1854-1886], 1:51.

10. Spencer W. Kimball, "Our own Liahona," *Ensign*, November 1976, Vol. 6, p.11.

11. Brigham Young, *Journal of Discourses*, vol. 150, 8:175; italics added.

12. Joseph Smith Jr., *History of The Church of Jesus Christ of Latter-day Saints,* ed. B. H. Roberts, 2d ed., rev., 7 vols. (Salt Lake City: Deseret Book, 1971), 3:385–87 (hereafter cited as *History of the Church*).

13. *Fox's Book of Martyrs*, edited by William Byron Forbush.

14. Brigham Young as quoted in *Encyclopedia of Mormonism*, 1-4 vols., edited by Daniel H. Ludlow [New York: Macmillan, 1992], 125.

15. Joseph Fielding Smith, *Doctrines of Salvation: Sermons and Writings of Joseph Fielding Smith,* ed. Bruce R. McConkie, 3 vols. (Salt Lake City: Bookcraft, 1954–56), 1:133–38; Bruce R. McConkie, *Mormon Doctrine,* 2d ed. (Salt Lake City: Bookcraft, 1966), 92–93.

16. C. Wade Brown, *The First Page of the Golden Plates*, (Orem, Utah: Granite Publishing, 2000), p. 25-32.

17. Brown, *First Page of the Golden Plates,* 25–32.

18. John A. Tvedtnes, review of Answering Mormon Scholars: A Response to Criticism of the book *Covering up the black hole in the Book of Mormon* by Jerald and Sandra Tanner, in FARMS Review of Books 6, no. 2, 1994: 235.

19. Milton R. Hunter, *Christ in Ancient America* (Salt Lake City: Deseret Book Co., 1959), 60.

20. See also Wayne A. Larsen, Alvin C. Rencher, and Tim Layton, "Who Wrote the Book of Mormon? An Analysis of Wordprints," *BYU Studies* 20 (spring 1980): 225–51.

21. Ethan Smith, *View of the Hebrews,* 2d ed. (1825), 168, 169.

22. Hugh Nibley, *The Prophetic Book of Mormon* (Salt Lake City: Deseret Book Co.; Provo: Foundation for Ancient Research and Mormon Studies, 1989), 200-202; some italics added.

23. John W. Welch, ed., *Reexploring the Book of Mormon* (Salt Lake City: Deseret Book Co.; Provo: Foundation for Ancient Research and Mormon Studies, 1992), 86.

24. See Robert Paul, "Joseph Smith and the Manchester New York Library," *BYU Studies* 22, no. 3 (1982): 340; Lucy Mack Smith, *History of Joseph Smith by His Mother Lucy Mack Smith,* notes and commentary by Preston Nibley (Salt Lake City: Bookcraft, 1979), 82.

25. *Contributor* 7, no. 8 (May 1886): 284.

26. Andrew Jenson, *Latter-day Saint Biographical Encyclopedia: A Compilation of Biographical Sketches of Prominent Men and Women in The Church of Jesus Christ of Latter-day Saints,* 4 vols. (Salt Lake City: Andrew Jenson History, 1901–36), 246.

27. B. H. Roberts to Heber J. Grant, March 15, 1923 [1922], quoted in Madsen, *B. H. Roberts,* 57–58.

28. Milton R. Hunter, *Archaeology and the Book of Mormon* (Salt Lake City: Deseret Book Co., 1956), 27.

29. "Pre-Columbian Horses from the Yucatan," *Journal of Mammalogy* 38, (1957): 278.

30. Matthew Roper, review of *Mormonism: Shadow or Reality?* by Jerald and Sandra Tanner, in FARMS Review of Books 4, vol. 4 (1992): 207.

31. John L. Sorenson, *An Ancient American Setting for the Book of Mormon* (Salt Lake City and Provo: Deseret Book Co., Foundation for Ancient Research and Mormon Studies, 1985), 297.

32. Sorenson, *Ancient American Setting,* 278.

33. Hunter, *Archaeology and the Book of Mormon,* 25–27.

34. Matthew Roper, review of Answering Mormon Scholars:

A Response to Criticism Raised by Mormon Defenders, by Jerald and Sandra Tanner, in FARMS Review of Books 9, no. 1 (1997): 174-175.

35. See *Saints' Herald* 31 (October 4, 1884): 644; *William Smith on Mormonism* (Lamoni, Iowa: Herald Steam Book, 1883), 12.

36. See "Sermon in the Saints' Chapel," Saints' Herald 31 (June 8, 1884): 644.

37. See Jack M. Lyon, Linda Ririe Gundry, and Jay A. Parry, eds., *Best-Loved Stories of the LDS People* (Salt Lake City: Deseret Book Co., 1997), 25.

38. See Michael D. Coe, *The Maya,* [London: Thames and Hudson, 1984], 148.

39. Roper, review of *Mormonism: Shadow or Reality?* 199.

40. Roper, review of *Mormonism: Shadow or Reality?* 199.

41. Roper, review of *Mormonism: Shadow or Reality?* 211.

42. Roper, review of *Mormonism: Shadow or Reality?* 187; italics added.

43. William J. Hamblin, review of Archaeology and the Book of Mormon, by Jerald and Sandra Tanner, in FARMS Review of Books 5, vol. 5 (1993): 261; italics added.

44. Howard W. Hunter, " No Man Shall Add or Take Away," *Ensign*, April 1981, Vol. 11.

45. Sheri L. Dew, *Go Forward with Faith: The Biography of Gordon B. Hinckley* (Salt Lake City: Deseret Book Co., 1996), 584.

46. Hunter, *Christ in Ancient America,* 60.

47. Donald W. Parry and Dana M. Pike, *LDS Perspectives on the Dead Sea Scrolls* (Provo: Foundation for Ancient Research and Mormon Studies, 1997), 215.

48. Parry and Pike, *LDS Perspectives on the Dead Sea Scrolls,* 215.

49. Richard Lloyd Anderson, *Understanding Paul,* (Salt Lake City: Deseret Book Co., 1983),320-321; italics added.

50. Joseph Fielding Smith, comp., *Teachings of the Prophet Joseph Smith* (Salt Lake City: Deseret Book Co., 1972), 345.

51. Joseph Fielding McConkie, *Answers: Straightforward Answers to Tough Gospel Questions* ([Salt Lake City: Deseret Book Co., 1998), 48–49.

52. Stanley B. Kimball, *Heber C. Kimball: Mormon Patriarch and Pioneer* (Urbana: University of Illinois Press, 1981), 85; Larry E. Dahl and Donald Q.Cannon, *Encyclopedia of Joseph Smith's Teachings* (Salt Lake City: Bookcraft, 1997), 414.

53. Smith, *Teachings of the Prophet Joseph Smith,* 339; Daniel H. Ludlow, *A Companion to Your Study of the Old Testament* (Salt

Lake City: Deseret Book Co., 1981), 339.

54. Bruce R. McConkie, *A New Witness for the Articles of Faith,* 231.

55. Robert L. and Rosemary Brown, *They Lie in Wait to Deceive: A Study of Anti-Mormon Deception,* ed. Barbara Ellsworth, vol. 1 (Mesa, Ariz.: Brownsworth Publishing Co., 1982).

56. Anderson, *Understanding Paul,* 97.

57. Wilford Woodruff, "The Discourses of Wilford Woodruff," *Deseret Weekly,* November 14, 1891.

58. Joseph Fielding Smith, *Answers to Gospel Questions,* 5 vols. (Salt Lake City: Deseret Book Co., 1957–66), 5:153; italics added.

59. Joseph Fielding Smith, *Church History and Modern Revelation,* 4 vols. (Salt Lake City: The Church of Jesus Christ of Latter-day Saints, 1946–49), 2:190–91.

60. *History of the Church,* 5:85, August 6, 1842.

61. *History of the Church,* 2:182.

62. *History of the Church,* 5:394, May 18, 1843; italics added.

63. Gerald N. Lund, *The Coming of the Lord* (Salt Lake City: Bookcraft, 1971), 54-56.

64. James E. Carver, *Answering an Ex-Mormon Critic* (Sandy, Utah: Mormon Miscellaneous, 1983), 11, 12.

65. Joseph Fielding Smith, *Church History and Modern Revelation,* 4 vols. (Salt Lake City: The Church of Jesus Christ of Latter-day Saints, 1946–49), 4: 144–45.

66. Smith, *Church History and Modern Revelation,* 4:145–48.

67. Orson Pratt, in *Journal of Discourses,* 16:5.

68. Smith, *Church History and Modern Revelation,* 3:26.

69. Smith, *Church History and Modern Revelation,* 3:31–32.

70. Smith, *Doctrines of Salvation,* 2:228; italics added.

71. Joseph Smith, Jr., "Is Man Immortal," *Improvement Era,* 1916. Vol. Xix, January 1916, No. 3.

72. James E. Talmage, *Articles of Faith* (Salt Lake City: Deseret Book Co., 1981), 77; italics added.

73. See Milton V. Backman Jr., *American Religions and the Rise of Mormonism* (place: publisher, year), 79.

74. LeGrand Richards, *A Marvelous Work and a Wonder* (Salt Lake City: Deseret Book Co., 1950), 338.

75. *History of the Church,* 4:211–12.

76. Smith, *Doctrines of Salvation,* 3:94; italics added.

77. Bruce R. McConkie, *The Mortal Messiah: From Bethlehem to Calvary,* 4 vols. (Salt Lake City: Deseret Book, 1979–81), 1:128.

78. John A. Tvedtnes, *Answering Mormon Scholars: A Response To Criticism of the Book,* 235; some italics added.

79. McConkie, *Mormon Doctrine,* 172; italics added.

80. Gordon B. Hinckley, "The Symbol of Christ," *Ensign,* vol. 5 (May 1975): 93.

81. Marion G. Romney, *Look to God and Live* (Salt Lake City: Deseret Book Co., 1971), 96–97.

82. *Student Manual 121–122* [Salt Lake City: Corporation of the President of The Church of Jesus Christ of Latter Day Saints, 1989], 107.

83. Richards, *Marvelous Work and a Wonder,* 265–71.

84. Bruce R. McConkie, *Doctrinal New Testament Commentary,* 3 vols. (Salt Lake City: Bookcraft, 1965–73), 2:500; bold in original.

85. Smith, *Doctrines of Salvation,* 2:158, 230; italics in original.

86. McConkie, *Mormon Doctrine,* 755.

87. Roper, review of *Answering Mormon Scholars: A Response to Criticism Raised by Mormon Defenders,* 215.

88. John W. Welch, ed., *Reexploring the Book of Mormon* (Salt Lake City Deseret Book Co.; Provo, Utah: Foundation for Ancient Research and Mormon Studies, 1992), 213.

89. Roper, review of *Answering Mormon Scholars: A Response to Criticism Raised by Mormon Defenders,* 140.

90. John W. Welch, ed., *Reexploring the Book of Mormon,* 143.

91. Noel B. Reynolds, ed., *Book of Mormon Authorship: New Light on Ancient Origins* (Provo: BYU Religious Studies Center, 1982), 51; italics added to text (not scriptures).

92. Milton R. Hunter, *Conference Report,* October 1954, 108.

93. George Reynolds and Janne M. Sjodahl, *Commentary on the Book of Mormon,* ed. and arr. Philip C. Reynolds, 7 vols. (Salt Lake City: Deseret Book Co., 1955–61), 2:331.

94. Reynolds and Sjodahl, *Commentary on the Book of Mormon,* 2:328.

95. Reynolds and Sjodahl, *Commentary on the Book of Mormon,* 2:324.

96. Reynolds and Sjodahl, *Commentary on the Book of Mormon,* 2:322.

97. Reynolds and Sjodahl, *Commentary on the Book of Mormon,* 2:323.

98. Reynolds and Sjodahl, *Commentary on the Book of Mormon,* 2:322.

99. LeGrand Richards, *A Marvelous Work and a Wonder*, 407-412.

100. LeGrand Richards, *A Marvelous Work and a Wonder*, 407-412.

101. B. H. Roberts, *A Comprehensive History of The Church of Jesus Christ of Latter-day Saints, Century One*, 6 vols. (Salt Lake City: The Church of Jesus Christ of Latter-day Saints, 1930), 331–33.

102. Lyon, Gundry, and Parry, *Best-Loved Stories of the LDS People*, 87.

103. Lyon, Gundry, and Parry, *Best-Loved Stories of the LDS People*, 114.

104. Lyon, Gundry, and Parry, *Best-Loved Stories of the LDS People*, 297–98.

105. James E. Talmage, *The House of the Lord* (Salt Lake City: Deseret Book Co., 1968), 111–12; italics added.

106. Joseph F. Smith, *Gospel Doctrine: Selections from the Sermons and Writings of Joseph F. Smith,* comp. John A. Widtsoe (Salt Lake City: Deseret Book Co., 1939), 499.

BIBLIOGRAPHY

Anderson, Richard Lloyd, *Understanding Paul* [Salt Lake City: Deseret Book Co., 1983], p. 97.

Backman Jr., Milton V., *American Religions and the Rise of Mormonism*, 1980, p. 79.

Brown, C. Wade, *The First Page of the Golden Plates* [Orem, UT, Granite Publishing, 2000], pp. 25-32.

Coe, *The Maya*, p. 148.

Contributor, Vol. 7 [October 1185-September 1886], vol. VII, May 1886, No. 8, p. 284.

Deseret Weekly, November 14, 1891.

Dew, Sheri L., *Go Forward With Faith: The Biography of Gordon B. Hinkley* [Salt Lake City: Deseret Book Co., 1996], p. 584.

Ensign, May 1975, p. 93.

Gundry, Linda Ririe, Lyon, Jack M., and Parry, Jay A., eds., *Best-Loved Stories of the LDS People* [Salt Lake City: Deseret Book Co., 1997], pp. 25, 87, 114, 297-98.

http://www.biology.washington.edu/fingerprint/dnaintro.html.

Hunter, Howard W., *The Teachings of Howard W. Hunter*, edited by Clyde J. Williams [Salt Lake City: Bookcraft, 1997], p. 59.

Hunter, Milton R., *Archaeology and the Book of Mormon* [Salt Lake City: Deseret Book Co., 1956], p. 25-7.

——. *Christ in Ancient America* [Salt Lake City: Deseret Book Co., 1959], p. 60.

——. *Conference Report,* October 1954, Morning Session, p. 108.

Jakeman, M. Wells, "An Unusual Tree of Life Sculpture from Ancient Central America," Bulletin of University Archaeological Society [March 1953], pp. 26-49.

Jenson, Andrew, *Latter Day Saint Biographical Encyclopedia: A Compilation of Biographical Sketches of Prominent Men and Women in the Church of Jesus Christ of Latter-day Saints*, 4 vols., [Salt Lake City], p. 246.

Journal of Discourses, 26 vols. [London: Latter-day Saints' Book Depot, 1854-1886], 1:51, 16:5-6.

Kimball, Spencer W., *Conference Report*, October 9, 1976, Week ending.

Kimball, Stanley B., *Heber C. Kimball: Mormon Patriarch and Pioneer*, p. 85; Standardized.

Lee, Harold B., *Conference Report,* October 1950, Third day Morning session, p. 129.

———. *The Teachings of Harold B. Lee*, edited by Clyde J. Williams [Salt Lake City: Bookcraft, 1996], p. 413.

Little, James A., *From Kirtland to Salt Lake City* [Salt Lake City: James A. Little, 1890], pp. 74-5.

Ludlow, Daniel H., *A Companion to Your Study of the Old Testament* [Salt Lake City: Deseret Book Co., 1981], p. 339.

Lund, Gerald N., *The Coming of the Lord* [Salt Lake City; Bookcraft, 1971], p. 56.

Madsen, Truman G., *B.H. Roberts and the Book of Mormon*, BYU Studies, vol. 19 (1978-1979), Number 3-Spring 1979, p. 440.

Maxwell, Neal A., General Conference, D 78:18, April 1988.

McConkie, Bruce R., *A New Witness for the Articles of Faith* [Salt Lake City: Deseret Book Co., 1976], pp. 345, 339.

———. *Doctrinal New Testament Commentary*, 3 vols. [Salt Lake City: Bookcraft, 1965-1973], 2:500.

———. Mormon Doctrine, 2nd ed. [Salt Lake City: Bookcraft, 1966], pp. 92-3, 172, 755.

———. *Mortal Messiah*, 1:128.

McConkie, Joseph Fielding, *Answers: Straightforward Answers to Tough Gospel Questions* [Salt Lake City: Deseret Book Co., 1998], pp. 48-9.

Parry, Donald W. and Pike, Dana M., *LDS Perspectives on the Dead Sea Scrolls* [Provo: Foundation for Ancient Research and Mormon Studies, 1997].

Paul, Robert, "Joseph Smith and the Manchester New York Library," Brigham Young University Studies, vol. 22, number 3-Summer 1982.

Relief Society Magazine, January 1948, p. 8.

Reynolds, George and Sjodahl, Janne M., Commentary on the Book of Mormon, edited and arranged by Philip C. Reynolds, 7 vol. [Salt Lake City: Deseret Book Co., 1955-1961], 2:331, 2;328, 2:324, 2:322, 2:323.

Reynolds, Noel B., ed., Book of Mormon Authorship: New Light on Ancient Origins [Provo: BYU Religious Studies Center, 1982], p. 51.

Richards, LeGrand, A Marvelous Work and Wonder [Salt Lake City: Deseret Book Co., 1950], pp. 339, 265-71, 412.

Roberts, B. H., A Comprehensive History of the Church of Jesus Christ of Latter-day Saints, 6 vols. [Salt Lake City: Deseret News Press, 1930], 3:331-33.

Romney, Marion G., Look to God and Live [Salt Lake City: Deseret Book Co., 1971], pp. 96-7.

Saints' Herald 31 (October 4, 1884): 644; William Smith on Mormonism, Lamoni, Iowa: Herald Steam Book, 1883.

Sermon in Saints' Chapel, Saint's Herald 31 (1884): 644.

Smith, Joseph, Encyclopedia of Joseph Smith's Teachings, edited by Larry E. Dahl and Donald Q. Cannon [Salt Lake City: Bookcraft, 1997], pp. 309-11; Compare pp. 358, 367.

———. History of the Church of Jesus Christ of Latter-day Saints, 7 vols., introduction and notes by B. H. Roberts [Salt Lake City: The Church of Jesus Christ of Latter-day Saints, 1932-1951], 3:386-87, 5:394, 2:182, 4:211-12.

———. History of the Church, vol. 5, August 6, 1842, p. 85.

———. History of the Church, vol. 4, p. 588.

———. History of the Church of Jesus Christ of Latter-day Saints, 7 vols., 2nd ed. Rev., edited by B. H. Roberts [Salt Lake City: The Church of Jesus Christ of Latter-day Saints, 1932-1951], 2:103-5.

———. Teachings of the Prophet Joseph Smith, selected and arranged by Joseph Fielding Smith [Salt Lake City: Deseret Book Co., 1976], pp. 339, 345.

Smith, Joseph Fielding, *Answers to Gospel Questions*, 5 vols. [Salt lake City: Deseret Book Co., 1957-1966], p. 5:154.

———. *Church History and Modern Revelation*, 4 vols. [Salt Lake City: The Church of Jesus Christ of Latter-day Saints, 1946-1949], 4:144-45, 4:145-48, 3:26, 3:31-32, 2:190-91.

———. *Doctrines of Salvation*, 3 vols., edited by Bruce R. McConkie [Salt Lake City: Bookcraft, 1954-1956], pp. 2:228, 2:158, 2:230, 3:94; vol. 1, pp. 133-38.

———. *Gospel Doctrine: Selections from the Sermons and Writings of Joseph F. Smith*, Compiled by John A. Widstoe [Salt Lake City: Deseret Book Co., 1939], p. 231.

Strong, *A Concise Dictionary of the Words in the Hebrew Bible*, p. 19.

Stuy, Brian H. ed., *Collected Discourses* 5 vols. [Burbank, California, and Woodland Hills, UT: B. H. S. Publishing, 1987-1992], 1.

Talmage, James E., *Articles of Faith* [Salt Lake City: Deseret Book Co., 1981], p. 77.

———. The House of the Lord [Salt Lake City: Deseret Book Co., 1968], pp. 111-12.

Tanner, Jerald and Sandra, *Archaeology and the Book of Mormon* [William J. Hamblin], FARMS Review of Books, vol. 5, 1993, pp. 235, 261.

———. *Answering Mormon Scholars: A Response to Criticism Raised by Mormon Defenders* [Matthew Roper], FARMS Review of Books, vol. 9, no. 1, 1997.

———. *Answering Mormon Scholars: A Response to Criticism of the Book* 236; FARMS Review of Books, vol. 6, No. 2, 1994.

———. *Mormonism: Shadow or Reality?* [Matthew Roper], FARMS Review of Books, vol. 4, 1992, pp. 207, 211, 187.

View of the Hebrews, 2nd edition, (1825), pp. 168-9.

Welch, John W., ed., *Reexploring the Book of Mormon* [Salt Lake City and Provo: Deseret Book Co., Foundation for Ancient Research and Mormon Studies, 1992], p. 143, 213.

Whitney, Orson F., Life of Heber C. Kimball, Collector's Edition [Salt Lake City: Bookcraft, 1992], pp. 446, 449-50.

——. *Life of Heber C. Kimball* [Salt Lake City: Kimball Family, 1888], p. 322.

"Who Wrote the Book of Mormon? An Analysis of Word Prints," *BYU Studies* 20 [Spring 1980], pp. 225-51.

Young, Brigham, Brigham Young Papers, Church Archives, February 5, 1852.

About the Author

Dr. David P. Bowman was born in California and raised in Idaho Falls, Idaho. His parents, Wildan and Jeniece Bowman, his wife Kimberly, and his family have always been a motivating factor in his life and have encouraged him to set high goals.

David served a sign-language and proselyting mission in the St. Louis, Missouri area. He then attended Ricks College and Brigham Young University, where he was awarded both academic and leadership scholarships. David attended medical school at Western University of Health Sciences in Los Angeles, California. His internship and residency were in Phoenix, Arizona, where he enjoyed doing a lot of missionary work.

Dr. Bowman's church callings have included ward missionary, stake missionary, and stake mission presidency.

Dr. and Mrs. Bowman love living in Idaho Falls, where they grew up together. They have three children: Jens, Jacob, and Anna. Dr. Bowman now practices medicine at his two offices, "Idaho Urgent Care" and "Clear Skin."

Dr. Bowman enjoys fishing, skiing, and spending time with his family.